"The veteran *New York Times* Supreme Court reporter charts the first term of the right-leaning, avowedly religious supermajority now on the bench. . . . For Supreme Court watchers, provocative; for civil libertarians, alarming."

—*Kirkus Reviews*

"Pulitzer-winner Greenhouse surveys the fallout from the death in 2020 of liberal feminist Ruth Bader Ginsburg and her replacement by Barrett. . . . Greenhouse incisively dissects the crucial struggle between doctrinaire conservatives Samuel Alito and Neil Gorsuch, and Chief Justice John Roberts, whose preferred strategy is to gradually change court jurisprudence through subtle rulings on low-profile cases. Distinguished by Greenhouse's vivid profiles of the justices and lucid unraveling of their knotty legal theories, this is a revelatory study of the Supreme Court in flux."

—*Publishers Weekly*

"She has crafted a quick history of the year of Amy Coney Barrett's confirmation to succeed Ruth Bader Ginsburg, which capped a three-decade project to move the judiciary in a conservative direction—and outlines the stakes in pending cases. *Justice on the Brink* is, in a way, an account of the politicization of a branch of government that has at least tried to *appear* apolitical."

—*Harvard Magazine*

"A Pulitzer Prize–winning journalist, Greenhouse for more than three decades has established herself as perhaps the most influential commentator on the Supreme Court. As suggested by her title, in this work she focuses on what may well be a truly pivotal shift in the mission and role of the court in our American democracy."

—*The National Book Review*

"Linda Greenhouse, one of America's most astute writers about the Supreme Court, has written a remarkable book that combines a riveting account of the legal arguments in pathbreaking cases—including cases involving religion, abortion, voting rights, and affirmative action—with compelling insights about how each of the nine justices resolved them. *Justice on the Brink* is invaluable for all citizens who want to understand the future of the court and the Constitution."

—JEFFREY ROSEN, president and chief executive officer,
National Constitution Center

"This is the book to read and reread for anyone wanting to understand what lies behind this pivotal time for American law and the legitimacy of American institutions."

—MARTHA MINOW, 300th Anniversary University Professor,
Harvard University, and former dean, Harvard Law School

Justice on the Brink: A Requiem for the Supreme Court (2021)

Just a Journalist: On the Press, Life, and the Spaces Between (2017)

The Burger Court and the Rise of the Judicial Right
(with Michael J. Graetz, 2016)

The U.S. Supreme Court: A Very Short Introduction (2012)

Before Roe v. Wade: *Voices That Shaped the Abortion Debate Before the Supreme Court's Ruling* (with Reva B. Siegel, 2010)

Becoming Justice Blackmun (2005)

JUSTICE ON THE BRINK

JUSTICE ON THE BRINK

A REQUIEM FOR THE SUPREME COURT

LINDA GREENHOUSE

RANDOM HOUSE
NEW YORK

2022 Random House Trade Paperback Edition

Copyright © 2021, 2022 by Linda Greenhouse

Published in the United States by Random House, an imprint and division of
Penguin Random House LLC, New York.

RANDOM HOUSE and the HOUSE colophon are registered trademarks of
Penguin Random House LLC.

Originally published in hardcover and in slightly different form in the
United States by Random House, an imprint and division of
Penguin Random House LLC, in 2021.

LIBRARY OF CONGRESS CATALOGING-IN-PUBLICATION DATA
Names: Greenhouse, Linda, author.
Title: Justice on the brink / Linda Greenhouse.
Description: New York, N.Y. : Random House, 2021. | Includes bibliographical
references and index.
Identifiers: LCCN 2021013364 (print) | LCCN 2021013365 (ebook) |
ISBN 9780593447949 (trade paperback) | ISBN 9780593447956 (ebook)
Subjects: LCSH: United States. Supreme Court—History. | Judges—
Selection and appointment—United States. | Ginsburg, Ruth Bader | Barrett,
Amy Coney. | Political questions and judicial power—United States.
Classification: LCC KF8742 .G743 2021 (print) | LCC KF8742 (ebook) |
DDC 347.73/26090512—dc23
LC record available at https://lccn.loc.gov/2021013364
LC ebook record available at https://lccn.loc.gov/2021013365

Printed in the United States of America on acid-free paper

randomhousebooks.com

2 4 6 8 9 7 5 3 1

Book design by Simon M. Sullivan

For Lizzy Longstreth, born in the middle of it all

THE YEAR WHEN IT HAPPENED

IT WAS A TIDAL WAVE crashing onto the constitutional shore, sweeping away what had once seemed rooted in legal bedrock. The right to abortion. Sensible limitations on gun ownership. Public schools free of religious ceremony. Deference by judges to policymakers' expertise.

The Supreme Court term that ended in June 2022 left many Americans reeling. How did it happen that "so few have so quickly changed so much," in the words of the three justices who dissented from the decision to overturn *Roe v. Wade* after nearly fifty years of legal abortion? How could a court that not long ago barred public prayer at high school football games and graduations as an unconstitutional "establishment" of religion now grant a public employee—a football coach—the right to commandeer the field for prayer at the fifty-yard line in the name of freedom of religion? Why in an era of recurring gun violence that left the country shaken to its core would the court strike down a law that required gun license applicants to show they had a valid reason for carrying a concealed weapon?

This was no simple tidal wave. It was a tsunami, the product of deep forces that traveled beneath the surface for years, gathering strength until it reached its destination: a conservative takeover of the Supreme Court so extreme that it outflanked the indisputably conservative chief justice, John Roberts.

This book tells that story.

Month by month, the court's conservative wing, now a supermajority with the arrival of a third Trump-appointed justice, planted the seeds that would burst into bloom in the following term, when the court finally commanded a distracted public's attention. The events of that foundational term are chronicled here in real time: Justice Ruth Bader Ginsburg's death in September 2020; her replacement on the eve of Election Day by Justice Amy Coney Barrett; the court's elevation of religion over public health; the addition to its docket of a Second Amendment case after a decade of silence on gun rights; its internal conflict over the flood of lawsuits through which Donald Trump's allies and lawyers sought to keep him in office.

And finally, with the term approaching its end, the justices' decision to insert the court once again into the abortion wars by granting a hearing to Mississippi's defense of an antiabortion law so obviously unconstitutional that the country's most conservative federal appeals court had declared it invalid.

The justices had turned down similar appeals from antiabortion states in the recent past, and Mississippi's appeal figured to hit still another dead end at the Supreme Court. But now things were different. As a candidate, Trump had boasted that *Roe v. Wade* would fall "automatically" if he had the chance to fill vacancies on the Supreme Court. In Amy Coney Barrett, the president found a woman with impeccable antiabortion credentials to replace a stalwart defender of reproductive rights. The court's announcement in May 2021 that it would hear *Dobbs v. Jackson Women's Health Organization* in its next term simply pulled back the curtain on a stage that was already set. "It was always about abortion," this book's May chapter reminds us.

Looking back from the perspective of the term that followed, it's clear that a real-time account of this single term became something more: a window not only on the court's own unprecedented transformation but also on how that court in turn transformed American law. Nearly all the decisions that defined the 2021–22 term had roots in choices the new supermajority made during the term before: not only the cases the justices accepted for review but also the signals they sent about the kinds of cases they would welcome as vehicles for future aggressive rulings.

In exercising its nearly unlimited power to set its own agenda, the court inevitably helps set the country's agenda as well, fostering conversation and debate about the issues the justices have put in play. That is hardly surprising, given the court's role in an ongoing dialogue with other organs of government and, through them, with the American people. What was exceptional in the 2020–21 term and the term that followed was the degree to which the questions in play threatened to destabilize long-standing social and political settlements. The court itself became the issue.

While the court presents itself protectively as simply the passive recipient of the legal problems the American public brings to its doorstep, anyone watching the behavior of the conservative justices could readily see a different reality. Justices Clarence Thomas and Samuel Alito in particular are unabashed in signaling to the conservative ecosystem that surrounds the court that they are ready to move the law if presented with the right vehicle.

In fact, the 2020–21 term opened with such a signal. The court refused to hear an appeal by a former Kentucky county clerk who sought immunity for her refusal to issue a marriage license to a same-sex couple in the immediate aftermath of the *Obergefell* decision in which the court recognized a constitutional right to same-sex marriage. The clerk, Kim Davis, claimed that her Christian beliefs prevented her from carrying out her duty to issue the license. Defying a judge's order, she was found in contempt of court and spent five days in jail.

The appeal as she presented it was procedurally flawed, and Justices Thomas and Alito agreed with the rest of the justices that the court should not accept it. The Supreme Court rejects the great majority of the appeals it receives, and ordinarily a rejection is simply that, neither explained nor elaborated upon. But Justices Thomas and Alito, who had both dissented in *Obergefell*, had a point to make. Davis's case, they wrote, "provides a stark reminder of the consequences of *Obergefell*." They added: "Davis may have been one of the first victims of this Court's cavalier treatment of religion in its *Obergefell* decision, but she will not be the last." The court had created a problem, they concluded, "that only it can fix."

Could there have been a more explicit Help Wanted ad for an *Obergefell* victim? Invitation noted and accepted, a new petition arrived at the court even before the next term began, filed by a Christian right litigating organization, Alliance Defending Freedom. Its client was a Colorado web designer who wanted to start designing custom wedding websites but who asserted that as a Christian, she could not in good conscience design such a website for a same-sex couple. She claimed a constitutional right to post a statement to that effect on her business's website in defiance of Colorado's antidiscrimination law. The state argued in opposition to her Supreme Court appeal (*303 Creative LLC v. Elenis*) that because she was not actually in the wedding website business, she had suffered no injury and her case failed the court's ordinary "ripeness" requirement. The justices accepted her appeal nonetheless, for decision during the 2022–23 term.

It requires no particular foresight to predict that although the country largely accepts same-sex marriage, with more than one million Americans now married to persons of the same sex, whether those with religious objections to such marriages are free to disobey a state's antidiscrimination law will be a topic of contentious conversation as the court considers this case.

How should the public understand a Supreme Court that seeks so openly to shape the law to its liking? Justice Thomas's observation, in his opinion concurring with the overturning of *Roe v. Wade*, that *Obergefell* and even the 1965 decision recognizing a constitutional right to contraception would logically be the next to fall got the country's attention. While many people reacted with surprise and alarm, Justice Thomas has in fact been issuing invitations and predictions of this sort for years. The difference is that after the court's reckless erasure of the right to abortion, we can no longer write off such predictions as dystopian fantasies.

Justice is indeed on the brink in the new legal landscape reshaped by an empowered Supreme Court and delivered to a startled country. And yet what occurred in the course of a few weeks in June 2022 should have come as no surprise. It had already happened, month by month, in the term you will read about in the following pages.

July 4, 2022

CONTENTS

THE CHOSEN ONE

THE LATE OCTOBER SKY HAD GROWN DARK, but the lights aimed at the White House were so bright that on the Truman Balcony it might have been high noon. She stood bathed in the glow, the president of the United States by her side, he bundled in a heavy coat against the evening chill and she in a short-sleeved black dress that brushed the top of her knees. Her light brown hair fell straight to her shoulders. She looked younger than her forty-eight years. Barely an hour earlier, by a near party-line vote of 52 to 48 (with all Republican senators except Susan Collins of Maine voting in favor and all the Democrats voting against), the Senate had confirmed her to a Supreme Court seat that had been empty for the mere five weeks since the death of the woman who had occupied it for twenty-seven years, Justice Ruth Bader Ginsburg.

Not for 151 years had the Senate confirmed a Supreme Court nominee without a single vote from the minority party. For the Democratic senators, who had refused on principle to show up for the Judiciary Committee vote, filling a Supreme Court vacancy on the very eve of a presidential election was an illegitimate exercise of power. But to Senator Mitch McConnell, Republican of Kentucky, the majority leader who during the past four years had shepherded more than two hundred of President Donald Trump's nominees to their life-tenured seats on the federal bench, it was the reason he was there.

Moments before climbing the stairs to the balcony, the newly confirmed nominee had stood on the South Portico of the White House in front of two hundred invited guests seated on the South Lawn. Her husband held a Bible as Justice Clarence Thomas administered the Constitutional Oath, required of all federal officials. She had chosen the court's most outspoken conservative, its only Black member, for this special honor. No other Supreme Court justices were present. In addition to the Constitutional Oath, federal judges also take the Judicial Oath, in which they promise to "do equal right to the poor and to the rich." Chief Justice John Roberts would administer that oath the next day in a discreet ceremony at the Supreme Court.

But there was nothing discreet about this night. The election was eight days away. In many states, voting was already under way, and some ten million Americans had already cast their ballot for president. The Truman Balcony tableau, Democrats would grumble the next morning, was the ultimate photo op, breathtaking in its audacity; the country had never seen anything like it. True enough. But on the other hand, was it really so astonishing? The country was witnessing something new, yes. But what was really on display was the culmination of a project launched years before, one that had been set on a path carefully planned, tended, and laid out for all to see—except, of course, that most people weren't looking, or, if they were, they mistook occasional setbacks for lasting defeat. It was a project to take back the Supreme Court, and the woman on the balcony was its instrument. She was Amy Coney Barrett, the chosen one.

THERE ARE FEW inevitable events in politics, but in retrospect it's tempting to see Amy Barrett's nomination to the Supreme Court as one of them. Long before President Trump's announcement of her selection in the White House Rose Garden on September 26—the celebratory event that became a notorious COVID-19 superspreader— he had made it clear that he would name her to the Supreme Court if he got the chance. When Justice Anthony Kennedy retired two years earlier, Judge Barrett, who had taken her seat only months before on the federal appeals court in Chicago, appeared on the president's short list for the vacancy. But Trump chose instead another appeals court judge, Brett Kavanaugh. "I'm saving her for Ginsburg," he explained, words intended to assure any disappointed members of his base that while the devoutly Catholic mother of seven had been passed over for this vacancy, she would not be overlooked the next time.

The question, of course—really the only question—was whether there would be a next time. Not since Richard Nixon had there been three Supreme Court vacancies in a president's first term. But no one could rule it out. The recent history of Supreme Court nominations was filled with the unexpected. Justice Antonin Scalia, revered on the right almost to the point of worship, had died unexpectedly in February 2016, near the start of President Barack Obama's final year in office. Barely an hour after word came of the justice's death, well before most Americans had even heard the news on that Saturday afternoon, Senator McConnell had declared that he would not permit the president to fill the vacancy. "The American people should have a voice in the selection of their next Supreme Court justice," McConnell said. "Therefore, this vacancy should not be filled until we have a new president."

It was an eyebrow-raising, norm-shattering proposition. While it was generally assumed that the Supreme Court confirmation door would close at some point during an election year, no one had questioned the propriety of filling a seat only a few months in. After all, Anthony Kennedy, President Ronald Reagan's eventual choice for the court after the prolonged battle that ended in the defeat of Robert Bork, was not confirmed until February 1988, another presidential election year. McConnell's challenge sounded like just so much bluster. But his word held. The Senate never gave a hearing to Obama's nominee, Merrick Garland, chief judge of the federal appeals court in Washington, D.C., a widely admired figure who had drawn praise in the past from leading Republicans, suddenly grown silent.

Eleven days after taking office, Trump nominated Neil Gorsuch, a judge on the federal appeals court in Denver, for the Scalia vacancy. When Democrats threatened a filibuster to protest filling what they deemed a stolen seat, the Republican majority changed the rules and abolished the filibuster for Supreme Court nominations. Gorsuch was confirmed by a vote of 54 to 45 (60 votes would have been required to break a filibuster) and took his seat in April 2017, in time for the final round of arguments in the 2016–17 term. His tenure as the court's junior justice was brief. Trump's second Supreme Court nominee, Brett Kavanaugh—like Merrick Garland a judge on the United States Court of Appeals for the District of Columbia Circuit, usually referred to as the D.C. Circuit—was confirmed to the Kennedy vacancy the next year.

Of the two appointments, Kavanaugh's was without doubt the more consequential. The substitution of the conservative Gorsuch for the conservative Scalia did not promise to change the court's precarious ideological balance. But whenever the basically conservative court had tilted toward the left in recent years, it was Anthony Kennedy who made the difference: establishing the right to same-sex marriage; preserving the right to abortion; giving "enemy combatant" prisoners at Guantánamo Bay access to federal court; refusing to shut the door on affirmative action. Justice Scalia was a dissenter in those cases, while Justice Kennedy was in the narrow majority in all of them, earning conservatives' scorn; typical was the appraisal by John O. McGinnis, a law professor at Northwestern University, who dismissed Kennedy as a justice "who spouted aphorisms worthy of fortune cookies rather than locating his reasoning in the original meaning of our fundamental law." Brett Kavanaugh, who had been Kennedy's law clerk, was deemed more ideologically reliable, a safe and confirmable choice for the high-stakes vacancy.

The next year passed without a retirement, and when the 2019–20 term ended on July 9 without a retirement announcement, it appeared that there would be no Supreme Court vacancy during the remainder of Trump's first term. The public was unaware that Justice Ginsburg, at eighty-seven the oldest member of the court and the senior member of its increasingly beleaguered liberal bloc, was fighting what would be the last of her numerous battles with cancer. The week after the term ended, the court's public information office issued a low-key statement in Justice Ginsburg's name on a quiet Friday afternoon, referring to "lesions on my liver" and "the success of my current treatment." To a reader accustomed to announcements about Justice Ginsburg's health and her increasingly frequent hospitalizations, this looked like business as usual.

Nine weeks later, on September 18, Ruth Ginsburg died of metastatic pancreatic cancer. Nina Totenberg of NPR reported the statement that the justice, during her final days, had dictated to her granddaughter Clara Spera: "My most fervent wish is that I will not be replaced until a new president is installed."

Justice Ginsburg was the best-known member of the court, and the country was stunned by her death and its implications, with Election Day six weeks away. In her final years, Ginsburg had become a cultural icon, tightly embraced by the left as the last hope of a Supreme Court hurtling to the right. She happily accepted the nickname "the Notorious RBG," borrowed from rap culture to signify the verbal toughness of her dissenting opinions and her personal toughness in repeatedly staring down mortality.

As darkness fell the Friday night of her death, hundreds gathered on the Supreme Court steps to pray from the liturgy of the Jewish Sabbath and to place flowers and lighted candles in a spontaneous memorial. Mourners carried homemade posters: . . . WHEN THERE ARE NINE, a reference to Ginsburg's standard answer to the question of when she would be satisfied with the number of women on the Supreme Court; THANK YOU FOR HOLDING ON AS LONG AS YOU DID. Two women, evidently having heard the NPR report, held up a big sign that read, in capital letters, HONOR HER WISH.

For Senator McConnell, this was a time not for mourning, but for business, and he was ready. The president was in the air, flying back from a campaign rally in Minnesota. The White House operator patched McConnell's urgent call through to Air Force One. As Josh Holmes, McConnell's former chief of staff, later told the PBS documentary program *Frontline*, the majority leader delivered a two-part message: "I'm going to put out a statement that says we're going to fill the vacancy" and "You've gotta nominate Amy Coney Barrett."

Why Amy Barrett? The answer was obvious, although as yet unspoken; there were motions to go through, after all. The fact was that by September 18, 2020, in every way that mattered, she was the perfect choice.

Certainly Ruth Ginsburg's replacement needed to be a woman; that much was obvious. But that fact alone didn't necessarily single out Amy Barrett. While Trump's judicial selections had been overwhelmingly male, there were at least a few women on the bench with the youth and the conservative credentials to merit being added to the list. But the truth was that there was no list. With the Florida electorate in mind, the White House put out word that the president was considering Barbara Lagoa, a Cuban American and the first Latina on the Florida Supreme Court, whom Trump had named the year before to a federal appeals court. Despite that public show of an actual search, the president never even interviewed Judge Lagoa. The selection process began and ended with Amy Barrett.

Neil Gorsuch and Brett Kavanaugh had been strikingly conventional choices for the Supreme Court. Any of the candidates whom Donald Trump defeated for the Republican presidential nomination might have selected either or both of them. Both had clerked on the Supreme Court. Both were creatures of the Beltway who had paid their dues in Republican politics and worked at high levels in the administration of President George W. Bush, Gorsuch in the Justice Department as principal deputy to the associate attorney general and Kavanaugh in the White House as staff secretary to the president, a weightier job than its title suggests. President Bush rewarded each with a federal appellate judgeship, and each had spent more than a decade on the bench. Their confirmations had been contentious for reasons external to their biographies, Gorsuch's because of what the Republicans had done to Merrick Garland in order to keep the seat open, and Kavanaugh's because of the crucial vacancy he had been named to fill. (An accusation of sexual misconduct as a teenager, which Kavanaugh vigorously denied, came late in the confirmation process, generating much heat and little light.)

Amy Barrett also clerked on the Supreme Court, but there the similarity ended. By traditional Republican standards, she was far from a conventional choice. She lacked the Ivy League credentials shared by every other sitting justice, all of whom were law graduates of either Harvard (John Roberts, Stephen Breyer, Elena Kagan, Neil Gorsuch) or Yale (Clarence Thomas, Samuel Alito, Sonia Sotomayor, Brett Kavanaugh.)

Barrett graduated from law school at the University of Notre Dame, having turned down an offer of admission from the higher-ranked University of Chicago Law School. "I'm a Catholic, and I always grew up loving Notre Dame," she explained years later, adding: "I really wanted to choose a place where I felt like I was not going to be just educated as a lawyer. I wanted to be in a place where I felt like I would be developed and inspired as a whole person." A commencement speech she gave there in 2006, nine years after her own graduation, made clear the distinctive view she held of her alma mater. "Keep in mind," she told the graduating students, "that your legal career is but a means to an end." That end, she explained, "is building the kingdom of God."

Compared with other recent Supreme Court nominees of both Republican and Democratic presidents, her résumé was thin. She had been a judge for a few months short of three years. She had practiced law only briefly, spending the two years following her clerkship as an associate in a Washington, D.C., law firm. She had never worked in government at any level. After her time in Washington, she returned to the shelter of Notre Dame and spent fifteen years on the law school's faculty.

It was in South Bend, Indiana, home of Notre Dame, where People of Praise, the unusual religious group in which she was raised, was founded in 1971 and still has its headquarters. Although it is nominally pan-Christian, some 90 percent of the group's seventeen hundred members are Catholic, participants in a charismatic renewal movement that emerged in the wake of Vatican II. Members view themselves as a tight-knit community of worship and mutual support, and they are expected to accept traditional gender roles within traditionally structured families. (Married women were originally known as "handmaids" until the Margaret Atwood novel gave the term an undesirable resonance.) Barrett's husband, Jesse, whom she met in law school, was also raised in the group. South Bend proved a welcoming place for the couple to settle and raise a big family. Barrett herself, who grew up in a suburb of New Orleans, was the oldest of seven children. She and Jesse proceeded to have seven of their own, five by birth along with a boy and a girl adopted from Haiti.

That Amy Barrett was Catholic was hardly unusual. Quite the contrary, in fact; she would be joining a court on which six of the eight justices were raised in the church: Chief Justice Roberts and Justices Alito, Sotomayor, Thomas, Kavanaugh, and Gorsuch, who grew up Catholic although he now worshipped with his wife and daughters in the Episcopal church. Kavanaugh and Gorsuch had even attended the same elite Jesuit all-boys school, Georgetown Prep, in suburban Washington, D.C., although being two years apart in age, they were not classmates. (All the Catholic justices but Alito attended Catholic schools.)

What was unusual was the public dimension to Barrett's Catholicism: not religion's role in her personal and family life, certainly a private matter, but her willingness during her pre-judicial career to attest to her adherence to Catholic doctrine on matters of public concern, abortion prominently among them. In 2013, on the fortieth anniversary of the Supreme Court's *Roe v. Wade* decision, which established the constitutional right to abortion, Barrett signed a statement placed in the Notre Dame student newspaper by the University Faculty for Life and the Notre Dame Fund to Protect Human Life. "In the 40 years since the Supreme Court's infamous *Roe v. Wade* decision, over 55 million unborn children have been killed by abortions," the statement read. "We faculty and staff at the University of Notre Dame reaffirm our full support for our University's commitment to the right to life, we renew our call for the unborn to be protected in law and welcomed in life, and we voice our love and support for the mothers who bear them."

Signing this statement was evidently neither required nor even expected of senior Notre Dame faculty members. The statement carried 106 signatures from across the university. Of the law school's more than thirty full professors, Amy Barrett was one of only six to sign and thus to deplore publicly the "infamous" Supreme Court decision.

The previous year, she had signed a statement criticizing the Obama administration for its implementation of the Affordable Care Act's requirement to include contraception coverage in employer-sponsored health plans. Religious orders and churches themselves were exempt from the mandate, and religiously affiliated organizations like colleges and the chain of nursing homes run by an order of nuns, the Little Sisters of the Poor, were demanding the same exemption. The Obama administration offered them instead a hands-off "accommodation" under which, without the employer's involvement, an organization's insurance provider would underwrite the coverage and inform employees of its availability.

The statement Barrett signed in opposition to this policy, under the headline UNACCEPTABLE, was drafted and circulated by the Becket Fund for Religious Liberty, a prominent organization that litigates against what it perceives as government incursions on the rights of believers. The statement labeled the Obama policy "a grave violation of religious freedom," adding: "It is an insult to the intelligence of Catholics, Protestants, Eastern Orthodox Christians, Jews, Muslims, and other people of faith and conscience to imagine that they will accept an assault on their religious liberty if only it is covered up by a cheap accounting trick." (The Becket Fund statement was an early salvo in the religious war against the Affordable Care Act's contraception mandate. This struggle reached the Supreme Court three times, culminating in one of the final decisions of the 2019–20 term. The court upheld the Trump administration's decision to grant an opt-out from the mandate for any employer who requested one, either for religious reasons or unspecified reasons of "conscience." The decision, *Little Sisters of the Poor v. Pennsylvania*, provoked Justice Ginsburg's final published opinion, a dissent in which she objected: "Today, for the first time, the Court casts totally aside countervailing rights and interests in its zeal to secure religious rights to the nth degree.")

Among other public statements Barrett signed before becoming a judge was a "Letter to Synod Fathers from Catholic Women," addressed to Pope Francis and the bishops convening at the Vatican in October 2015 to conduct a "Synod of Bishops on the Family." This letter expressed "our love for Pope Francis, our fidelity to and gratitude for the doctrines of the Catholic Church, and our confidence in the Synod of Bishops as it strives to strengthen the Church's evangelizing mission." It added:

> We give witness that the Church's teachings—on the dignity of the human person and the value of human life from conception to natural death; on the meaning of human sexuality, the significance of sexual difference and the complementarity of men and women; on openness to life and the gift of motherhood; and on marriage and family founded on the indissoluble commitment of a man and a woman—provide a sure guide to the Christian life, promote women's flourishing, and serve to protect the poor and most vulnerable among us.

In 2016, the University Faculty for Life, of which she was then a member, unanimously passed a resolution condemning Notre Dame's decision to give Vice President Joe Biden the Laetare Medal, awarded annually to "an American Catholic in recognition of outstanding service to Church and society." How could the vice president meet that qualification, the group demanded, when he "has for decades conspicuously rejected Church teaching about life" by supporting the right to abortion? The resolution continued: "Saying that Mr. Biden rejects Church teaching could make it sound like he is merely disobeying the rules of his religious group. But the Church's teaching about the sanctity of life is *true*" (emphasis in original).

Biden had received the medal two weeks earlier. The resolution asked that it be rescinded. Awarding it to Biden was "a scandalous violation of the University's moral responsibility," the resolution asserted. "In past years, Notre Dame awarded the Laetare Medal to persons who spoke truth to power. This year, Notre Dame has chosen to honor power at the expense of truth."

To a member of the general public reading these statements, it may have mattered little that one participant happened to be an obscure law professor. But Don McGahn was not a disinterested observer. He was a Notre Dame graduate himself, serving as Donald Trump's White House counsel. In that capacity, he was also the administration's chief judge-picker, and he had dozens of appeals court seats to fill, positions the Senate had prevented President Obama from filling. One was an Indiana seat on the Seventh Circuit, which is based in Chicago and covers Illinois, Indiana, and Wisconsin. President Obama had attempted to fill that seat by nominating Myra Selby, the first woman and first African American to serve on the Indiana Supreme Court. The Senate's Republican majority had never given her a hearing, so the seat was available to Don McGahn. The Trump administration was less than four months old when Amy Barrett's nomination was announced on May 8, 2017.

During her hearing before the Senate Judiciary Committee that September, the question of religion loomed large, as it did on the dockets of federal courts around the country. Republican-controlled state legislatures were enacting dozens of antiabortion measures, many now being challenged in court. *Roe v. Wade* itself was seen as increasingly vulnerable. Multiple courts were also dealing with the ongoing religious challenges to the Affordable Care Act's contraception mandate. There were also cases brought by vendors—bakers, photographers, florists—who were raising religious objections to providing goods and services for celebrations of the same-sex marriages that the Supreme Court had authorized in the *Obergefell* decision in 2015.

Democratic senators were openly skeptical about whether Professor Barrett could set aside her deep religious commitments and, as a judge, address such questions with an open mind. Her assurances that she could failed to persuade Senator Dianne Feinstein of California, the committee's ranking Democrat. Senator Feinstein asked her: "Why is it that so many of us on this side have this very uncomfortable feeling that—you know, dogma and law are two different things. And I think whatever a religion is, it has its own dogma. The law is totally different. And I think in your case, professor, when you read your speeches, the conclusion one draws is that the dogma lives loudly within you, and that's of concern when you come to big issues that large numbers of people have fought for years in this country."

Feinstein's words proved a gift to the Republican Party, provoking an immediate and sustained backlash. Op-ed commentary portrayed the senator, and by extension all the Democrats, as anti-Catholic, even anti-religion. "The notion that Catholics are so beholden to Rome as to be incapable of rendering independent judgment in public office has a long, sordid history," Sohrab Ahmari, a writer for *Commentary* magazine, wrote in a *New York Times* op-ed days after the Judiciary Committee hearing. Coffee mugs and T-shirts sold in Catholic bookstores and over the Internet bore the words "The dogma lives loudly within *me*." When Don McGahn spoke at Barrett's Seventh Circuit investiture ceremony, held at Notre Dame, he took the occasion to quip: "We now affectionately call her Judge Dogma."

This was one way, but hardly the only way, to look at Senator Feinstein's comment. What, exactly, was wrong with what the senator said? A nominee to a powerful life-tenured position had made her religious commitments a central part of her public persona. The job she was seeking required, on a regular basis, the exercise of judgment in cases with powerful claims on both sides. Why shouldn't a senator want to know how a judicial nominee's own conscience, her own sense of right and wrong, would factor into the judgments on the kinds of cases roiling the federal courts? And why should the role of the Catholic church, having injected itself deeply into politics, be off-limits as a topic for questions by politicians?

Some weighty voices did indeed make that point. Cathleen Kaveny, a prominent Catholic law professor and theologian at Boston College, published an op-ed in *The Washington Post* under the headline NO, DIANNE FEINSTEIN IS NOT AN ANTI-CATHOLIC BIGOT. "To say 'No Catholics (or Muslims or Jews or secular humanists) need apply' would indeed be a constitutionally prohibited religious test," Kaveny wrote. She continued:

But the Constitution cannot reasonably be read to prohibit asking a candidate for public office how her moral commitments would affect her public service. Religious believers don't get a free pass.

Whether progressive or conservative, Catholic positions on matters of morality and public policy have significant implications for the legal framework governing American life. It is legitimate for citizens to bring those commitments with them into the public square. But it is also fair for others to ask hard questions about what that will mean.

American Catholics can't say, on the one hand, that our faith has a public dimension—important implications for our public policy and law—and cry foul, on the other, when fellow citizens challenge us about those implications. We can't have it both ways. That's to be neither a conscientious Catholic nor a public-spirited American.

In retrospect, Dianne Feinstein's clumsy question might have been the best thing that happened to Amy Barrett in her first venture into the public spotlight. People who would scarcely have noticed a Seventh Circuit appointment amid the chaos of Trump's early months in office now knew her name. The meme of Catholic martyrdom that was now attached to that name overwhelmed the competing narrative offered by Cathleen Kaveny and a handful of others. It resonated powerfully with the theme of Christian victimhood that Donald Trump had so successfully exploited during his rise to power. It isn't necessary to claim that it influenced her confirmation to the Seventh Circuit, a foregone conclusion in any event. But beyond doubt it helped make her next chapter inevitable.

BEGINNING YEARS EARLIER, there was another contributor to Amy Barrett's trajectory: the Federalist Society.

Many people first heard of "Fed Soc," as insiders call the organization, during the 2016 presidential campaign, when candidate Donald Trump credited it with providing lists of properly vetted conservative lawyers and judges from which he pledged to select his judicial nominees. Once in office, President Trump did as he had promised and rarely, if ever, deviated from the Fed Soc–approved lists. During his time in office, the organization's annual banquet, held in late fall in Washington, D.C., was a triumphant affair. "Thank you from the bottom of my heart for your support and prayers," Neil Gorsuch told the group at its November 2017 banquet, the first following his confirmation to the Supreme Court. Brett Kavanaugh received a standing ovation from the more than two thousand guests when he showed up at the banquet the following year, shortly after his bitter confirmation fight. It was during Gorsuch's victory-lap banquet that Don McGahn addressed the group. The claim that the Trump administration had "outsourced" judicial selection to the Federalist Society was "completely false," McGahn told the black-tie crowd, adding: "I've been a member of the Federalist Society since law school—still am. So, frankly, it seems like it's been insourced."

Although new on the public stage in 2016, the Federalist Society was no newcomer, and being in a position to pick judges for the new president was simply the payoff of the long strategic vision that had guided it since its founding in 1982. Its plan from the beginning was to identify and nurture future generations of conservative law students, young men and women who in fifteen or twenty years would form the pool from which conservative judges would be chosen.

The organization was started by a small group of law students at Yale and the University of Chicago resentful of the scarcity of conservative voices in their respective student bodies and on their faculties. Their timing was perfect: The Reagan administration, at the height of its power, had begun to place on the federal courts conservative law professors, many of them quite young, whose theories may well have been outside the mainstream at a faculty workshop but who were now in a position to change the legal conversation. The significance of growing the pool of future judges was clear. The students who organized the group's first conference, held at Yale in April 1982, attracted a star-studded lineup of advisers and mentors, including Robert Bork, who was already a Reagan-appointed federal appeals court judge, and

Antonin Scalia, who was soon to become one. Theodore Olson, an assistant attorney general who later served in the George W. Bush administration as solicitor general, was also an early supporter.

A sometimes unruly mix of social conservatives, big business conservatives, and libertarians, united by a feeling of having wandered too long in the wilderness of legal academia, the group grew quickly through chapters in law schools around the country. Soon it began to attract substantial financial support from conservative foundations with money to spend and eagerness for creative new ventures. Morton Blackwell, a longtime conservative political organizer who had recently established the Leadership Institute to train conservative activists, addressed that first conference. As *Politico Magazine* reported in a 2018 article titled "The Weekend at Yale That Changed American Politics," Blackwell outlined the project: "How to get the right people into the study of law. How to get into the right law school. How to succeed as a conservative in law school. Law student participation in politics and government. How to get better people on law faculties. How to get a good clerking job. How to become a judge. How to make sure the right people get to be judges." (Nearly four decades later, on December 30, 2020, Blackwell would reappear as one of nineteen self-identified "conservatives" who signed an open letter calling on the Senate at its January 6 session to refuse to certify Joe Biden's Electoral College victory.)

Blackwell's speech to the first Federalist Society conference provided a road map for what the political scientist Steven M. Teles in his 2008 book, *The Rise of the Conservative Legal Movement*, called a conservative countermobilization. And it succeeded beyond expectations. In their 2013 book, *The Federalist Society: How Conservatives Took the Law Back from Liberals*, Michael Avery and Danielle McLaughlin observed that "every single federal judge appointed by President George H. W. Bush or President George W. Bush was either a member or approved by members of the society."

Amy Coney was not a member of the Federalist Society in law school; that came later. She did not so much choose Fed Soc as it chose her. She was exactly the kind of person the society's founders had been looking for fifteen years before. That she was female was a plus; Fed Soc was becoming self-conscious about being overweighted with young men. Even better, she was a self-identified conservative who proclaimed her fidelity to a theory of constitutional interpretation known as originalism.

Although its name connoted deep historic roots, originalism was of recent vintage, hatched in the network of conservative organizations that served as the intellectual incubators of the Reagan Revolution. Embraced by Robert Bork, the failed Supreme Court nominee, and Antonin Scalia, who ascended to the Supreme Court from the D.C. Circuit in 1986, the theory held that the only legitimate way to interpret the Constitution's words was according to their original meaning. Scalia was scathing about the notion that constitutional meaning might evolve as society arrived at new understanding of concepts like equality and liberty. His was no "living" Constitution, he often proclaimed, but rather one that was "dead, dead, dead."

In a 2019 talk at Hillsdale College, a Christian college in Michigan, Amy Barrett traced her own journey toward originalism. "I wasn't familiar when I entered law school with originalism as a theory," she told the students. "I found myself as I read more and more cases becoming more and more convinced that the opinions that I read that took the originalist approach were right."

Not all members of the Federalist Society described themselves as originalists. But to be an originalist in the mid-1990s, when Barrett was in law school, was to place oneself in the heart of the Fed Soc comfort zone. Combined with her impressive academic record—she graduated summa cum laude and first in her class—Barrett's endorsement of originalism made her a prime candidate for conservative faculty members looking to propel star like-minded students into competition for top judicial clerkships. Two former Scalia clerks on the Notre Dame faculty, Patrick Schiltz and William Kelley, recommended her to Judge Laurence Silberman, a Reagan appointee on the D.C. Circuit who in turn often placed his clerks in the Supreme Court chambers of his former colleague Justice Scalia. Her path was now set. One of her other law school mentors, John Garvey, a professor with whom she wrote a law review article on the moral quandary faced by Catholic judges in death penalty cases, recommended her to Justice Scalia with a single sentence: "Amy Coney is the best student I ever had."

For the Federalist Society, adding more conservatives to law school faculties was indispensable for the larger project of growing the next generations of conservative law students and future judges; the success of that ultimate goal depended on a network of mentors and sponsors embedded in the nation's law schools. Her talent and interests made Amy Barrett a highly plausible candidate to fill such a role. But the day had passed when a would-be law professor could jump from a Supreme Court clerkship directly onto a law school's tenure track. Most law clerks, even those with academic ambitions, took jobs at law firms, a good way to pay off student loans and acquire some experience in law practice. To enter academia, however, even someone with a Supreme Court law clerk's credentials had to compile a portfolio of published or at least publishable legal writing to show to a faculty's hiring committee, a difficult task given the grueling schedule of an associate in a law firm. To help fill the junior faculty pipeline, Harvard, Yale, Columbia, Chicago, and other law schools established fellowships to give young lawyers time and resources to make the transition from law practice to legal academia.

In 1997, the conservative Olin Foundation, working with the Federalist Society, set up a fellowship program as a separate track for young conservative lawyers to prepare to enter the teaching market. The yearlong fellowship came with a stipend, an office at a law school, and ongoing feedback and support from the senior faculty members affiliated with the program. Acceptance, as with the other fellowship programs, was highly competitive. Steven Teles's book on the conservative legal movement includes a list of the first thirty-one Olin fellows, 1997 to 2006, all but ten of whom had found teaching positions by the time the book was published in 2008.

Amy Barrett received one of the Olin fellowships in 2001, following her clerkships and a subsequent two years as a law firm associate. She spent her fellowship year at George Washington University's law school. Harvard Law School graduates dominated the fellowship in its early years, accounting for nine of the first thirty-one. She stands out on the list as a graduate of Notre Dame. Nearly all the others were graduates of higher-ranked law schools, including Yale, Columbia, Chicago, and the Universities of Michigan and Virginia; legal academia is nothing if not elitist. As happened with her initial clerkship application to Judge Silberman, who ordinarily considered only applicants from the top law schools, people were happy to make exceptions for Amy Coney Barrett. When her fellowship year was over, she returned to South Bend. The Notre Dame law faculty that had sent her off to Washington as a favored graduate now embraced her as a colleague.

Her connection to the Federalist Society continued and deepened. She became a popular speaker at law school Fed Soc chapters around the country, during both her teaching years and her time on the Seventh Circuit. Harvard, the University of Michigan, Duke, Washington & Lee, Tulane, Stanford, and Indiana University in both Indianapolis and Bloomington were among the law school campuses she visited. She was, as she had been from the start, a Fed Soc star.

AMY BARRETT'S APPEARANCE on the Truman Balcony was the last the country would see of the new Supreme Court justice for many months. The court building had been closed to the public due to the COVID-19 pandemic since March. The justices no longer conducted their business in public, or even face-to-face behind closed doors. They heard cases over the telephone, without video, enabling Justice Ginsburg to take part in a day of arguments back in May from her room at the Johns Hopkins Hospital in Baltimore. The justices' twice-weekly private conferences, their communal lunches on argument days, all the normal attributes of court life were in suspension. Instead of assembling on the bench on decision days to announce their rulings to the public in person, the justices left it to the court clerk's office to post the opinions on www.supremecourt.gov, one at a time, at ten-minute intervals.

Invisible as she was, Justice Barrett's presence was palpable none-theless during the opening months of her tenure, before she had written a word. As cases arrived at the court from Trump allies trying to overturn the result of the presidential election, all eyes were on her, albeit virtually. When she provided a fifth vote in support of religious groups challenging COVID restrictions on in-person worship services, there could be no debate about the difference her arrival was making; when Justice Ginsburg was alive, a similar case just months earlier came out 5 to 4 the other way. Chief Justice Roberts had been in the majority then. Now he was a dissenter.

Almost exactly two years earlier, Roberts had delivered a highly unusual rebuke to President Trump after the president lashed out at an "Obama judge" who had ruled against him. "We do not have Obama judges or Trump judges, Bush judges or Clinton judges," the chief justice had said in a written statement that made headlines.

As the strange pandemic year of death and renewal came to an end, was John Roberts perhaps wondering whether that statement, uttered in such defiant confidence, was really still true? He was sixty-five years old, in his sixteenth year as chief justice of the United States, and he could anticipate another ten years at least, possibly fifteen or more. History had long since symbolically affixed his name to the door: the Roberts court. Could history change its mind? Was it just possible that historians of the future would judge this year to have been the dawn of the Trump court?

The chapters that follow, chronicling the life of the Supreme Court from July 2020 to July 2021, are an initial effort to answer that question.

JUSTICE ON THE BRINK

CHAPTER ONE

JULY · THE TRIUMPH OF JOHN ROBERTS

JUST AS BASEBALL FANS RELISH STATISTICS, so do Supreme Court watchers: how often a justice votes with the majority, how often in dissent, how often allied with this colleague or that one. With the numbers, a portrait takes shape to reveal a justice's power and role on the court. For Chief Justice Roberts, the portrait that emerged from the term that ended on July 9, 2020, was one of triumph.

Of the term's fifty-three cases decided with signed opinions—an unusually low number, due to the postponement of cases scheduled for argument early in the COVID-19 shutdown—he was in dissent in only two, fewer than any of his colleagues and his own record low for his fifteen years on the court. The easiest way to keep track of the court during the term's nine months was simply to look for John Roberts, finding him in the majority in decisions on presidential immunity, immigration policy, religion, abortion, protections for LGBTQ employees, and nearly everything else.

He managed at crucial moments to navigate across the court's ideological divide. He maintained the court's focus when the COVID-19 pandemic drove the justices from their chambers and their courtroom, leaving them to hear cases not on a fancy Internet platform but over their home telephones. And as important as anything else was this: Under a hot election-year spotlight, he kept the Supreme Court out of trouble. After the court handed down its last decisions on

July 9, two weeks later than usual, he was entitled to feel both relief and pride.

It might so easily have been otherwise, as he surely knew. Had the 2016 presidential election turned out as most people expected, a President Hillary Clinton would have filled the Scalia vacancy, and Roberts would have found himself facing the prospect of near irrelevance. Ruth Bader Ginsburg, as the senior justice among five liberals on the court, would have been able to shape the course of events, leaving the chief justice a bystander.

Of course, not every Supreme Court case turns on ideology. Most do not; during the term that included the 2016 election, the court decided more than half its cases unanimously. But when ideology matters, it matters greatly. The loss of a reliable conservative majority would have doomed two projects on which Roberts, with Scalia as a reliable ally, was making steady progress. Those two projects lay at the center of the national conversation, indeed at the heart of the country's struggle to define itself during the opening decades of the twenty-first century. One involved race, the other religion. Roberts's long-term plan was to change how the Constitution understood both, and now, with Donald Trump having filled the Scalia and Kennedy vacancies, he was in a position to achieve his goal.

There had not been a case concerning racial equality on the docket for the 2019–20 term, but that was an anomaly—a fortunate one for any chief justice interested in his court's keeping a low profile, given the urgent racial reckoning that shook the country following the police killing of George Floyd, an unarmed Black man, in Minneapolis on May 25. Race would certainly be back, and Roberts was ready, even though he might not have been aware that an important new Voting Rights Act case had arrived at the court in April, filed by Arizona Republicans seeking to limit the use of the Voting Rights Act of 1965 to attack measures that result in suppressing the vote. It would be early fall before the petition made its way to the justices for action.

The debate over public policy concerning race—voting rights and affirmative action, to which he referred, dismissively, as "racial balancing"—had drawn Roberts's interest since his earliest days as a lawyer. In 1981, direct from a Supreme Court clerkship, he had joined the Reagan administration, where he was an eager participant in the administration's program to dismantle or at least curtail race-conscious policies across the government and in the private sector as well. Serving first as a special assistant to Attorney General William French Smith and later as a lawyer in the White House counsel's office, he wrote strongly worded memos marshaling opposition to efforts under way in Congress to renew an expiring section of the 1965 Voting Rights Act and to restore another section that a 1980 Supreme Court decision had undercut. These internal memos came to light in 2005 when President George W. Bush nominated Roberts to be chief justice, and they provided what little substance there was to the Democrats' tepid opposition to his confirmation.

On becoming chief justice, John Roberts had moved quickly to convert his long-held views into law. A case known by the shorthand *Parents Involved* reached the court during his first term and presented just such an opportunity. Formerly segregated public school systems in Louisville and Seattle had emerged from years of federal court supervision after achieving what the courts deemed an acceptable level of racial integration. Each city was determined to protect that hard-won accomplishment from the demographic pressures of resegregation driven largely by housing patterns. Each had adopted student assignment plans that took a child's race into account in considering a request to attend or transfer to a particular school; if an application threatened to upset a school's racial mix, it would be denied. In each city, white parents whose requests had been denied brought a lawsuit claiming that their children were victims of racial discrimination.

These were not the first such lawsuits. All had failed, the lower courts accepting the argument that plans like these were justified as a way to prevent backsliding into racial isolation. Ordinarily, the Supreme Court agrees to hear only those cases that reflect disagreement among the lower courts, on the premise that only the Supreme Court can resolve a "conflict in the circuits" and provide a binding national rule. Despite the conspicuous absence of a conflict, the justices agreed to hear the appeals from the Louisville and Seattle parents, consolidating them for a single argument during the 2006–07 term on whether, even for the purpose of preserving integration, the overt consideration of race violated the Constitution's guarantee of equal protection. The court's answer, overturning two federal appeals courts, was that it did. The vote was 5 to 4.

Roberts assigned himself the majority opinion. Explaining why the student assignment plans were unconstitutional, he wrote that the school systems' interest in avoiding resegregation was not sufficiently "compelling" to justify a racially conscious remedy. The court's equal protection precedents provided that only a "compelling interest" could excuse a government policy that took race into account. To proclaim that a formerly segregated school system had no compelling interest in avoiding a return to racial isolation was a bold move, further than Roberts needed to go to justify his position. The court's precedents require that in addition to serving a compelling interest, a race-conscious policy must also be "narrowly tailored," that is, it can be no broader than necessary to accomplish the purpose. A government body that fails the narrow tailoring test can go back to the drawing board to achieve its goal by other means. But a finding of "no compelling interest" means that the goal itself is illegitimate.

Three of the conservative justices who had cast their votes with Roberts at the justices' private conference signed his opinion, but the fourth, Anthony Kennedy, refused. Of course "a compelling interest exists in avoiding racial isolation," Kennedy declared in his separate opinion. His view was that the case presented simply a narrow tailoring problem: The school systems should be required to try alternatives, such as redrawing school attendance zones, that did not require taking an individual student's race into account.

Roberts's refusal to concede the legitimacy of the school systems' goal had driven away a natural ally, a justice who in two decades on the court had never upheld a government policy that counted people by race. In losing Kennedy, he gave up the chance to speak for a majority; he "lost the court," as the expression goes when a justice starts out writing a majority opinion but ends up falling short. True, the court had invalidated the challenged assignment plans, but it did so in a way that failed to clarify, much less change, the law.

The mystery was why Roberts behaved as he had. Was he simply determined, no matter the cost, to lay down a marker for what he had long believed, that the government should basically get out of the race business? Or did he misjudge the dynamic of a court that he had known well as an advocate but where he was still a newcomer as a justice?

Roberts was certainly not alone in his dislike of policies that, in sorting people by race, conferred benefits on minorities at the expense of whites who had not personally been guilty of racial discrimination. That was one way of describing the question presented by a Supreme Court case that galvanized the country during Roberts's second year of law school. *Regents of the University of California v. Bakke* began as a lawsuit by a rejected white applicant to a new state medical school. The school had set aside sixteen of the one hundred places in the entering class for members of racial minorities. The school's goal was to do its part to counter the entrenched racial discrimination that for too long had prevented too many talented young Black people from pursuing careers in medicine. But the disappointed white applicant, Allan P. Bakke, argued that simply because of his race, he had been deprived of the chance to compete for every available seat in the class.

The Bakke case divided the country and split the Supreme Court quite literally in half. Four justices declared the racial quota to be unconstitutional and another four found it justified. The solitary and controlling opinion was written by Justice Lewis F. Powell, who said that the fixed quota was unconstitutional but that a university could take race into account through a less rigid admissions process in order to achieve the benefits of diversity.

The Bakke case was decided in June 1978. By the summer of 1980, when Roberts began his Supreme Court clerkship for William Rehnquist, who was then an associate justice, the debate over affirmative action, racial set-asides, and other race-conscious public policies was if anything more heated than ever. Rehnquist was firmly on the anti-affirmative-action side of this debate. The term before Roberts began his clerkship, Rehnquist had issued a stinging dissent from a decision that upheld a collective bargaining agreement in the steel industry that set aside for Black employees half the places in a special training program. *United Steelworkers of America v. Weber* was not a constitutional case. Rather, it required interpreting Title VII of the Civil Rights Act of 1964, which prohibits racial discrimination in employment. Ruling in a class action lawsuit brought on behalf of white steelworkers, the Supreme Court majority held that the broader purpose of Title VII was to attack the history of job discrimination, and that a program entered into by a voluntary agreement between the company and the labor union served that purpose by opening an avenue to advancement for Black workers who had been shut out of similar opportunities. Rehnquist denounced the majority opinion as a "tour de force" worthy of George Orwell's *1984* for taking language that meant one thing and giving it the opposite meaning.

The court had no major race-related case on its docket during Roberts's clerkship year. Whether his association with Rehnquist, who became a lifelong mentor, helped form his attitude toward race-conscious policies or simply reinforced them is unclear. But what is clear is that his ideas were very much in sync with those at the highest levels of the Reagan administration when he finished his clerkship and began his career as a lawyer.

WHILE A CHIEF justice automatically receives the privileges of seniority, Roberts was still very much the new man on the block by the time *Parents Involved* was decided in June 2007. Before his arrival in September 2005, there had not been a vacancy on the court since President Bill Clinton named Stephen Breyer to succeed Harry Blackmun in 1994. The intervening eleven years marked the longest period of membership stability on the court since the 1820s. After so much time together, the justices, while not exactly a family, understood one another and had achieved a level of comfort that comes from familiarity.

Roberts was sworn in on September 29, 2005, with the term set to begin on October 3. Such an abrupt arrival would have been awkward in any event, but there was an added factor: The members of the court were still mourning—genuinely mourning, not simply in the officially prescribed sense—the loss of Chief Justice William Rehnquist, who had died of thyroid cancer over the Labor Day weekend. In his public manner, Rehnquist came across as aloof and unapproachable. But his colleagues knew a different man, one who enjoyed practical jokes and musical theater, an amateur painter and would-be mystery writer who was scrupulously fair in distributing the court's workload. He was deeply conservative in his approach to the law; that was a given. But colleagues across the ideological spectrum held him in high esteem. Ruth Ginsburg, who referred to him fondly as "my chief," described him after his death as "the fairest, most efficient boss I ever had."

Had Rehnquist been alive to hear Ginsburg's appraisal, he would have appreciated its sly humor: The chief justice is most definitely not any justice's boss. His is one vote out of nine. The other justices, each confirmed by the Senate just as he was and also enjoying life tenure, decidedly do not work for him. The chief justice enjoys certain customary prerogatives, such as assigning the majority opinions in cases in which he is in the majority. But success in the role is at least as dependent on personality as it is on a formal job description.

At his death, Rehnquist was eighty years old and had served on the court for thirty-two years, becoming chief justice at almost the exact midpoint. John Roberts was fifty, the youngest chief justice since John Marshall. (It was evident just how relatively young he was when the senior associate justice, John Paul Stevens, administered the oath of office; Stevens was already on the court when Roberts had shown up twenty-five years earlier to clerk for then Associate Justice Rehnquist.)

In a sense, John Roberts was an accidental chief justice. President George W. Bush had named him to the D.C. Circuit just two years earlier. (The first President Bush had nominated him to the D.C. Circuit in 1992, at the unusually young age of thirty-seven, but the Democrats in the Senate blocked his confirmation.) In July 2005, the president nominated him to Justice Sandra Day O'Connor's associate justice seat after the court's first female justice surprised nearly everyone, including her own colleagues, with her decision to retire. Roberts had argued dozens of Supreme Court cases both as a deputy solicitor general in the Department of Justice and in private practice. A graduate of Harvard College, where he majored in history and graduated summa cum laude in three years, and of Harvard Law School, where he was managing editor of the law review, his academic credentials were impeccable. So too, for this particular Republican president, were his political credentials. During the contested aftermath of the 2000 presidential election, Roberts had gone to Florida to help the Bush legal team in the fight for the state's crucial electoral votes.

But while he was a natural choice for O'Connor's seat, his relative youth and limited judicial experience made him a less obvious candidate to be chief justice. The position might well not have gone to him had President Bush had more time to decide. But with Rehnquist dying so close to the start of the term, and with Roberts fully vetted and about to appear for what promised to be a trouble-free Senate confirmation hearing, the choice was easy. (The O'Connor seat went eventually to Samuel Alito.)

Roberts's performance before the Senate Judiciary Committee was a sure-handed crowd pleaser that set him on a path to confirmation by a vote of 78 to 22. His opening statement evoked a rural Midwestern upbringing, far from the Ivy League roots he would share with most of the justices who would soon be his colleagues. "I think all of us retain from the days of our youth certain enduring images," he told the senators. "For me those images are of the endless fields of Indiana stretching to the horizon, punctuated by an isolated silo or a barn."

No doubt the young John Roberts had seen such sights, perhaps on family drives through the countryside. But in fact, he and his three sisters grew up not on a farm but in an upscale and well-manicured Chicago suburb. His father was an executive at Bethlehem Steel, and there were many families like his in Long Beach, Indiana, then as now a nearly entirely white community. As recounted in Joan Biskupic's

2019 biography, *The Chief,* those who knew him recall him as a serious child and outstanding student.

Roberts was a familiar figure to the members of the court. Before becoming a judge, he had thrived in the elite ranks of the Supreme Court bar and was widely considered one of the best Supreme Court advocates of the day. In oral argument, his style was low-key, never showy, his untold hours of preparation enabling him to speak with ease and without notes. The justices appreciated his skill, and several offered public praise for his nomination. But they were slow to warm to him as a colleague, in part because change was hard after so many years of stability and because Roberts quickly assumed the role of chief justice rather than that of a deferential newcomer. And he perhaps had more to learn than he expected. One lesson, as the *Parents Involved* debacle demonstrated, was that goals are often better reached through indirection and over time than by direct and immediate confrontation.

Roberts took that lesson to heart and soon was able to apply it with great effectiveness. The year after *Parents Involved,* the question of the constitutionality of the Voting Rights Act of 1965, the same law at which the young John Roberts had taken aim during his Reagan administration days, reached the court. The act's Section 5 required jurisdictions with histories of obstructing minority voters to get federal approval before changing any election procedure. (The new case from Arizona that arrived on the court's docket in April 2020 concerned a different section of the law, Section 2, which has nationwide scope.) The formula that determined which states or parts of states would be covered by this "preclearance" requirement was contained in the act's Section 4. Most of the covered jurisdictions were in the South and were deeply resentful of what they regarded as federal overreach. Section 5 had originally been enacted as a temporary measure needing periodic renewal. Congress renewed it in 2006 by an overwhelming bipartisan vote for a period of twenty-five years.

A small Texas utility district challenged the preclearance requirement as beyond the scope of Congress's constitutional authority. It was the most serious challenge in decades to any of the nation's core civil rights statutes, and a major ruling was widely anticipated. But that was not what Roberts delivered in June 2009. Joined by seven other justices, he said there was no need to decide the constitutional question because the utility district appeared in any event to qualify for an exemption from Section 5. "The importance of the question does not justify our rushing to decide it," Roberts wrote.

His opinion was a short sixteen pages and appeared at first glance as a conventional application of a doctrine known as constitutional avoidance, under which the court refrains from deciding a constitutional question if a case can be resolved through statutory interpretation. But the opinion was in fact a rhetorically loaded invitation to other jurisdictions to bring a challenge to Section 5 that could not so easily escape review, and Roberts offered a strong hint of the court's receptivity to such a case. Yes, Section 5 had been useful, he wrote, but "things have changed in the south." Black citizens were no longer being kept from the polls. The regime of federal oversight that made sense in 1965 now looked outdated. The preclearance requirement, he warned, "imposes current burdens that must be justified by current needs."

Roberts's language, about as subtle as a billboard, raised the question why four liberal justices signed on without comment. It couldn't be that they failed to understand the chief justice's message. Perhaps they assumed, or hoped, that by the time the next case arrived, Congress would have taken the hint and revised the Section 4 formula to target only those jurisdictions whose questionable records were recent rather than long ago. More likely, seeing the writing on the wall, the liberal justices decided that quietly signing the opinion was their best option. The decision would at least buy some time.

Not surprisingly, the court's invitation proved irresistible. The plaintiff in the case that reached the court in 2012 was Shelby County, Alabama, and the outcome was predictable. This time, the vote was not 8 to 1 but 5 to 4. Roberts drove to the heart of the matter, picking up the precise language from his earlier opinion about burdens, current needs, and changes in the South. Congress's failure to update the statute doomed it, he wrote: "Our country has changed, and while any racial discrimination in voting is too much, Congress must ensure that the legislation it passes to remedy that problem speaks to current conditions." He delivered a stern lecture to Congress, reminding it that three years earlier, "we expressed our broader concern about the constitutionality of the Act." He continued: "Congress could have updated the coverage formula at that time, but did not do so. Its failure to act leaves us today with no choice."

Blame Congress, in other words, not the court. By invalidating the Section 4 formula, the decision as a technical matter left the iconic Section 5 intact. But everyone knew that the same political reality that had precluded any substantial updating of the formula for the past forty years would prevent any effort now. A crucial provision of the Voting Rights Act was, for all intents and purposes, a nullity. The court had killed it obliquely rather than directly, but it was still dead.

The decision, *Shelby County v. Holder*, provoked one of Ruth Bader Ginsburg's most powerful dissenting opinions. Speaking for herself and Justices Breyer, Sotomayor, and Kagan, she read her dissent from the bench to underscore the significance of what had occurred. Her opinion contained a long list of discriminatory voting practices that the preclearance process had intercepted very recently. "Throwing out preclearance when it has worked and is continuing to work," she said, "is like throwing away your umbrella in a rainstorm because you are not getting wet." Southern governors and legislatures responded quickly to the decision by reimposing practices that had been blocked and by enacting new ones, including extensive voter ID requirements. Things indeed had changed in the South, now once again free to suppress the votes of those whom the politicians in power did not care to see at the polls.

Roberts had learned his lesson well: Think big, but start small. Life tenure meant there was no need to rush. For a strategic justice, time was a reliable friend.

THE FRUITS OF that lesson were visible in Roberts's success in the 2019–20 term. The term's religion cases, in particular, demonstrated his progress on a long-range project, achieved by planting seeds that would in time take root and blossom. When it came to religion, the project involved reinterpreting—one might say weaponizing—the Constitution's Free Exercise Clause, turning it from its historic role as a shield that protected believers from government interference into a sword that vaulted believers into a position of privilege.

Throughout American constitutional history, there has been tension between the two religion clauses of the First Amendment, the Establishment Clause and the Free Exercise Clause. Broadly speaking, the Establishment Clause prevents the government from endorsing or (depending on the precedent) coercing a religious practice or viewpoint, while the Free Exercise Clause requires the government to leave believers free to practice their faith. What happens when a believer claims a right under the Free Exercise Clause that, if granted, would require the government to take action that the Establishment Clause would seem to forbid?

To Roberts's mentor, Chief Justice Rehnquist, it was incumbent on the court to find "room for play in the joints" between the two clauses. In one of Rehnquist's last major opinions, *Locke v. Davey*, the court considered a tuition scholarship program that the state of Washington had established for post-secondary education. The state, not wanting to spend public money on training people for religious office, deemed students studying for the ministry to be ineligible for the scholarship. A ministerial student claimed that the Free Exercise Clause required his inclusion in the program. The court said no. Rehnquist explained that while the Establishment Clause would permit the state to subsidize ministerial study if it chose, the Free Exercise Clause could not be interpreted to require the state to do so.

That 2004 opinion exemplified Rehnquist's "play in the joints." But with conservative religion on the march in the ensuing decade, his compromise-infused construct had come to look like an artifact from a simpler age. The structure was unstable, the joints weak. Roberts would weaken them further.

As with the voting rights case, he proceeded in two steps. The first step came in late 2015, when an appeal arrived from Trinity Lutheran

Church in Columbia, Missouri. Out of context, the facts made the case look trivial. Missouri awarded grants for rehabilitating playground surfaces using scrap rubber from old tires. Cash for the program was limited, and schools had to submit applications. Because the Missouri constitution prohibited directing state money to religious schools, the state refused to consider Trinity Lutheran's application for a grant to resurface its nursery school playground. The lower courts, analogizing the church's position to that of the ministerial student in *Locke v. Davey*, rejected its Free Exercise Clause argument.

The Supreme Court ruled for the church. In his majority opinion, Roberts said the lower courts' reliance on *Locke v. Davey* was misplaced. "Davey was not denied a scholarship because of who he *was*," Roberts wrote. "He was denied a scholarship because of what he proposed to *do*—use the funds to prepare for the ministry. Here, there is no question that Trinity Lutheran was denied a grant simply because of what it is—a church." Missouri was in effect demanding that the church "renounce its religious character" in order to qualify for a grant, Roberts said: "The exclusion of Trinity Lutheran from a public benefit for which it is otherwise qualified, solely because it is a church, is odious to our Constitution."

The vote was 7 to 2, leaving only Sonia Sotomayor, joined by Justice Ginsburg, to object:

> To hear the Court tell it, this is a simple case about recycling tires to resurface a playground. The stakes are higher. This case is about nothing less than the relationship between religious institutions and the civil government—that is, between church and state. The Court today profoundly changes that relationship by holding, for the first time, that the Constitution requires the government to provide public funds directly to a church. Its decision slights both our precedents and our history, and its reasoning weakens this country's longstanding commitment to a separation of church and state beneficial to both.

How could the other two liberal justices, Kagan and Breyer, not have seen this case as Sotomayor and Ginsburg saw it? Perhaps Roberts mollified them with the unusual footnote he added to his opinion: "This case involves express discrimination based on religious identity with respect to playground resurfacing. We do not address religious uses of funding or other forms of discrimination."

Really? The Supreme Court was invoking high constitutional principle simply in the service of playground resurfacing? Justices Gorsuch and Thomas wouldn't buy it. Perhaps the footnote might lead the public to assume the decision was limited to playgrounds or, more broadly, to children's health and safety, but "such a reading would be unreasonable, for our cases are 'governed by general principles, rather than ad hoc improvisations,'" Gorsuch wrote. His quotation was from a Rehnquist opinion, clearly intended to tweak Roberts. "And the general principles here," Gorsuch went on, "do not permit discrimination against religious exercise—whether on the playground or anywhere else."

Roberts found his opportunity to put the *Trinity Lutheran* decision to work in the 2019–20 term. The new case was from Montana, which like Washington State in *Locke v. Davey* and Missouri in *Trinity Lutheran* had carved religion out from a general benefit program. In this instance, it was a tax credit that parents could use for private school tuition. Montana's constitution, like that of many other states, had a "no aid" provision that prohibited "any direct or indirect appropriation or payment" of public funds to religious schools. For that reason, the Montana Department of Revenue ruled that the tax credit could not be used for religious school tuition. The state supreme court upheld that ruling, and then went further. On the ground that there was no way effectively to police how parents would use the benefit, it invalidated the entire program, for religious and secular private schools alike.

The Institute for Justice, representing families who wanted to use the tax credit for their children's religious school tuition, appealed to the U.S. Supreme Court. The institute is a libertarian organization with an active docket of cases, long a leader in the campaign for publicly funded vouchers that parents can use for tuition at nonpublic schools. Its interest is not in religious education as such, but in nonpublic education of any kind. The Institute for Justice had won a major Supreme Court victory in 2002 when the court held that it did not violate the Establishment Clause to allow publicly financed vouchers to be used for parochial school tuition. The court had been bitterly divided on the question, with four justices in dissent. The law, however, was now clear. But the Montana case went further. It presented the precise "play in the joints" question that Rehnquist had anticipated: Given that the Establishment Clause *permitted* indirect public subsidy of religious schools, did the Free Exercise Clause *require* it?

Yes, it did, the court now ruled in *Espinoza v. Montana Department of Revenue*. The vote was 5 to 4. Roberts faced two obstacles in writing an opinion on behalf of the religious school parents. The first was that, with the program shut down for all schools, it was hard to point to discrimination of the kind he had found "odious" in *Trinity Lutheran*. Roberts probed beneath the surface of the apparent nondiscrimination. The state court's "error of federal law," he said, was failing to recognize that the Montana constitution's "no aid" provision itself violated the Free Exercise Clause; the tax credit should not have been withheld from the religious schools in the first place.

Roberts's second challenge was the odd footnote in the *Trinity Lutheran* case. Taken at face value, it appeared to limit that decision to discrimination in state funding for resurfacing playgrounds with old tires. No, Roberts said, what the footnote actually did was disavow a ruling on the "religious uses of funding," and the Montana case was perfectly consistent with that. Just like *Trinity Lutheran*, this case presented a question of "status" and not of "use"; the religious schools were being disqualified because of their identity as religious schools, not because of anything they would be doing with the state's money. "A state need not subsidize private education," Roberts wrote. "But once a state decides to do so, it cannot disqualify some private schools simply because they are religious."

The four dissenters challenged the logic of Roberts's argument. Of course the issue was more than just "status," Breyer argued. It was religious "use" just as it had been in *Locke v. Davey*, where the question was not the ministerial student's identity but the use to which he wanted to put the state scholarship. Breyer pointed out that nearly all the private schools in Montana were religious schools, and that in 2018, the program's last year, 94 percent of the scholarship money had gone to religious school tuition. The whole purpose of religious education was to transmit the faith to the next generation, he observed: "And the upshot is that here, as in *Locke*, we confront a state's decision not to fund the inculcation of religious truths."

Certainly the five justices in the majority, all of whom had Catholic upbringings and four of whom had attended Catholic secondary schools, could understand Breyer's point. Roberts himself was a graduate of a small all-boys Catholic boarding school, La Lumiere, in La Porte, Indiana, where attendance at daily chapel and Sunday mass was required. That the majority in the Montana case consisted of five Catholics while the dissent comprised three Jews (Ginsburg, Breyer, and Kagan) and a nonpracticing Catholic (Sotomayor) was surely noteworthy. Yet following the decision on the last day of June 2020, there was an almost complete absence of public comment on the court's glaring religious divide. Gender, race, ethnicity, sexual orientation—all were now fair game in discourse about public figures. Religion, as Senator Feinstein had learned when she tripped on the subject during Amy Coney Barrett's first confirmation hearing, remained the last taboo.

HOW HAD THERE come to be a majority of Catholics on the U.S. Supreme Court? Just as the court had been all-white and all-male for most of its history, so too had it been almost all-Protestant, a fact long accepted without question or even much attention. The first Catholic justice was Chief Justice Roger Taney in 1836. Following his death in 1864, there was a gap of thirty years, but beginning in the twentieth century, there was always at least one Catholic on the court. Sometimes there were two, along with the occasional Jew. (The first Jewish justice was Louis Brandeis in 1916; there were no Jews on the court during the twenty-four years between Abe Fortas's departure in 1969 and Ruth Bader Ginsburg's arrival in 1993). The pattern of solitary

Catholic justices changed dramatically in the mid-1980s. Eight of the fifteen Catholic justices ever to serve have been appointed since then, beginning with Ronald Reagan's appointment of Antonin Scalia in 1986. Seven of the eight—all but Sotomayor—were named by Republican presidents.

A hypothetical feel-good explanation for the evolution of a Catholic Supreme Court might be that the prejudice that once limited Catholics' participation in public life had disappeared by the 1980s. The actual explanation is more political and more cynical, summarized in one word: abortion. Beginning with the Republican Party platform that Ronald Reagan ran on in 1980, and continuing until the party's failure in 2020 to adopt any platform, the Republican Party pledged itself and its presidential candidates to, as the 1980 platform put it, "work for the appointment of judges at all levels of the judiciary who respect traditional family values and the sanctity of human life." In other words, a president's duty was to appoint judges who would overturn *Roe v. Wade*. Even in an era that has seen the shredding of so many norms, a president still cannot probe a potential Supreme Court nominee for a commitment to that goal. Catholicism became a proxy for the answer a nominee couldn't give to the question a president couldn't ask.

The impact of this transformation has been dramatic. After the 2019–20 term ended, two law professors, Lee Epstein of Washington University in St. Louis and Eric Posner of the University of Chicago, traced the court's handling of religion cases since the mid-twentieth century. From the start of the Warren court in 1953 until the end of the Rehnquist court in 2005, individuals claiming a religious right prevailed about half the time. There was little difference during this period between justices appointed by Republican presidents, who ruled for the religious claim 56 percent of the time, and those appointed by Democrats, at 47 percent.

But since the advent of the Roberts court, religious claims have prevailed nearly 90 percent of the time, and the voting patterns of the court's Republican- and Democratic-appointed justices have diverged sharply. "Of all the justices who have sat on cases since 1953," Epstein and Posner wrote in a *New York Times* op-ed describing their findings, "those who voted most often for the religious side belonged to the current conservative bloc on the court: Brett Kavanaugh (100 percent), Neil Gorsuch (100 percent), Clarence Thomas (94 percent), John Roberts (93 percent) and Samuel Alito (93 percent)." Support among the liberal justices for the religious claim varied from a high of 73 percent for Elena Kagan to Ruth Ginsburg's 21 percent. "The Roberts court has been the most polarized on religious issues in the seven decades, and probably ever," the authors concluded.

Of the term's three religion cases, *Espinoza v. Montana Department of Revenue* was the only one that Roberts chose to write for himself. He assigned Alito to write the opinion of a case on whether religious institutions were bound by the nation's laws that prohibit discrimination in employment. The court had already ruled that churches and other religious employers were entitled to claim a "ministerial exception" from laws that generally apply in the nation's workplaces. But the scope of that exception, first addressed in an opinion Roberts had written in 2012, was unclear. As was so often the case, that seemingly narrow Roberts opinion would prove a launching pad for a later, more far-reaching ruling.

The phrase "ministerial exception" appears nowhere in federal law. It was an invention of lower court judges over a number of years as cases reached the federal courts from employees of churches and religious schools who were asserting their rights under the federal laws that prohibit employment discrimination on the basis of race, sex, age, and disability. The lower courts reasoned that under the Free Exercise Clause, houses of worship had to be free to choose their clergy, while under the Establishment Clause, the government could not interfere with internal church governance. Under this analysis, the religion clauses were not in tension; they both pointed in the same direction.

In 2012, the Supreme Court endorsed this reasoning and applied it to reject the disability claim of a fourth grade teacher at a Lutheran school who lost her job following a long-term medical leave. She had taught both a general fourth grade curriculum and a religion class, and she led students in daily prayer. Although she was not ordained, the school held her out as a minister; she had received specialized religious training, and in Lutheran terms she was a "called" teacher, entitled to a "diploma of vocation."

Roberts assigned himself the opinion. "The church must be free to choose those who will guide it on its way" is how he explained the court's conclusion. He framed the decision in *Hosanna-Tabor Evangelical Lutheran Church and School v. Equal Employment Opportunity Commission* as a narrow one, emphasizing the teacher's quasi-ministerial status. "Today we hold only that the ministerial exception bars such a suit," he wrote. "There will be time enough to address the applicability of the exception to other circumstances if and when they arise." That assurance undoubtedly went far in accounting for the fact that the decision was unanimous.

But how narrow was it really? What did Roberts mean by declaring that "the church must be free"? What was the reference to "the church" doing in a case presented as a dispute between a particular church and one of its employees? Winnifred Fallers Sullivan, a scholar of law and religion at Indiana University, asked those questions in a critical analysis of the *Hosanna-Tabor* decision in her book *Church State Corporation* (University of Chicago Press, 2020). Not surprisingly, the Constitution makes no reference to "church," Sullivan observed; a country founded on the notion of disestablishment had no "church" to refer to. "How precisely does a disestablished church still have a legal public existence?" she asked. And how does the court justify giving priority to the rights of the "legal fiction of the church" over the statutory rights of individuals?

Those questions went unanswered during the eight years it took for the ministerial exception to return to the court. There were two cases, consolidated for one opinion under the caption *Our Lady of Guadalupe School v. Morrissey-Berru*. Each case was brought by an elementary school teacher at a Catholic school, two different schools in the Los Angeles area. One plaintiff, who was in her sixties when the school refused to renew her contract, sued for age discrimination. The other claimed disability discrimination when she was dismissed after informing the school that she would need time off for treatment for breast cancer. Neither had religious training. They taught a general curriculum plus a religion class that they taught from a prescribed workbook. The federal appeals court in Los Angeles compared the teachers' credentials and role with those of the teacher in the *Hosanna-Tabor* case. Finding no basis for concluding that the teachers were serving a ministerial function, it refused to consider *Hosanna-Tabor* a relevant precedent. The teachers were entitled to proceed with their claims.

That was a mistake, the Supreme Court held. Roberts assigned the opinion to Alito. These teachers, like the teacher in *Hosanna-Tabor*, were "entrusted with the responsibility of instructing their students in the faith," Alito wrote. It was their function that mattered, not their lack of religious credentials and titles. *Hosanna-Tabor* applied in full to shield the schools from the teachers' lawsuits. In his opinion, Alito observed that "the religious education and formation of students is the very reason for the existence of most private religious schools." This was a surprising observation, given that in the Montana case the previous week, the court had disclaimed any relevance for what actually went on inside a religious school.

The vote was 7 to 2, with only Justices Sotomayor and Ginsburg in dissent. Sotomayor's opinion accused the majority of "rewriting *Hosanna-Tabor*." The court had "traded legal analysis for a rubber stamp," she said, allowing religious schools "to discriminate widely and with impunity for reasons wholly divorced from religious beliefs." More than one hundred thousand secular teachers at religious schools were now stripped of their statutory protection against employment discrimination, Sotomayor noted.

The new decision not only failed to answer the questions raised eight years earlier by Roberts's opinion in *Hosanna-Tabor*, it amplified them, walling off from the reach of civil law an ever-expanding domain where religion prevailed and where the cost to individuals went unacknowledged. So it was, too, in the third of the term's religion cases.

Little Sisters of the Poor v. Pennsylvania was the final chapter in a dispute that had been raging since soon after passage of the Affordable Care Act in 2010. That law, and the regulations the Obama administration issued to implement it, required employers to provide group health policies that included, without a co-pay, all federally approved contraceptives. The regulations exempted churches themselves from the requirement, but not nonprofit religious organizations. Those were offered an accommodation: At their request, their insurers would remove contraception from the employer's plan and provide the coverage directly to the employees, without the employer's further involvement.

In the *Hobby Lobby* case in 2014, the Supreme Court ruled by a 5-to-4 vote that the administration had to make a similar accommodation available to closely held for-profit corporations owned by individuals with religious objections to birth control. Hobby Lobby itself was a national chain of craft stores with some one thousand employees. In his majority opinion, Justice Alito offered the reassurance that female employees would still get their cost-free contraceptives and that the burden on women "would be precisely zero." If there was a basis for his certainty, he did not reveal it.

The religious nonprofits, meanwhile, found inadequate the very accommodation that the court in the *Hobby Lobby* case held up as a standard for how to respect religious objections to the contraception mandate. What the religious nonprofits wanted was nothing less than a complete exemption. Their complaint was based on the religious concept of complicity: that the act of telling their insurers that they wanted the coverage dropped would simply shift the source of the coverage but wouldn't free them from complicity in the sin of having facilitated their employees' use of birth control. Mobilized by religious right litigating organizations, including most prominently the Becket Fund for Religious Liberty, dozens of religiously affiliated colleges, nursing homes, and other nonprofits brought lawsuits in courts around the country. By the spring of 2016, when a consolidated group of seven of these cases was ready for the Supreme Court to decide, Justice Scalia had died and the eight remaining justices were unable to reach a decision. Instead, in an unusual and unanimous ruling, the court sent the cases back to the lower courts and told the two sides to work out a compromise.

The religious groups would not move from their position that even saying no was too much to ask of them. By the time Donald Trump became president, it was clear that no compromise was possible. In short order, his administration issued new rules, offering a complete opt-out to even publicly traded companies that claimed either a religious or an undefined "moral" objection to contraception. Federal appeals courts on both coasts blocked the new rules, finding them invalid under basic principles of administrative law. As the case reached the Supreme Court in the 2019–20 term, religion as such had been reduced to a subtext. It was now an administrative law case. Had the administration followed the correct procedures in issuing the new rules? Had it provided an adequate explanation when it supplanted the previous precisely drawn regulations with its broad-brush exemptions?

Administrative law is the bread and butter of the Supreme Court's docket: whether federal agencies are acting within their authority, whether they have solicited and been attentive to public input, whether they have explained themselves adequately. Administrative law is where the citizen meets the government. It was one of Ruth Ginsburg's specialties, and she liked to quote a line from Felix Frankfurter's opinion in a case from 1943: "The history of liberty has largely been the history of observance of procedural safeguards." The cases are often important without capturing the attention of a broad public. There are exceptions. One, in the previous term, concerned whether the president had properly added a citizenship question to the 2020 census. Roberts had written an opinion shutting down the plan on the ground that the administration had not been truthful about its motive. "The evidence tells a story that does not match the explanation," he wrote.

And now there was another exception. People noticed the contraception case, thanks in part to its framing by the energetic public relations team at the Becket Fund for Religious Liberty. The fund's client was an order of nuns with a perfect name for the publicity campaign that enveloped the case: the Little Sisters of the Poor. The order ran nursing homes that served the elderly poor, imposing no religious test for employment. It had been one of the original plaintiffs that challenged the Obama accommodation for religious nonprofits. In this phase of the case, it was allied with the Trump administration in defending the full exemption that the Trump rules had granted.

The real-world issues in the case were obvious despite its packaging as an administrative law case. Would the court ignore the promise Alito had made in the *Hobby Lobby* case and permit the nuns' attenuated complicity claim to deprive the women in their diverse workforce of a health benefit to which they were entitled?

The Becket Fund understandably kept the public focus on the nuns, not their female employees. Its press strategy portrayed the nuns as victims, as unwilling conscripts in a government-sponsored contraception master plan. "The federal government doesn't need nuns to help it distribute contraception," said one press release distributed on the eve of the Supreme Court argument in May. Of course, the Obama administration had not required the nuns to "help" in any normal sense of that word; the whole point of the accommodation was to make sure that religious employers did not have to "help," that all they had to do was inform their insurers that they didn't want to do anything. That was a point easily lost. On the morning of the argument, the Becket Fund's Facebook page featured a virtual rally for the Little Sisters that invited people to join the nuns in praying the rosary.

Clarence Thomas's opinion upholding the Trump rules was a fairly conventional voyage through the administrative law thicket. The rules were "free from procedural defects," he concluded. As a rallying cry, that left quite a bit to be desired, so on the last of the opinion's twenty-six pages, Thomas made sure that the narrative that had been constructed for the Little Sisters would live permanently in the pages of United States Reports, the official compendium of Supreme Court decisions. It was regrettable, Thomas said, that the Little Sisters, "like many other religious objectors, have had to fight for the ability to continue in their noble work without violating their sincerely held religious beliefs."

The vote was 7 to 2, although Thomas's opinion spoke for only five. Justices Kagan and Breyer declined to sign. In a separate opinion, they wrote that although the Trump rules had now cleared one hurdle, an outcome they agreed with, administrative law offered other lines of attack, to be explored in other cases that were still pending in the lower courts. The two justices' distaste for the rules was clear, and they sought in their opinion to provide a road map for the ongoing litigation.

It was left to Ruth Ginsburg, in a dissenting opinion that Justice Sotomayor joined, to speak for the women who would be affected by the ruling. "Today, for the first time," she wrote, "the court casts totally aside countervailing rights and interests in its zeal to secure religious rights to the nth degree." The date was July 8. It was to be her final published opinion.

WHEN THE COURT heard telephonic argument in the *Little Sisters* case, Ginsburg had dialed in from her hospital room. Whether she suspected that the term might be her last, she and the other justices knew that the *Little Sisters* case and the other religion cases of the term would in no sense be the court's last word. In February, the court had agreed to hear a case from Philadelphia on whether the Free Exercise Clause entitled a Catholic social service agency to keep its contract with the city while defying an ordinance that barred city contractors from discriminating on the basis of sexual orientation. Catholic Social Services, a private nonprofit organization, received millions of dollars from Philadelphia to recruit and screen potential foster parents for children in the city's care. After Philadelphia learned that the agency was refusing to consider placements with same-sex couples, the city declined to renew its contract. The agency sued and lost in the lower courts.

Fulton v. City of Philadelphia was another Becket Fund case. The fund brought the case in the name of three "heroic foster moms," as its press release described the women who had served as foster parents for multiple children placed by Catholic Social Services and who wanted to continue in that role. The question the case raised was a deep and familiar one: When does religion provide an off-ramp from a law intended to apply to everyone? The court would schedule argument in the fall.

The three religion cases fitted neatly into the chief justice's long-term project. But the court's lone abortion case assuredly did not. The case that arrived on the court's docket in early 2019 was not one that he had been looking for. Although he was less outspoken than Scalia had been or than Thomas still was, Roberts's dissatisfaction with the court's abortion jurisprudence was obvious. He dissented in 2016 from a decision that struck down a Texas law requiring doctors who performed abortions to have admitting privileges at a nearby hospital. While Texas had defended the measure as protective of women's health, expert testimony at trial showed that the requirement imposed an unnecessary burden that, far from protecting women's heath, would result in closing perhaps half the abortion clinics in Texas. In his majority opinion in *Whole Woman's Health v. Hellerstedt*, Justice Breyer weighed the law's nonexistent "benefit" to women's health against the limits it placed on women's access to abortion. This balancing exercise showed the law to impose an "undue burden," Justice Breyer said, making it unconstitutional within the meaning of *Planned Parenthood of Southeastern Pennsylvania v. Casey*, the court's 1992 precedent that established the "undue burden" standard as the test of an abortion restriction's constitutionality.

Like Texas and other states with antiabortion legislative majorities, Louisiana had also imposed an admitting privileges requirement, which a federal district court had declared unconstitutional shortly before the Supreme Court's decision in the Texas case. Although the two laws were identical, meaning that Louisiana's law was just as unconstitutional as the Texas law, Louisiana continued to defend its law in the United States Court of Appeals for the Fifth Circuit. That court, which sits in New Orleans, covers both Louisiana and Texas. Its decision upholding the Texas law had just been overturned by the Supreme Court in *Whole Woman's Health*.

Nonetheless, the Fifth Circuit, long one of the most conservative of the thirteen federal appeals courts, proceeded to uphold the identi-

cal Louisiana law. It did so on the basis of a largely fictional narrative
about differences between the two states and the purported lack of
energy the Louisiana doctors had shown in seeking admitting privileges. (One of the doctors had been trying for five years, and others
for many months, without success, as Judge John deGravelles, the
federal district judge who presided over a six-day trial, chronicled in
his opinion invalidating the law. Judge deGravelles called the law "an
inapt remedy for a problem that does not exist." The Fifth Circuit
panel overturned the district court opinion without explaining why it
was ignoring the trial judge's findings.)

The only way to process the Fifth Circuit's decision was as a shocking act of defiance by a federal appeals court. Roberts understood that
no matter what he thought about abortion in general or *Whole Woman's Health* in particular, he could not allow the Fifth Circuit to get
away with thumbing its nose at the Supreme Court. The case first
arrived at the Supreme Court in early 2019 as an emergency request
by the June Medical abortion clinic for a temporary stay of the Fifth
Circuit decision to give the clinic time to prepare its Supreme Court
appeal. Without the stay, the clinic asserted, there would be a single
doctor legally entitled to perform abortions left in all of Louisiana. A
stay requires five votes, not the usual four required to grant a case for
review. The vote in *Whole Woman's Health*, with Scalia's seat still unfilled, had been 5 to 3, with Kennedy joining the liberal justices. Now,
with Kennedy gone, the four liberals alone could not stop the Louisiana law from taking effect.

Roberts joined them. He could hardly have done otherwise. It
would have been unthinkable for the chief justice of the United States
to permit a defiant lower court ruling to take effect before the Supreme Court even had the chance to review it. Four justices dissented:
Thomas and Alito, who like Roberts had dissented in *Whole Woman's
Health*, and the two new justices, Gorsuch and Kavanaugh. By the
time *June Medical Services v. Russo* was argued in March 2020, the stay
had been in effect for more than a year.

Roberts's vote to grant the stay was not a commitment to a position
on the merits. He needed to find a way to thread the needle: to re-

mind the Fifth Circuit of its place in the judicial hierarchy without personally embracing the very precedent he would criticize the appeals court for defying. He met that challenge by providing a fifth vote to overturn the Fifth Circuit while not signing the opinion in which Breyer, who had written the majority opinion in *Whole Woman's Health* four years earlier, applied not only the holding but the analysis he had used in that case. Roberts's separate opinion now relegated Breyer to speaking for a plurality.

In his opinion concurring only "in the judgment," Roberts made clear that he was not retreating from his dissent from *Whole Woman's Health*. This made his invocation of stare decisis, the rule of standing by precedent, more than a little puzzling. "The legal doctrine of *stare decisis* requires us, absent special circumstances, to treat like cases alike," he said by way of explanation for his vote. "The Louisiana law imposes a burden on access to abortion just as severe as that imposed by the Texas law, for the same reasons. Therefore Louisiana's law cannot stand under our precedents."

Roberts could have stopped there. That he went further into a lengthy critique of Breyer's opinions in both *Whole Woman's Health* and *June Medical* placed his deep unease with the court's abortion jurisprudence in sharp relief. Breyer had constructed *Whole Woman's Health* as an explication of the "undue burden" standard the court had adopted for evaluating restrictions on access to abortion in the *Casey* decision in 1992. While that decision had preserved the constitutional right to abortion, it had left important questions unanswered, including how a court would be able to tell whether a particular burden was "undue." One way, Breyer wrote in *Whole Woman's Health*, was to weigh a regulation's asserted benefit against the burden it imposed. If the benefit was slight and the burden onerous, the regulation imposed an undue burden. It came down to a question of context and proportionality. Because abortions almost never required hospitalization, the benefit to women's welfare of the admitting privileges requirement was negligible. And because hospital credentialing committees were reluctant to grant privileges to doctors who performed abortions, the burden was substantial: It would close clinics. The Texas

and Louisiana laws thus imposed an undue burden and were unconstitutional.

Roberts objected to the weighing of benefits and burdens. How
could a court appraise the supposed benefit from an abortion restriction? he asked. "There is no plausible sense in which anyone, let alone
this court, could objectively assign weight to such imponderable values," he wrote. "Pretending that we could pull that off would require
us to act as legislators, not judges." His complaint seemed founded in
a misunderstanding of how the majority in *Whole Woman's Health* had
analyzed the problem. Stephen Breyer, the empiricist among the justices, was not evaluating "imponderables." Rather, he took at face
value that state's claim that it had enacted the regulation for the sake
of protecting women's health, and he examined that claim in light of
evidence on the safety of abortion, the rarity of complications requiring hospitalization, and the fact that any woman requiring hospital
treatment would receive care regardless of whether the doctor who
performed the abortion had admitting privileges.

Roberts insisted that the only factor courts should examine was
whether a challenged regulation imposed a "substantial burden" on
women's access to abortion, not whether the state's rationale held up.
It was at least possible to interpret his language as authorizing, or
perhaps inviting, courts to shrug off even a demonstrably specious
rationale for restricting abortion. "Burden" then became an absolute
rather than relative term. If women had to wait longer, travel farther,
navigate bureaucratic obstacles in order to exercise their constitutional right to terminate a pregnancy—well, if at the end of the day
they got their abortion, by what measure could a court deem the burden undue if it was precluded from inquiring into the state's reasons
for constructing the obstacle course? And if reasons were irrelevant,
didn't that mean that any reason would do? "Any reason" implied the
most minimal level of constitutional scrutiny, known as "rational
basis" review, and in *Roe v. Wade* and ever since, the court had always
demanded more.

There was considerable ambiguity in Roberts's sixteen-page separate opinion, enough to lead some lower court judges to declare that

because *Whole Woman's Health* evidently no longer commanded a majority of the Supreme Court, it was no longer binding. Other judges argued that, to the contrary, a Supreme Court decision always remains binding precedent until the Supreme Court says otherwise. And so the question lingered in the air as the term came to an end: When the next abortion case arrived, or the case after that, would the court indeed, as so many had hoped and so many others feared, at last say otherwise?

A BLOCKBUSTER TURN TO THE CENTER LED BY A CHIEF JUSTICE AT CENTER STAGE was the headline *The New York Times* gave to the article by its Supreme Court correspondent, Adam Liptak, wrapping up the term. The theme echoed across the mainstream media: that a court on which Donald Trump had placed two justices had, thanks to the chief justice, not veered sharply to the right. The court had not permitted the president to shield his financial records from inquiry by a New York City prosecutor. It had not permitted Trump to erase the Obama administration's protections for the "Dreamers," young unauthorized immigrants who had been brought to the country as children. Surprising many, it had interpreted the major federal civil rights statute that prohibits sex discrimination in employment to extend to gay, lesbian, and transgender employees.

Neil Gorsuch wrote that opinion for a 6-to-3 majority. An avowed "textualist" when it came to interpreting statutes, Gorsuch believed that the language of a law was all that mattered. In enacting Title VII of the Civil Rights Act of 1964, Congress had prohibited discrimination on account of sex. "An employer who fires an individual for being homosexual or transgender fires that person for traits or actions it would not have questioned in members of a different sex," he wrote. "Sex plays a necessary and undisguisable role in the decision, exactly what Title VII forbids." That the drafter of Title VII would most likely not have expected this outcome made no difference, Gorsuch insisted: "But the limits of the drafters' imagination supply no reason to ignore the law's demands. When the express terms of a statute give us one answer and extratextual considerations suggest another, it's no contest. Only the written word is law, and all persons are entitled to its benefit."

The decision, and the fact that Gorsuch had written for the majority, shocked the political right. "An alien appears to have occupied the body of Justice Neil Gorsuch as he wrote Monday's opinion in *Bostock v. Clayton County*," a *Wall Street Journal* editorial began. (Trump's other appointee, Brett Kavanaugh, dissented, as did Thomas and Alito.) That was just the beginning of the conservative outcry that peaked as the term came to an end. A senator from Missouri, Josh Hawley, who had clerked for Roberts during the 2007–08 term, gave a speech on the Senate floor that he then published under the title "Was It All for This? The Failure of the Conservative Legal Movement." In the speech, Hawley—not yet as well known as he would become six months later for his effort to overturn the result of the presidential election—took aim at the *Bostock* decision, which he derided as "a piece of legislation" undeserving of the textualist label. Hawley's real theme was what he saw as the consequence of the decision for those with religious objections to equal treatment for LGBT individuals. His speech was a dirge about the fate of religious conservatives on the public stage:

> The bargain has never been explicitly articulated, but religious conservatives know what it is. The bargain is that you go along with the party establishment, you support their policies and priorities—or at least keep your mouth shut about it—and, in return, the establishment will put some judges on the bench who supposedly will protect your constitutional rights to freedom of worship, to freedom of exercise. That's what we've been told for years now. . . . I question how judges who hold to this philosophy ended up on the bench. I question the bargain that people of faith have been asked to hold to for all of these years.

Gorsuch, completing his third term on the court, may not have been accustomed to criticism of this sort from the right. John Roberts certainly was. His votes upholding the Affordable Care Act in 2012 and 2015 provoked attacks that bordered on the vicious. During the 2016 presidential campaign, Donald Trump called him a "disaster" and a "disgrace." After the term ended, Vice President Mike Pence called him merely "a disappointment to conservatives." The theme from the right this time was that Roberts had abandoned conservative principles in a "self-defeating attempt to make the court appear non-political," the conservative Harvard law professor Adrian Vermeule and Varad Mehta, a cultural historian, wrote in *The Washington Post*.

Inside the court, carping was directed at Roberts from the conservative justices. Although the justices became invisible to the public after the court closed its building in March, published dissents from the conservatives left a paper trail of bitterness. One particular sore point concerned guns. Since the *Heller* decision in 2008 reinterpreted the Second Amendment as protecting the individual right to keep a handgun at home for self-defense, the court had declined to elaborate further. What about guns outside the home, carried openly or concealed? What about crossing state lines with a lawfully owned firearm? The court regularly refused to grant Second Amendment cases, to the mounting frustration of Justices Thomas and Alito, who complained regularly that the court was turning the Second Amendment into a "second-class right."

Finally, the court had agreed to hear a Second Amendment case, one that looked like an easy winner for the pro-gun side. It was a challenge to a New York City ordinance that prohibited licensed gun owners from taking their weapons outside the city to a shooting range or a second home. Although the city had succeeded in defending the ordinance in the lower courts, the Supreme Court was clearly hostile territory, and an adverse decision could well go further than invalidating a single quirky local law. So after the justices agreed to hear the New York State Rifle & Pistol Association's appeal, the city repealed the ordinance, rendering the case moot.

At least, that was the city's obvious intent, but Justices Thomas, Alito, and Gorsuch did not want to let the case go. It was simply too inviting a vehicle. After extensive briefing on the mootness issue, the justices heard argument in December 2019. It wasn't until late April that the court issued a two-page unsigned opinion declaring the case moot, accompanied by Alito's thirty-one-page dissenting opinion. Joined by Thomas and Gorsuch, he argued that the case was not moot because, among other reasons, the gun owners might be entitled to damages covering the period when the city was infringing their Second Amendment rights. Alito was obviously steaming. He mocked the city for having defended the ordinance in the lower courts on the ground of public safety, a rationale that "evaporated" once the Supreme Court agreed to hear the case.

Still, it appeared that the court would add a new Second Amendment case to its docket. Ten cases had come in during the months the New York case was pending, and, as is typical, these were put on hold to await the New York decision. Surprisingly, after a six-week delay, the court denied all ten. Thomas filed a nineteen-page dissent from the denial of one of the group, a case from New Jersey that challenged that state's particularly high bar for a license to carry a gun outside the home. "Rather than prolonging our decade-long failure to protect the Second Amendment, I would grant this petition," Thomas, joined by Kavanaugh, wrote in *Rogers v. Grewal*.

The other cases were denied without comment, leaving unclear what precisely had happened inside the black box that is the weekly private conference at which the justices discuss pending business. But clearly there were four justices—Thomas, Alito, Kavanaugh, and Gorsuch—eager, or at least willing, to take up a Second Amendment case, and it takes only four votes to grant review. But four votes to grant are useless, even self-defeating, without the prospect of five votes to prevail on the merits. That suggests that Roberts had withheld his vote and that his hand was behind the mootness disposition in the New York case, an outcome that blocked what had seemed an easy path to expanding the Second Amendment. There would be no Second Amendment case in the 2019–20 term. But the cases would keep coming. John Roberts was not the only one who knew how to play a long game.

HAVING ALREADY PROFOUNDLY disrupted life at the court, COVID-19 became an unexpected source of tension late in the term. Churches began to bring cases challenging government orders that limited attendance at worship services in order to prevent spreading the virus. The first case arrived in May from the South Bay United Pentecostal Church in Chula Vista, California. Governor Gavin Newsom's order limited church attendance to 25 percent of capacity or one hundred worshippers, whichever was lower. Seeking an injunction, the church was represented by the Thomas More Society, a Chicago-based organization that most frequently represented antiabortion protesters. Its argument was that because retail stores, restaurants, and other businesses were not subject to a similarly strict occupancy cap, the governor's order discriminated against religion in violation of the Free Exercise Clause.

Under the court's practice, a motion for an injunction or a stay of a lower court decision requires five votes. Justices Thomas, Alito, Gorsuch, and Kavanaugh voted with the church. Roberts did not. He planned to issue an order denying the injunction, and, as is typical when the court denies such requests, he did not plan to add any comment to the order. But then Kavanaugh circulated a dissenting opinion. "The Church and its congregants simply want to be treated equally to comparable secular businesses," he wrote. The occupancy cap on religious services, he said, "indisputably discriminates against religion, and such discrimination violates the First Amendment." Thomas and Gorsuch signed Kavanaugh's opinion; Alito, while noting that he was also in dissent, neither signed nor wrote separately.

Now the court's internal dispute was in the open for all to see. Roberts decided that Kavanaugh's loose allegations of discrimination could not go unrebutted. In an opinion labeled "concurring in denial of application for injunctive relief," he made it clear that Kavanaugh had mischaracterized the governor's order. In fact, Roberts observed, "similar or more severe restrictions apply to comparable secular gatherings, including lectures, concerts, movie showings, spectator sports, and theatrical performances, where large numbers of people gather in close proximity for extended periods of time."

Roberts said the question of what limitations to impose during a health crisis "is a dynamic and fact-intensive matter subject to considerable disagreement." Decisions made by politically accountable officials "should not be subject to second-guessing by an unelected federal judiciary, which lacks the background, competence, and expertise to assess public health and is not accountable to the people." And in a direct swipe at Kavanaugh, he closed with "The notion that it is 'indisputably clear' that the government's limitations are unconstitutional seems quite improbable."

Another case arrived as the term was ending in July. It was from a church in Nevada, Calvary Chapel Dayton Valley, represented by Alliance Defending Freedom, a national litigating organization known for clients who claim religious reasons for discriminating against LGBT individuals. Nevada had capped church services at fifty people, and the church, claiming a Free Exercise violation, sought an injunction to permit it to seat ninety. The four justices again fell one vote short.

Alito, no longer silent, filed a dissenting opinion. He complained that in capping casinos, bowling alleys, and other entertainment venues at 50 percent of capacity, while limiting religious services to fifty people regardless of capacity, the state "blatantly discriminates against houses of worship." He added that "preventing congregants from worshipping will cause irreparable harm"—"irreparable harm" being a main criterion for granting an injunction. Alito left unaddressed the question of whether the church might have added a second service to accommodate the additional forty congregants.

Thomas and Kavanaugh signed Alito's opinion. Gorsuch wrote separately. "The world we inhabit today, with a pandemic upon us, poses unusual challenges," he wrote. "But there is no world in which the Constitution permits Nevada to favor Caesars Palace over Calvary Chapel."

This time, John Roberts said nothing. He had the upper hand. He could wait.

Or could he?

CHAPTER TWO

AUGUST–SEPTEMBER · AN ENDING AND A BEGINNING

IN MIDSUMMER, with COVID cases surging again nationwide and the daily death toll approaching one thousand, yard signs adorned with Justice Ginsburg's image appeared in front of homes and businesses in the Adams Morgan neighborhood northwest of Capitol Hill. The text read: RBG WORKS LESS THAN 5 MILES FROM HERE. IF YOU WON'T WEAR A MASK TO PROTECT YOUR FRIENDS AND FAMILY, DO IT TO PROTECT RBG.

The signs were a project of the Adams Morgan Business Improvement District, a quasi-governmental organization looking for ways to promote mask wearing to stop the spread of COVID-19. In the diverse and ever-gentrifying Adams Morgan, the RBG pitch was sure to appeal. After appearing in local media, photos of the signs went modestly viral. Justice Ginsburg's friends, knowing that she rarely ventured onto the Internet, mailed pictures of the signs to her Watergate apartment for her amusement.

Ruth Ginsburg's problem wasn't COVID, however. It was, once again, cancer. Pancreatic cancer had returned the previous year after an unusually long interval of ten years since her initial diagnosis and surgery in 2009. It was Stage IV this time, with metastases to the liver. A cure was not in the picture for the eighty-seven-year-old justice. Because immunotherapy had proved unsuccessful, it was now a matter of keeping the cancer "at bay" with chemotherapy, as Ginsburg put it in a low-key statement issued in her name in mid-July by the court's public information office. It was a matter of time.

Throughout her life, cancer had been Ginsburg's near-constant companion. Her mother, Celia Bader, died of cervical cancer at the age of forty-seven, two days before Ruth's high school graduation. Her husband, Martin, survived testicular cancer when the two were newlywed law students. He was to die of a spinal tumor in 2010, in the fifty-sixth year of their marriage. Ginsburg herself underwent surgery for colon cancer in 1999 and for lung cancer in 2018. Although strangers who saw her often remarked on how small and frail she looked, she remained remarkably vigorous through all these trials, with a schedule of travel and speaking that would have exhausted many younger and healthier people. She often attended opera and other musical performances and usually worked late into the night. She called her personal trainer, Bryant Johnson, "the most important person in my life" after her family; his book, *The RBG Workout: How She Says Strong . . . and You Can Too!*, published in 2017, described the energetic twice-weekly workouts he led her through. (A video of Ginsburg going through her exercise routine with Stephen Colbert— and at age eighty-five outlasting the *Late Show* host—was something of an Internet sensation in 2018.)

Even in her final weeks, she was looking to the future. After her funeral in September, Justice Stephen Breyer returned to his chambers for the first time in weeks and found a card she had sent him to mark his birthday on August 15, when he turned eighty-two. "To my younger colleague, stay cool and well," the eighty-seven-year-old justice had written. "I order you to have a happy birthday." She had enclosed a photo of herself, adding the words: "We'll get together when this epidemic is over and we'll see an opera and life will go on."

Calls for Ginsburg to retire had started during Barack Obama's first term as president. The argument was that she most likely would not outlast a Republican president if one were to win the White House in 2012 and serve two terms. Randall Kennedy, a law professor at Harvard, made this argument explicit in a widely noticed essay he published in *The New Republic* in April 2011. For good measure, he threw in Stephen Breyer, at the time a healthy seventy-two. The two justices "need to act soon," Kennedy wrote. "If they wait much beyond the end of this Supreme Court term, the Republicans will delay confirmation, praying for an upset in the presidential election."

Professor Kennedy offered the experience of Justice Thurgood Marshall, for whom he had clerked, as a "cautionary tale." Although in poor health, Marshall had hung on until his condition left him no choice. His retirement in June 1991 gave President George H. W. Bush the opportunity to name as his successor Clarence Thomas, placed on the D.C. Circuit eighteen months earlier to await just that contingency. "Now, if Justice Ginsburg departs the Supreme Court with a Republican in the White House," Randall Kennedy wrote, "it is probable that the female Thurgood Marshall will be replaced by a female Clarence Thomas."

It was one thing for a Supreme Court justice's detractors to call for retirement or even impeachment. But the public calls by a justice's ideological allies to urge retirement for the good of the country were highly unusual, a symptom of a polarized court in hyperpartisan times. Neither Ginsburg nor Breyer responded publicly. Quite quickly, Breyer's name fell out of the conversation, and a renewed round of retirement calls during Obama's second term focused exclusively on Ginsburg. By then, it was clear that the unceasing drumbeat was getting under her skin. "So tell me who the president could have nominated this spring that you would rather see on the court than me?" she demanded of the journalist Joan Biskupic during an on-the-record interview in July 2014. Two years later, in the summer of the 2016 presidential election year, Ginsburg expressed her confidence in the Supreme Court's future with Hillary Clinton in the White House. "It's likely that the next president, whoever she will be, will have a few appointments to make," she said with a smile to Mark Sherman of the Associated Press. When the reporter raised the prospect that the winner might be Donald Trump rather than Clinton, Ginsburg responded: "I don't want to think about that possibility, but if it should be, then everything is up for grabs."

The second-guessing of Ginsburg's decision to remain on the

bench continued even after her death on September 18. If anything, it grew louder as it became clear that the Republican-controlled Senate was actually going to do the unthinkable and install her replacement with just weeks to go before Election Day. The criticism was at once completely fair and unduly harsh. Ginsburg was hardly the only one to believe that Hillary Clinton would succeed Barack Obama as president, an assumption embraced by nearly the entire Eastern establishment and reflected in most opinion polls. Nor was she incorrect to worry that the Republican Senate would block an effort by Obama to name someone equally liberal to take her place; even before the Republicans captured the Senate in 2014, the availability of the filibuster for Supreme Court nominations would have given Republicans the upper hand in blocking any nominee of whom they disapproved.

As the years went on, there was a further point to consider: Had Ginsburg yielded to the advice to retire during Obama's first term, the court and the country would have been without her voice for the decade during which she came to embody resistance to the Supreme Court's increasingly conservative turn. It was during those crucial years that her powerful dissenting opinions, the most important of which she delivered from the bench, earned her the "Notorious RBG" sobriquet, bestowed by the 2015 book *Notorious RBG: The Life and Times of Ruth Bader Ginsburg* by Irin Carmon and Shana Knizhnik. The court had other liberal dissenters during those years, of course. But it was Ginsburg—feminist, grandmother, iron-willed survivor— who inspired women to dress their young daughters for Halloween in mini judicial robes with fanciful lace collars, and Ginsburg whose life story was told in children's books with titles like *I Dissent: Ruth Bader Ginsburg Makes Her Mark*.

None of this had been even remotely foreseeable during her first fifteen years on the Supreme Court bench; had she retired when the men told her to (women's voices were almost never part of this particular chorus), none of it would have happened. It wasn't so much that Ginsburg had changed as that the court and the culture had changed around her. For the three years between Sandra Day

O'Connor's retirement in 2006 and Sonia Sotomayor's arrival in 2009, Ginsburg was the only female justice as the court was wrenched further to the right by O'Connor's replacement, Samuel Alito. She spoke out in dissent on abortion and discrimination cases that would almost certainly have come out differently had the moderate O'Connor remained on the court.

Despite having preached the virtues of collegiality for her entire judicial career, Ginsburg now grasped the dissenting opinion as a platform from which to speak over the court's head to engage the public directly. (A Harvard law professor, Lani Guinier, attached to the practice of the oral dissent the word "demosprudence"—a jurisprudence of the people—to signify that not only courts, but social movements as well, engage in lawgiving.) It's clear in retrospect that Ruth Ginsburg in dissent provided something the culture needed: someone to call out, with the gravitas bestowed by age and position, what was happening to the court in vivid and readily understood language—the "umbrella in a rainstorm" image of her Shelby County dissent. One can debate whether having a rock star justice is good for the Supreme Court. But there is no doubt that for the last ten years of her life, Ruth Bader Ginsburg was a rock star.

HER ROUTE TO that exalted final chapter was a most unlikely one. She grew up in financially straitened circumstances in Brooklyn and attended Cornell University on a scholarship. Already married and the mother of a young daughter, she entered Harvard Law School in the fall of 1956. The school did not exactly welcome women: There were only nine in a class of 552 students. Ginsburg quickly shot to the top of the class, winning a coveted place on the law review. When her husband, Martin, took a job in New York City, she transferred to Columbia Law School for her third and final year.

Although she was tied for first in the graduating class, she received no job offers. Law firm partners didn't want women as colleagues, and judges didn't want female law clerks. She finally secured a federal district court clerkship after one of her professors threatened the judge with never recommending another student to him unless he hired her.

This was the world that greeted Ruth Ginsburg—and, on the opposite coast a few years earlier, the world that had greeted Sandra Day O'Connor, who graduated near the top of her Stanford Law School class and was offered only secretarial positions. There was no law against sex discrimination, and even the most liberal judges in the country had never interpreted the Constitution's guarantee of equal protection as having anything to do with women. This was the world that the young Ruth Ginsburg set out to change.

From her position as the first director of the American Civil Liberties Union's Women's Rights Project in the mid-1970s, she argued six cases before the Supreme Court and won five of them. Her goal was at once simple and profound: not simply to eliminate practices that discriminated against women, but to break the bonds of stereotype that assigned women and men to separate roles based on assumptions about their capacities and needs. She sought to liberate men as well as women from what she called "sex-role pigeonholing." To open the eyes of the nine men of the Supreme Court, none of whom had ever sat with a female colleague, she brought cases with sympathetic male plaintiffs, such as the young widower who wanted to be his child's caretaker and who sought the survivor benefits that the Social Security system bestowed only on widows. In another case, a female Air Force officer who earned more than her husband claimed the housing and other benefits to which a man in her position would have been entitled on the assumption that husbands were the primary breadwinners.

Few of her cases were the stuff of headlines. But one case at a time, Ruth Ginsburg persuaded the justices of the Supreme Court to create something completely new: a constitutional jurisprudence of sex equality. Some called her the Thurgood Marshall of the women's rights movement, an admiring reference to Marshall's strategic choice and presentation of cases in his litigation campaign for the NAACP Legal Defense and Educational Fund that led to the landmark *Brown v. Board of Education* in 1954.

Before Jimmy Carter became president in 1977, only eight women had ever held lifetime appointments on the federal courts. Determined to diversify the bench, Carter appointed forty-one women, members of Ruth Ginsburg's generation who had spent professional lifetimes breaking barriers. In 1980, his final year in office, Carter named Ginsburg to the D.C. Circuit. She would soon be joined there by Antonin Scalia, appointed by a president, Ronald Reagan, who had a priority of his own: to fill the federal bench with young conservative academics. Ginsburg and Scalia formed a bond over their shared love for opera, a decades-long friendship undimmed by their very different views of the law and, in particular, the meaning of equality.

Ginsburg's nomination to the Supreme Court by President Bill Clinton in 1993 drew only three negative votes in the Senate despite her unequivocal embrace during her confirmation hearing of the constitutional right to abortion as "something central to a woman's life, to her dignity"—a reminder, perhaps, that the country and the court were not always engulfed by the polarizing politics of abortion.

The court that Ginsburg joined was notably more conservative than the one she had argued before. President Reagan had named Antonin Scalia to the Supreme Court in 1986 after a four-year tenure on the D.C. Circuit. President George H. W. Bush had named Clarence Thomas to succeed Thurgood Marshall. Opportunities for a junior justice on the liberal side of the court's spectrum to write important majority opinions were scarce. But the opportunity came to Ginsburg in 1996 in a case that was a near-perfect next chapter to her earlier victories as a litigator. The Clinton administration had sued the state of Virginia for refusing to admit women to the state-supported Virginia Military Institute. The school's alumni network formed an important part of Virginia's power structure, and women had begun inquiring about admission—347 of them in the previous two years, in fact, none of whom had received a response.

Virginia argued that women were unsuited for the school's "adversative" method of creating "citizen-soldiers" by subjecting students to grueling physical and mental challenges. This was, of course, precisely the stereotypical assignment of gender roles the eradication of which had been at the heart of Ruth Ginsburg's project. Her opinion cited a number of her own victories. Virginia's burden was to show an "exceedingly persuasive justification" for its exclusion of women, and it had failed. "'Inherent differences' between men and women, we have come to appreciate, remain cause for celebration," Ginsburg wrote in her majority opinion, "but not for denigration of the members of either sex or for artificial constraints on an individual's opportunity." While most women might not choose to subject themselves to VMI's style of education, she concluded, "generalizations about 'the way women are,' estimates of what is appropriate for *most women*, no longer justify denying opportunity to women whose talent and capacity place them outside the average description." The vote was 7 to 1, with her friend Nino Scalia the only dissenter. (Clarence Thomas, whose son had attended VMI, recused himself.)

Issued years before her voice raised in dissent made her "notorious," *United States v. Virginia* remained Ginsburg's most important majority opinion. In February 2017, she visited the Virginia Military Institute for the first time. Female cadets numbered 194 of the seventeen-hundred-member student body. Before Ginsburg spoke, a 2003 graduate, Lara Tyler Chambers, herself the daughter and granddaughter of VMI graduates, presented the justice with her battle ring. "I gave it to her to thank her for battling for us," Chambers said.

PRESIDENT BILL CLINTON spent nearly three months during the spring of 1993 deciding whom to name to the Supreme Court to replace Justice Byron White, a John F. Kennedy appointee who announced his retirement on March 20. It took until June 14 for Clinton to nominate Ruth Bader Ginsburg.

It took Donald Trump three days to choose her successor, from the Friday of Ginsburg's death to the Monday when he met with Amy Coney Barrett and offered her the job. When Trump made the formal announcement the following Saturday, September 26, Ginsburg had not yet been buried.

How did the Senate majority leader, Mitch McConnell of Kentucky, justify filling a Supreme Court vacancy six weeks before a presidential election when he had refused four years earlier to let President Obama fill a vacancy with nearly nine months to go before Election Day? The answer is that he couldn't. Nor did he have to. He had the votes—53 Republican senators—and, having abolished the filibuster in order to confirm Neil Gorsuch in 2017, all he needed was a simple majority. Breaking a filibuster requires sixty votes. Gorsuch was confirmed by a vote of 54 to 45. The vote to confirm Brett Kavanaugh the following year was 50 to 48. With Vice President Mike Pence available to break a tie, McConnell knew that he could lose three members of his caucus and still prevail. Everyone else knew that too, although discipline in the Senate Republican caucus was such that it was almost unthinkable that three Republicans would defy their leader.

Such explanation as he offered began by noting that the White House and the Senate had been in opposite hands in 2016. That made it appropriate, he said, to wait and let the public decide which of the two parties it wanted to put in charge of making this important appointment. By electing Donald Trump and retaining Republican control of the Senate, McConnell argued in a statement issued the night of Ginsburg's death, the public had given the president a mandate. "Americans reelected our majority in 2016 and expanded it in 2018 because we pledged to work with President Trump and support his agenda, particularly his outstanding appointments to the federal judiciary," McConnell said, adding: "Once again, we will keep our promise. President Trump's nominee will receive a vote on the floor of the United States Senate."

The Senate's Democratic minority leader, Chuck Schumer of New York, also had something to say on the night of Ginsburg's death: "The American people should have a voice in the selection of their next Supreme Court justice. Therefore, this vacancy should not be filled until we have a new president." For anyone with a memory of what happened four years earlier, that statement sounded eerily familiar. And with reason: Word for word, it was what McConnell had said on February 13, 2016, hours after the world learned of Justice

Scalia's death. On September 18, 2020, it was Chuck Schumer's grim joke.

Of course, "until we have a new president" now had a different meaning. President Obama, having served two full terms, had not been on the ballot in 2016, whereas in 2020, Republicans were hoping not for a new president but for the reelection of the incumbent. By early fall, that outcome was looking uncertain, making quick action all the more imperative. Trump had been lagging in the polls all summer, and shortly after Labor Day, FiveThirtyEight's national average showed Joe Biden with a lead of more than seven points. Biden was leading in five key states that Trump had carried in 2016: Michigan, Wisconsin, Pennsylvania, Florida, and Arizona. (Biden would go on to win all but Florida.)

Trump himself had something to say about his prospects. In rambling remarks to a meeting of Republican state attorneys general on September 23, the president let the world know that he planned to use the Supreme Court as a reelection insurance policy. "I think this will end up in the Supreme Court and I think it's very important that we have nine justices," he said. "I think this scam that the Democrats are pulling, it's a scam, this scam will be before the United States Supreme Court and I think having a four–four situation is not a good situation. I think it's very important to have a ninth judge."

The "scam" Trump was referring to was the expansion of mail-in balloting. In response to the pandemic, many states had relaxed barriers to absentee voting, some even sending ballots to all voters regardless of whether a voter had requested one. For months, Trump had been warning, without evidence, that mail-in ballots were rife with fraud. These repeated warnings, in addition to complaints about the procedures that mostly Democratic election officials had invoked to expand access to absentee voting, became the central theme in Trump's effort to undermine public confidence in the election. Lawsuits brought by Republican state officials, including legislators, to challenge the legitimacy of the expanded access were already making their way to the Supreme Court.

Trump had not yet announced his nominee, but word was starting to leak, and Amy Barrett was now the center of attention. From her confirmation to the Seventh Circuit three years earlier, the Senate Judiciary Committee already had an extensive file, including her speeches and the articles she had written as a law professor. These were starting to circulate around Washington, taking on new relevance.

Drawing particular attention during the days surrounding Barrett's nomination was an essay she published in 2017 in the journal *Constitutional Commentary* under the title "Countering the Majoritarian Difficulty." The title was a play on words. The actual phrase, "the counter-majoritarian difficulty," has little if any meaning to the general public but has been a favorite topic of debate in legal academia ever since it was coined by a Yale law professor, Alexander Bickel, in the early 1960s. It expresses a dilemma at the heart of the power of judicial review: the ability of courts composed of unelected judges to overturn legislation enacted by democratically elected legislatures. The "counter-majoritarian difficulty" poses the question of how democratic theory justifies judicial intervention on behalf of minority interests.

Barrett's essay approached this topic at a remove; it was a review of a book by another law professor, Randy Barnett, a libertarian whose main concern was the legitimacy not of judicial review but of government itself. His claim to fame was as the chief architect of the constitutional attack on the Affordable Care Act, an attack that in the 2012 Supreme Court decision *NFIB v. Sebelius* came very close to bringing down President Obama's principal legislative achievement. Chief Justice Roberts's vote had saved the statute on his singular theory that even though, as Barnett had argued, Congress lacked authority under the Commerce Clause to penalize people for not buying health insurance, the financial penalty could nonetheless be upheld and enforced as a tax under Congress's power to levy taxes.

Roberts's role as the savior of Obamacare had infuriated the political right. Prominent conservatives accused him of having sold out his constitutional principles to save his court from the backlash that would have occurred if five Republican-appointed justices, by invoking a novel theory of a constitutionally constricted Congress, had taken down a Democratic president's proudest accomplishment. (This would be the first time conservatives would feel betrayed by Roberts, but not the last.)

What made Amy Barrett's article the subject of interest, and—to Democrats—concern, was that she made clear her own disapproval of the chief justice's vote. "In *NFIB v. Sebelius*, the inspiration for Barnett's book," she wrote, "Chief Justice Roberts pushed the Affordable Care Act beyond its plausible meaning to save the statute." She went on for several pages, including such observations as "If the majority did not enact a 'tax,' interpreting the statute to impose a tax lacks democratic legitimacy." Finally, recalling Justice Scalia's dissenting opinion, she wrote:

> For Justice Scalia and those who share his commitment to uphold text, the measure of a court is its fair-minded application of the rule of law, which means going where the law leads. By this measure, it is illegitimate for the Court to distort either the Constitution or a statute to achieve what it deems a preferable result.

Although her tone was mild and academically appropriate, the force of Barrett's criticism was hard to miss. While it was of course noteworthy that Chief Justice Roberts was presumably about to be joined by a new colleague who had called him out as insufficiently committed to the rule of law, that was not the source of the Democrats' worries. Rather, what lent urgency to the Democrats' concern was that a new challenge to the Affordable Care Act was pending at the Supreme Court, with argument already scheduled for a week after Election Day.

The case, *State of California v. State of Texas*, stemmed directly from the Roberts opinion upholding the insurance mandate's penalty as a tax. In December 2017, as part of a major bill revising parts of the tax code, Congress reduced to zero the penalty for not buying health insurance. The bill left the rest of the Affordable Care Act untouched, but Texas and seventeen other Republican-dominated states filed suit claiming that the reduction to zero rendered the law unconstitutional. The states' theory was that since the Supreme Court had upheld the penalty only by deeming it a tax, the law could not stand now that there was no longer a tax. Since the insurance mandate was only one part of a complex thousand-page statute, the states had to explain why, if they were correct about the mandate, its invalidation should bring down the entire Affordable Care Act. Their argument was that the mandate was such an intrinsic part of the statute that it was "inseverable" from all the rest, making the entire law unconstitutional.

Concerned that the Trump administration would refuse to defend the law—an assumption that proved correct—California and a group of other blue states intervened in the case to counter the plaintiffs' arguments. The intervening states argued that in setting the penalty at zero, Congress had retained the option of raising it someday and, in any event, had not eliminated it; even with a zero penalty, the health insurance mandate was still a constitutional part of the statute. But, they asserted, even if the mandate provision was unconstitutional, the rest of the law remained valid.

At the heart of the dispute between the two blocs of states was the question of "severability." This question was hardly novel. It comes up whenever a court invalidates a portion of a multipart statute. The Supreme Court has deemed severability to be a question of congressional intent: Would Congress have enacted the law without the invalidated section?

In 2010, when Congress passed the Affordable Care Act, the answer would most likely have been no. Health economists had warned that the Affordable Care Act's insurance markets, which prohibited pricing based on an individual's health history and barred discrimination against people with preexisting medical conditions, could not function without requiring everyone to have health insurance, and without penalizing those who did not. The experts believed the insurance market would collapse because healthy individuals would not participate, leaving insurers to require ever higher premiums to cover the expenses of their ever more medically needy customers. The mandate was widely viewed as essential to the survival of Obamacare's insurance market, and the penalty was seen as essential to the operation of the mandate.

But experience in the intervening years proved otherwise. The Affordable Care Act turned out to be popular, and even after Congress set the penalty at zero, healthy people kept signing up for insurance. Clearly, the mandate was no longer essential, if it ever had been. And, the California group observed, that was the judgment Congress had made in 2017, when it set the penalty at zero while leaving the rest of the law fully in effect. Given that severability was a matter of congressional intent, these states argued, Congress's intent was clear: It wanted the Affordable Care Act to survive.

A federal district judge in Fort Worth agreed with the entirety of the Texas argument, declaring the mandate inseverable and the Affordable Care Act unconstitutional in all respects. On appeal, the United States Court of Appeals for the Fifth Circuit agreed that the mandate was now unconstitutional. But it sent the case back to the district court for reconsideration of the severability question, instructing Judge Reed O'Connor to "employ a finer-toothed comb" and to conduct a "more searching inquiry into which provisions of the Affordable Care Act Congress intended to be severable from the individual mandate." Both the Texas and California groups appealed to the Supreme Court. The justices agreed in March to hear both cases, consolidating them for a single argument.

Cases accepted that late in the term are always carried over for argument during the opening months of the next term. With the first Monday in October fast approaching, there was every reason to think that the seat now draped in black wool crepe—a custom the court was observing in Justice Ginsburg's honor despite plans to continue operating remotely—would be filled by Amy Coney Barrett in time for the November argument.

PRESIDENT TRUMP INTRODUCED his nominee to the country from the White House Rose Garden on the afternoon of Saturday, September 26. The previous day, Ruth Bader Ginsburg had lain in state

at the Capitol, her flag-draped coffin resting on the Lincoln cata-
falque. Her actual funeral would not be until the following week. She
was the first woman to receive the honor of lying in state, and only the
second Supreme Court justice; the first was William Howard Taft,
who before becoming chief justice had been president.

The more than two hundred people in the Rose Garden included
leaders of the religious right along with administration officials, family members, and Republican senators. There were no Democratic
senators in attendance. The guests sat in tightly packed rows, with
few wearing masks. Amy Barrett herself had tested positive for the
coronavirus over the summer, experiencing only mild symptoms; her
husband had also had a positive COVID test but had been asymptom-
atic. For others, including the president and First Lady, two United
States senators, the White House press secretary and three members
of her staff, the former governor of New Jersey, and the president of
Notre Dame, the gathering turned out to be a "superspreader event,"
as Dr. Anthony Fauci later described its consequences.

The Rose Garden has provided a natural backdrop for presidential
events of this sort. It was where, twenty-seven years earlier, on a sunny
June day in 1993, President Clinton had introduced Ruth Bader
Ginsburg, his first Supreme Court nominee. In her brief remarks,
Ginsburg, sixty years old at the time, brought the president to tears
when, speaking of her mother, who had died decades earlier, she said,
"I pray that I may be all that she would have been had she lived in an
age when women could aspire and achieve and daughters are cher-
ished as much as sons."

Trump introduced his nominee as "really fantastic," "a woman of
remarkable intellect and character." He then pivoted to the personal:
"Her family is a core part of who Amy is. She opened her home and
her heart and adopted two beautiful children from Haiti. Her incred-
ible bond with her youngest child, a son with Down syndrome, is a
true inspiration. If confirmed, Justice Barrett will make history as the
first mother of school-aged children ever to serve on the U.S. Supreme Court. That's good." While Barrett's motherhood would not
be unique among Supreme Court justices—Sandra O'Connor was the

mother of three sons, and Ruth Ginsburg had a son and a daughter—it would become a near-constant theme during her confirmation hearing, raised by Republican senators who had no real questions to ask but who needed something to say when their turn came to face the nominee or, more precisely, the television cameras.

Before he finished, Trump could not resist serving up a few of the sound bites that the Supreme Court seemed to trigger for him. "Rulings that the Supreme Court will issue in the coming years will decide the survival of our Second Amendment, our religious liberty, our public safety, and so much more," he offered. "To maintain security, liberty, and prosperity, we must preserve our priceless heritage of a nation of laws, and there is no one better to do that than Amy Coney Barrett."

In her own brief remarks, Barrett paid homage to Ginsburg, noting that "the flag of the United States is still flying at half-staff in memory of Justice Ruth Bader Ginsburg to mark the end of a great American life." She talked about her admiration for the "warm and rich friendship" that Ginsburg and her own mentor, Justice Scalia, had maintained despite their very different perspectives. "I clerked for Justice Scalia more than twenty years ago," she continued, "but the lessons I learned still resonate. His judicial philosophy is mine, too. A judge must apply the law as written. Judges are not policymakers, and they must be resolute in setting aside any policy views they might have."

"His judicial philosophy is mine, too." Pregnant with meaning, it was the most substantive line of the afternoon's proceeding, a carefully crafted statement of self-definition. As the satisfied crowd, which included Scalia's widow, Maureen, streamed from the Rose Garden into a crowded White House reception, it hung in the virus-laden air, a prophecy awaiting fulfillment.

CHAPTER THREE

OCTOBER · WAITING FOR JUSTICE BARRETT

IN MID-OCTOBER, the court issued an order that read, in its entirety:

ORDER IN PENDING CASE
20A53 SCARNATI, JOSEPH B., ET AL. V. BOOCKVAR, SEC. OF PA, ET AL.

The application for stay presented to Justice Alito and by him referred to the Court is denied.

Justice Thomas, Justice Alito, Justice Gorsuch, and Justice Kavanaugh would grant the application.

What, if anything, was the general public to make of this? To call the order opaque was an understatement. Someone had asked the Supreme Court, in a case that somehow related to Pennsylvania, to stop a particular decision from taking effect, and the court had said no.

Yet to anyone following the election cases that had begun to flow into the court as Election Day 2020 approached, the court might as well have posted this order in neon lights. Even without knowing the particulars, chances were high, given the respondent's SEC. OF PA title, that this was an election case. It wasn't necessary to know that Joseph B. Scarnati III was president pro tem of the Pennsylvania Senate and a Republican, or that Kathy Boockvar, a Democrat, was the commonwealth secretary, a position known in most states as the secretary of state. Whatever the details, what really mattered was the second sentence of the order: The eight justices of the Supreme Court, awaiting Amy Coney Barrett's confirmation, were split.

In half.

In an election case.

The order further revealed that whatever the precise issue, Chief Justice Roberts was on one side and the four other conservative justices were on the other. Those four had tried to give the Pennsylvania Republicans whatever it was they were asking for, but they lacked the fifth vote necessary to grant a stay.

When the court denies an application for a stay or another type of emergency relief, it isn't necessary for the justices who voted for a different outcome to identify themselves, and often they do not. By choosing to attach their names to this order, the four dissenters were sending a clear message: President Trump was right. He needed his ninth justice.

BY STATUTE, THE Supreme Court's term begins on the first Monday in October. In 2020, that was October 5, meaning that by October 19, the date of the Pennsylvania order, the court had been in session for an unusually busy two weeks.

With the pandemic surging, the justices were still conducting arguments by telephone, with no timetable for returning to in-person sessions. With interested members of the public listening via a link from C-SPAN, Chief Justice Roberts opened the new term by acknowledging Justice Ginsburg's death. "We at the court will remember her as a dear friend and treasured colleague," he said. Each of the eight justices, plus Anthony Kennedy and David Souter from retirement, had issued a public statement the day after Ginsburg's death. "The world is a better place for her having lived in it," Stephen Breyer said.

One of the more deeply personal statements came from Clarence Thomas, whose brief tenure on the D.C. Circuit had overlapped with Ginsburg's. He was "heartbroken," Justice Thomas said. "The most difficult part of a long tenure is watching colleagues decline and pass away. And the passing of my dear colleague Ruth is profoundly difficult and so very sad. I will dearly miss my friend." The shortest came from David Souter, eleven years into his retirement in New Hampshire. "Ruth Ginsburg was one of the members of the court who achieved greatness before she became a great justice," Souter wrote. "I loved her to pieces."

News from the court is ordinarily scarce during the opening weeks of a new term. While the justices immediately begin hearing arguments in cases carried over from the previous spring, decisions in those cases won't appear for weeks or even months. The action this October, and there was plenty of it, came not in granted or argued cases, but rather in cases the justices turned down or in response to urgent requests for what the court calls emergency relief.

Davis v. Ermold was one of hundreds of petitions denied on the term's opening day, included on a list that printed out to fifty-four pages. For the most part, these were cases that had arrived too late for consideration before the summer recess. By contrast, *Davis v. Ermold* had been on the docket for months. The petition had arrived at the court in January and had been scheduled for the justices' consideration seven times during the spring and early summer. But the court took no action, and the petition ended up along with nearly a thousand others on the gigantic "summer list" that provides the first assignment for the new crop of law clerks, who must plow through it and identify cases worthy of their bosses' consideration.

Along with the great majority of petitions on the summer list, *Davis v. Ermold* appeared fated to die the quiet death that comes with "certiorari denied." But Justices Thomas and Alito had other plans. Although, along with the rest of the court, they had not voted to hear the case, they decided to call attention to it with a "statement respecting the denial of certiorari" to be attached to the opening day order list. It was a statement they had reason to expect would jump off the page.

The Davis in the petition's caption was Kim Davis. It was a name plucked from the headlines of five years before, when, as the county clerk of Rowan County, Kentucky, she stopped issuing marriage licenses. The court's same-sex marriage decision, *Obergefell v. Hodges*, was barely a day old when three couples, including two same-sex couples, presented themselves in Davis's office to obtain marriage licenses. She explained that as a Christian, she could not allow herself to become complicit, by her signature, in a marriage she regarded as sinful. To avoid being accused of discrimination, she had decided to simply stop performing one of her legal duties, and would not be issuing marriage licenses to anyone.

As gay couples all over the country celebrated the *Obergefell* decision by formalizing their relationships, the Christian right embraced Kim Davis as a martyr. Refusing to back down in the face of a judge's order to do her job, she spent five days in jail for contempt of court and then traveled to Washington, D.C., to accept a "cost of discipleship" award from the Family Research Council, an evangelical group that calls itself "pro-marriage and pro-life." There, although she was an evangelical Protestant rather than a Catholic, she met with Pope Francis.

The fifteen-minute visit was arranged at the Vatican's diplomatic mission by Archbishop Carlo Maria Viganò, the papal nuncio, on the day the pope addressed a joint session of Congress. Francis was reportedly furious when he later learned who Davis was and realized that he had been used for political purposes not his own. For her part, Davis flaunted the meeting, telling ABC News that "just knowing the pope is on track with what we're doing, and agreeing, you know, kind of validates everything." Days later, the Vatican put out a highly unusual statement, declaring in the official English translation that "The Pope did not enter into the details of the situation of Mrs. Davis and his meeting with her should not be considered a form of support of her position in all of its particular and complex aspects."

This was the stuff of headlines, and Kim Davis's name was still widely recognizable nearly five years later. In her Supreme Court appeal, she was seeking immunity from a suit for damages that one of the same-sex couples had filed. Davis and her lawyers at Liberty

Counsel, a Christian right litigating organization, were invoking the doctrine of "qualified immunity," which shields public officials from the consequences of violating an individual's constitutional rights if the specific right at issue has not been clearly defined. Both the federal district court and the United States Court of Appeals for the Sixth Circuit rejected this defense, finding that, following the *Obergefell* decision, the right to same-sex marriage was perfectly clear.

By any objective measure, Davis's petition did not meet the criteria for Supreme Court review. The lawsuit had not yet gone to trial, a fact that usually weighs heavily against the chances of "getting a grant." An even more negative factor was that with its focus on the immunity doctrine, the petition itself didn't squarely present the religious freedom claim that had made Davis famous. Thomas and Alito acknowledged these deficiencies, explaining in their statement why they had not voted to grant the case. "This petition implicates important questions about the scope of our decision in *Obergefell*, but it does not cleanly present them," the two wrote.

So why wasn't that the end of the matter? The two justices' concession made their further discussion of the case entirely gratuitous. That much was clear, but it was also clear that Kim Davis's very name on the cover of her petition offered Thomas and Alito something they had spent five years waiting for. They had finally found an *Obergefell* "victim."

Both had dissented in *Obergefell* in opinions that warned that the decision would, as Thomas put it, lead to "ruinous consequences for religious liberty." By October 2020, those consequences had come to seem evanescent at worst. But Davis's petition gave the two justices the chance to replay their predictions of doom. "Davis may have been one of the first victims of this Court's cavalier treatment of religion in its *Obergefell* decision," they wrote, "but she will not be the last. Due to *Obergefell*, those with sincerely held religious beliefs concerning marriage will find it increasingly difficult to participate in society without running afoul of *Obergefell* and its effect on other antidiscrimination laws." The petition, they continued, "provides a stark reminder of the consequences of *Obergefell*. By choosing to privilege a novel constitutional right over the religious liberty interests explicitly protected in the First Amendment, and by doing so undemocratically, the court has created a problem that only it can fix."

"That only it can fix"? Were these two justices really suggesting that the court should revisit its 2015 decision and call it a mistake? The idea seemed outlandish; according to census figures released in late 2019, more than one million Americans were now legally married to partners of the same sex. And yet the court's math made the justices' suggestion perhaps not so far-fetched. The vote in *Obergefell* had been 5 to 4. Justice Kennedy, who wrote the majority opinion, was now gone, replaced by Brett Kavanaugh. Ruth Bader Ginsburg had also voted in the majority, and her empty seat, it appeared, was shortly to be filled by a deeply religious social conservative of Donald Trump's choosing. At the least, the Thomas-Alito statement was an invitation to anyone with a religious objection to same-sex marriage to bring the court a better case. If not a declaration of war, it was a vow of continued non-surrender.

As the justices were well aware, the court was a month away from hearing a case that did present a clash between a religious liberty claim and a nondiscrimination obligation. In *Fulton v. City of Philadelphia*, scheduled for argument the day after the presidential election, on November 4, the court was being asked to decide whether a Catholic social service agency, under contract with the city to find homes for foster children, was entitled as a matter of religious freedom to violate Philadelphia's antidiscrimination ordinance by refusing to consider same-sex couples as potential foster parents. The case carried the potential of a major revision of the court's Free Exercise Clause jurisprudence, which now, at least nominally, required governmental neutrality toward religion. It invited the court to embrace formally the position that the current majority had been edging toward in its recent decisions: that neutrality was no longer sufficient, and that the Free Exercise Clause instead entitled religious claims to a place of privilege above all others.

BY OCTOBER, GOVERNMENT responses to the COVID pandemic were generating legal questions that, while not completely novel, were arising in new contexts. The court had already encountered COVID in the context of religion, and beginning in May it had narrowly rejected claims by churches in California and Nevada to exemptions from public health limitations on in-person gatherings. The Pennsylvania election case that produced the 4–4 tie was another COVID case. The state supreme court, citing the pandemic in addition to the troubled state of the U.S. Postal Service, had ordered election officials to count ballots as long as they arrived within three days after Election Day. In its request to the justices for a stay, the Republican-controlled legislature maintained that the state court, which happened to have a Democratic majority, had infringed the prerogative that the U.S. Constitution gave exclusively to state legislatures.

This was in fact a highly contested interpretation of the Election Clause of Article I, section 4, of the U.S. Constitution, one that a majority of the U.S. Supreme Court had never embraced. But it was gaining ground in Republican legal circles. Republicans were frustrated by the willingness of state courts—many, as in Pennsylvania, with Democratic majorities—to find ways around rigid voting rules and deadlines in order to enable as many people as possible to have their votes count. And this theory of state legislative exclusivity appeared to be gaining traction within the Supreme Court as well.

While partisan struggles over election procedure were playing out in growing numbers of states, Governor Greg Abbott of Texas had a particular target of opportunity in mind: abortion. By executive order early in the pandemic, he imposed a temporary ban on abortions, claiming as his rationale a shortage of hospital beds and personal protective equipment in the state. This made no sense, because as the Supreme Court had found when it struck down the state's hospital admitting privileges requirement in 2016, abortion almost never requires hospitalization. That the Texas ban also applied to medication abortion, which involves taking two pills without surgical intervention, showed the ostensible rationale to be a fraud.

A federal district judge, unsurprisingly, enjoined the ban. It was equally unsurprising that the Fifth Circuit, the country's most consistently antiabortion federal appeals court, overturned the district court injunction. Planned Parenthood and other abortion providers appealed to the Supreme Court, but before the court could act, the state relented and allowed the ban to expire. The providers withdrew their petition, but they later asked the justices to vacate the Fifth Circuit's decision as moot, so that it could not be invoked as a precedent in a future public health emergency. The court granted the request in a brief, unanimous order in January 2021.

While more flagrant than most, Governor Abbott's executive order was an example of a familiar phenomenon known as abortion exceptionalism, the singling out of abortion for health-related restrictions more onerous than those imposed on medical procedures of equivalent or even greater risk. At the same time, another episode of abortion exceptionalism was unfolding on the national stage. The subject was the Food and Drug Administration's regulation of medication abortion.

Medication abortion involves two drugs taken in sequence. Since 2000, when the FDA first approved the procedure, it had required the first drug, mifepristone, to be dispensed in person by a medical provider in a healthcare setting. The woman could leave the office and take the drug at home, but she first had to receive in-person instruction, advice about possible risks, and a consent form to sign before leaving the office. Other drugs are subject to similar rules, but early in the pandemic, recognizing the widespread closures of medical offices, the FDA lifted other in-person requirements. It kept the rule for mifepristone. The American College of Obstetricians and Gynecologists, along with other medical organizations and a reproductive justice organization called SisterSong, went to federal district court in Maryland, where the FDA is located, for an injunction to require the agency to treat the abortion drug as it was treating other drugs during the public health emergency.

In July, U.S. District Judge Theodore D. Chuang agreed with the plaintiffs that under the circumstances of the pandemic, the in-person rule imposed an undue burden on women's access to abortion. He issued a nationwide injunction under which the abortion drug still had to be dispensed directly by medical professionals—it would not be available, for example, for pickup at pharmacies—but doctors would be able to mail or otherwise deliver it directly to their patients. When the Fourth Circuit refused the Trump administration's request for a stay pending appeal, the administration went to the Supreme Court. Jeffrey B. Wall, the acting solicitor general, told the justices that any problem of access to the drug was attributable to the pandemic itself and was not the FDA's problem to solve.

The administration's brief cited the Supreme Court's 1980 decision that upheld the Hyde Amendment, a budgetary provision that excludes abortion coverage from the federal Medicaid program. If a woman could not afford to pay for an abortion, the court had said then, her real problem was not the Hyde Amendment but poverty, a problem that the government didn't create and had no obligation to correct. Invoking that precedent in the FDA case, the administration's lawyer reminded the court that "the government need not remove obstacles to abortion access that are not of its own creation."

After the government filed its application for a stay, on August 26, six weeks passed without word from the court. On October 8, an unusual order emerged that revealed the depth of the fissure in the court's conservative bloc. The one-paragraph order was unsigned. It was obviously the result of an intricate compromise by which Chief Justice Roberts held the support of Gorsuch and Kavanaugh. The government's application was neither granted nor denied. Rather, the court would hold it "in abeyance," with the explanation that "without indicating the Court's views on the merits of the District Court's order or injunction, a more comprehensive record would aid this Court's review." The order invited the administration to go back to the district court with a new motion "to dissolve, modify, or stay the injunction, including on the ground that relevant circumstances have changed." In other words, had the pandemic situation improved since the district court's ruling in July? Were more medical offices now open? "The District Court should rule within 40 days of receiving the Government's submission," the order concluded.

Alito could barely contain his fury. "There is no legally sound reason for this unusual disposition," he wrote, joined by Thomas in a dissenting opinion that was four times the length of the order itself. While he did not call out the chief justice by name, Roberts was clearly his target as he rehashed the court's internal disputes months earlier over COVID-related limits on indoor worship services. "The free exercise of religion," Alito wrote, "has suffered previously unimaginable restraints, and this Court has stood by while that has occurred." He quoted Roberts's opinion from the first of the COVID religion cases in May, in which the chief justice had written that unelected judges, lacking "the background, competence, and expertise to assess public health," should not second-guess the judgment of experts. In the FDA case, Alito continued, the district judge "took a strikingly different approach" and, rather than deferring to the experts at the FDA, "saw the pandemic as a ground *for expanding the abortion right* recognized in *Roe v. Wade*" (emphasis in original).

"Under the approach recently taken by the Court in cases involving restrictions on First Amendment rights," Alito concluded, "the proper disposition of the Government's stay application should be clear: grant. But the Court is not willing to do that. Nor is it willing to deny the application. I see no reason for refusing to rule."

From the outside, it was hard to know what had set off Alito's tirade: religion, abortion, or his ill-concealed personal animus toward the chief justice. Probably all three. The 2020–21 term was only three days old, and already the bonds of civility that had united the justices in grief over their colleague's death seemed ready to snap.

THE TERM'S FIRST order in an election case came in an appeal brought by Republican officials in South Carolina who wanted to restore the state's long-standing requirement for a witness to sign an absentee voter's ballot. The state legislature had debated whether to suspend the witness requirement during the pandemic but did not make a change. A group of Democrats led by Kylon Middleton, an African American minister from Charleston, brought a lawsuit arguing that for voters who lived alone or who were avoiding contact with others during the pandemic, the witness requirement imposed a burden on the right to vote. A federal district judge agreed and granted a preliminary injunction suspending the requirement. The refusal by the United States Court of Appeals for the Fourth Circuit to grant the state's request for a stay enabled thousands of South Carolina voters to mail in their ballots without a second signature.

By the time the state's appeal reached the Supreme Court, some twenty thousand mail-in votes had been cast, presenting the justices with two questions: whether to grant the stay that the state sought and, if so, whether to make the stay retroactive, requiring thousands of people to vote again after getting a new ballot and finding a witness to sign it. All eight justices voted to grant the stay, but the majority refused to make it retroactive. The unsigned order provided that "any ballots cast before this stay issues and received within two days of this order may not be rejected for failing to comply with the witness requirement." Thomas, Alito, and Gorsuch wanted to go further and make the stay retroactive. They did not give a reason, noting only that they "would grant the application in full."

Each of the election cases, it seemed, presented a different facet of the problem of how a state's election apparatus should respond to a public health emergency. Each raised the question of which government agency should make that determination: federal court, state court, state election official, state legislature. A case from Alabama involved curbside voting, an accommodation that several Alabama counties had provided in the past to make it easier for people with disabilities to vote in person. The Centers for Disease Control and Prevention, in fact, was now recommending this practice. While Alabama law neither provided for it nor prohibited it, Alabama's secretary of state announced that curbside voting would be prohibited. Represented by several civil rights organizations, five voters, some disabled and some elderly, filed suit and won an injunction in federal district court. The United States Court of Appeals for the Eleventh Circuit refused the state's request for a stay pending appeal, and Alabama turned to the Supreme Court.

The court gave Alabama its stay, offering no explanation in an unsigned order. Justices Sotomayor, Kagan, and Breyer dissented, with Sotomayor writing at length for the three. She quoted from the district court testimony of one of the plaintiffs, Howard Porter, Jr., "a Black man in his seventies with asthma and Parkinson's Disease," who observed that his ancestors had given their lives for the sake of voting. "And while I don't mind dying to vote," Mr. Porter had testified, "I think we're past that—we're past that time."

A case from Wisconsin presented a deadline extension issue. A federal district judge had ruled that mail-in ballots would count as long as they were received by six days after Election Day. The Seventh Circuit had granted a Republican request for a stay, and the Democratic National Committee appealed to the Supreme Court, asking the justices to lift the stay. The court refused by a vote of 5 to 3, with Justices Kagan, Breyer, and Sotomayor dissenting. This time, both sides had something to say, filing a total of thirty-five pages of opinions. The most illuminating opinion, and the shortest, was the single paragraph that Chief Justice Roberts filed to explain how he reconciled two votes that appeared directly to contradict one another: his vote in the Pennsylvania case to permit a court-ordered deadline extension to remain in effect, and now his vote just a week later to block the court-ordered extension in Wisconsin.

The difference lay in the identity of the decision maker. In the Pennsylvania case, it was the state's supreme court that had ordered the extension, while in Wisconsin, the order had come from a federal judge. To the chief justice, the distinction was crucial. "While the Pennsylvania applications implicated the authority of state courts to apply their own constitutions to election regulations," he explained in the Wisconsin case, "this case involves federal intrusion on state lawmaking processes." He continued: "Different bodies of law and different precedents govern these two situations and require, in these particular circumstances, that we allow the modification of election rules in Pennsylvania but not Wisconsin." It was a distinction that would prove critical in the months to come.

The court issued the Wisconsin order on October 26, the day of Amy Coney Barrett's Senate confirmation. While she had taken her seat, albeit virtually, by the time the court issued two final preelection orders two days later, she did not participate. The court's public information office, in response to questions, made clear that this was not because she had recused herself but rather "because she has not had time to fully review the parties' filings."

One of those cases was from North Carolina. It was another deadline extension case, but with a difference: The six-day extension for receipt of mailed ballots had been ordered not by a judge but by the state's Board of Elections. Republican legislative leaders failed to persuade the Fourth Circuit to block the extension and came to the Supreme Court seeking an injunction. By a vote of 5 to 3, the court turned the Republicans down. Justices Thomas, Alito, and Gorsuch dissented. Clearly, they had not bought the distinction the chief justice had just made in the Wisconsin case between state and federal intervention. Gorsuch, in a dissenting opinion that Alito also signed, embraced the notion that under both the North Carolina and U.S. constitutions, the legislature was entitled to the last word.

The other case was from Pennsylvania. The Pennsylvania Republicans were back. Having failed by the 4-to-4 tie vote earlier in the month to get a stay of the state supreme court's deadline extension, they had now filed a formal petition challenging the extension and were asking the justices to expedite the petition's consideration. Without being expedited, the petition would not come up for the justices' review until December at the earliest.

But it was too late. All eight justices voted to deny the motion to expedite, even Alito, who wrote that although the petition itself "calls out for review by this Court," he had to "reluctantly conclude that there is simply not enough time at this late date to decide the question before the election." Thomas and Gorsuch signed Alito's statement. This was not necessarily the end of the Pennsylvania case, Alito warned, noting that the petition itself was still alive although not expedited. He observed that the state had ordered county boards of elections to segregate all ballots cast during the three-day extension period, "so that if the State Supreme Court's decision is ultimately overturned, a targeted remedy will be available." Election Day was six days away and Amy Coney Barrett was now on the Supreme Court.

The cases arising from the COVID pandemic presented the Supreme Court with a kind of judicial stress test. The justices, operating remotely and in a tightly compressed time frame, lacked the safety valve that casual daily interactions and weeks of quiet negotiation ordinarily provide a multimember court. While even in normal times, justices don't casually drop in on one another's chambers, they eat lunch together in their private dining room during weeks when the court is hearing arguments. The rule at lunch is not to talk business, the idea being that people who disagree about the Constitution can nonetheless find common ground in the latest production at the Kennedy Center.

Lacking the familiar elements of daily life at the court, the justices were necessarily thrown back on their sense of what mattered most. Law alone offered no definitive answer to the questions the pandemic brought to the court's door. In a public health crisis of historic dimension, what values should the court vindicate and in what voice should it speak? Where to strike the balance, for example, between a community's desire for congregate worship and the experts' call for restrictions on public gatherings? When does a pandemic justify, or require, rewriting long-standing election rules that are usually unobjectionable but that now threaten to keep voters from the polls? And the overarching question in a system built on federalism and the separation of powers: Who decides?

The answers not only divided liberal justices from conservatives but fractured the court's conservative bloc. The pandemic cases drove to the surface rifts that revealed a court fumbling toward a new center of gravity. As the month ended, the chief justice still held the center. In fact as well as name, it was still the Roberts court. The ground beneath his feet was shifting, to be sure. The question, as the month ended and the newest justice took her seat, was how long it would be before it crumbled.

IN 1995, WHEN she was just an assistant professor of law—not yet dean of Harvard Law School or a justice of the Supreme Court—Elena Kagan published an essay titled "Confirmation Messes, Old and New." She was sharply critical of the Senate for having permitted the Supreme Court confirmation process to become "a vapid and hollow charade, in which repetition of platitudes has replaced discussion of viewpoints and personal anecdotes have supplanted legal analysis." The Senate had abandoned its proper role, she complained: "When the Senate ceases to engage nominees in meaningful discussion of legal issues, the confirmation process takes on an air of vacuity and farce, and the Senate becomes incapable of either properly evaluating nominees or appropriately educating the public."

Well said. But fifteen years later, when President Barack Obama nominated her to succeed Justice John Paul Stevens, Kagan played the game as it had evolved, declining to answer the few substantive questions that senators threw her way. The takeaway from her seventeen hours of senatorial interrogation was an exchange with Senator Lindsey Graham. He asked Kagan, who was then serving in the Obama administration as solicitor general, about the foiled bombing of a commercial airliner the previous Christmas Day. What was she doing that day? the South Carolina Republican asked. "You know, like all Jews, I was probably at a Chinese restaurant," Kagan replied. "Good answer," said the senator, who voted for her confirmation.

There were no similar light moments during Amy Coney Barrett's confirmation hearing, but the absence of substance was entirely familiar. In fact, Barrett invoked as a precedent Elena Kagan's refusal to answer substantive questions. Senator Dianne Feinstein, the Judiciary Committee's ranking Democrat, noted that Barrett's mentor, Justice Scalia, had dissented in 1992 in *Planned Parenthood v. Casey*, the case that reaffirmed the constitutional right to abortion the court had established nineteen years earlier in *Roe v. Wade*. "Do you agree with Justice Scalia's view that *Roe* was wrongly decided?" Feinstein asked.

"So, Senator, I do want to be forthright and answer every question so far as I can," Barrett replied. "I think on that question, I'm going to invoke Justice Kagan's description, which I think is perfectly put. When she was in her confirmation hearing, she said that she was not going to grade precedent or give it a thumbs-up or thumbs-down, and I think in an area where precedent continues to be pressed and litigated, as is true of *Casey*, it would actually be wrong and a violation of the canons for me to do that as a sitting judge." Her reference was to the canons of judicial conduct. Feinstein tried again and got the same answer.

The hearing opened October 12, and senators questioned Barrett for two days. The Democratic senators' anger permeated the proceedings. Confirmation was foreordained, and the Democrats, helpless to stop it, were determined to exact whatever political price they could from the unseemly rush to fill the vacancy. The weapon they deployed was Barrett's 2017 law review article criticizing the Roberts opinion that had saved the Affordable Care Act back in 2012. Their point was that if Barrett was confirmed, she would be seated in time for the latest challenge to Obamacare, *California v. Texas*, scheduled for argument on November 10. An enemy of the statute, as they portrayed her, would have a seat at the table at a crucial moment.

The Democratic senators did everything they could to emphasize the human stakes in the case. The Trump administration was asking the court to invalidate the entire statute, and each senator told stories of individual constituents whose preexisting conditions would cause the loss of their insurance and thus of their medical lifeline if the justices followed Trump's road map. As they spoke, the Democrats displayed oversized posters with photographs of these constituents. The stories were heartrending: brain tumors, car accidents, children clinging to life, real people about to be thrown back into the jungle that was the American healthcare system before Obamacare. Each account ended with a reminder to whoever might be listening that these individuals' only hope was the fact that it was the Affordable Care Act that had saved them by abolishing lifetime caps on coverage and prohibiting insurance companies from refusing to insure people with preexisting medical conditions.

Amy Barrett had an answer for this, one that she repeated throughout the hearing: That's not this case. As she told first Senator Feinstein and then the others, "It's not a challenge to preexisting conditions coverage or to the extreme maximum relief from a cap." That was true, as Senator Dick Blumenthal told her: "Technically you're correct. But—it's a big 'but'—if the trial court is upheld and there's no severability, the entire act goes down."

The Connecticut Democrat's reference was to the heart of the argument in the upcoming case. The case turned on whether the law's requirement for individuals to buy insurance, which the Roberts opinion in 2012 had upheld as a valid exercise of Congress's power to levy taxes, was still valid now that Congress had reduced to zero the penalty for not buying insurance. A decision that the "individual mandate" had become unconstitutional would be of little moment; the American public had embraced Obamacare and no longer needed a push to sign up for it. The real question was whether invalidating the mandate would leave the rest of the law standing—whether the mandate was "severable" from the remainder of the statute—or whether part or even all of the Affordable Care Act would have to fall along with the mandate. Although the nominee was reluctant to acknowledge it, the potential implications of the case were every bit as grave as the Democrats claimed.

Senator Chris Coons of Delaware made the point most explicitly. Congress had voted and failed to overturn the Affordable Care Act seventy times, he observed. "So now on the eve of the election, I believe President Trump is making a last-gasp attempt to get the Supreme Court to do it for him. He can't do it through the democratic process. He can't do it administratively. He's going to try and do it with one more challenge."

A handful of times during the hearing, Barrett departed from her script to defend herself, and this was one. "I want to emphasize, just given this last line of questions that you're asking," she told Coons, "that I am standing before the committee today saying that I have the integrity to act consistently with my oath and apply the law as the law, to approach the ACA and every other statute without bias. And I have not made any commitments or deals or anything like that. I'm not here on a mission to destroy the Affordable Care Act. I'm just here to apply the law and adhere to the rule of law."

Another such moment came in response to another question from Senator Coons, this one about the election. The president, Coons said, "has been, I think, unfortunately, very, very clear about what he hopes for from a Supreme Court nominee." He continued: "Just days after Justice Ginsburg passed, the president was asked why there was such a rush to fill her seat before the election. And he responded, and I quote: 'We need nine justices. You need that with the millions of ballots that they'—and he meant the Democrats—'are sending. It's a scam. It's a hoax. You're going to need nine justices.' The next day he told reporters again, he doubled down, 'I think this'—and he means the election from the context—'will end up in the Supreme Court. It's very important. We must have nine justices.'"

Coons continued: "Our president has also been asked whether he'll commit to a peaceful transition if he loses the election. He's been asked directly and repeatedly. And instead of responding in the way we'd expect of any leader of the free world, with a clear and simple yes, he's tried to sow confusion and distrust in the potential results. So, Your Honor, I'm concerned that what President Trump wants here couldn't be clearer. That he's trying to rush this nomination ahead so you might cast a decision, a vote, in his favor in the event of a disputed election. And he's doing his level best to cast doubt on the legitimacy of an election in which literally millions of votes have already been cast, most of them by mail."

The senator asked Barrett to commit to recusing herself from "any case arising from a dispute in the presidential election results three weeks from now." Barrett would not make that commitment. She would consider recusal if and when the time came. Meanwhile, she said, "I certainly hope that all members of the committee have more confidence in my integrity than to think that I would allow myself to be used as a pawn to decide this election for the American people."

There was another reason for the Democrats' strategy beyond getting voters to focus on the potential loss of Obamacare as the result of Barrett's confirmation. The emphasis on healthcare gave the Democratic members of the Judiciary Committee something to talk about other than the nominee's religion.

During the hearing on Barrett's nomination to the Seventh Circuit in 2017, Senator Feinstein's questions about her commitments as a devout Catholic had sparked a backlash, one that was carefully cultivated by the religious right and seriously damaging to the Democrats. The Democratic leadership had clearly decided not to let that happen again, and the Judiciary Committee Democrats showed rare discipline in following their marching orders to stay away from religion.

For their part, the Republicans on the committee had not received the Democratic memo. They came prepared—overprepared—to defend Barrett against an attack that never came. It started with the opening round of questioning by the committee's chairman, Lindsey Graham. "I'm glad President Trump chose you," Graham told her. "And really, before the people of the United States is a very basic question: Is it okay to be religiously conservative? Is it okay to be pro-life in your personal life? It clearly is okay to be progressive and be pro-choice and seek a seat on the Supreme Court. I think resoundingly yes. And here's why your nomination is so important to me. In my world, to be a young conservative woman is not an easy path to take."

Referring to Senators Joni Ernst of Iowa and Marsha Blackburn of Tennessee, Graham continued: "We have two women on this committee. They can talk about it better than I. So I want to thank President Trump for choosing you, and I will do everything I can to make sure that you have a seat at the table." And Graham wrapped up his half hour of questioning with "God bless you."

Senator Josh Hawley of Missouri bore down even more heavily. "I'm not aware," he told Barrett, "of any law or provision of the Constitution that says if you are a member of the Catholic church and adhere to the teachings of the Catholic church or you have religious convictions in line with those of your church teaching, that you're therefore barred from office. Are you aware of any constitutional provision to that effect?"

Whatever Barrett thought about the preposterous lead-up to Hawley's question, she continued to play the role of demure witness. "I would think the Religious Test Clause would make it unconstitutional," she said.

Having prepared to battle a nonexistent foe, Hawley pressed on. "Well, let me just ask you about the Test Clause, since you bring it up. Article Six says 'No religious test shall ever be required as a qualification to any office or public trust under the United States.' Can you just give us your sense as a constitutional expert, scholar, judge now, of the significance of Article Six for our constitutional scheme?"

Barrett dutifully replied: "The Religious Test Clause prohibits this body, prohibits the government generally, from disqualifying people from office because of their religious beliefs."

Hawley, like Barrett a former Supreme Court law clerk, continued with his oddly patronizing line of questions. "And there's no indication from the Constitution that religious believers are second-class citizens in any way, is there?" he asked.

"Well, the Free Exercise Clause certainly suggests to the contrary," Barrett answered.

There was more of this, but finally Hawley overreached and made it impossible for the nominee to give the platitudinous response he clearly wanted. "Let me ask you about attempts to disfavor religious believers on the basis of faith," he said. "Is it your understanding, can a government at any level, federal government, state government, municipality, whatever, can they treat religious believers differently? Can they single them out for disfavor versus a nonreligious group? Is that permissible in our constitutional order?"

Too much the law professor and judge to descend to Hawley's level, Barrett suggested nuance where the senator sought simplicity. "Well, Senator Hawley, that's a complicated question because there's a lot of doctrines surrounding that, and there aren't bright line rules. And so that question would come up in a case with facts and it would require the whole judicial decision-making process. So it's not a hypothetical that I can answer." Hawley changed the subject.

SENATOR LINDSEY GRAHAM had been right about one thing. Amy Coney Barrett had indeed become a role model for young religious women. "A New Feminist Icon" was how Erika Bachiochi, a self-described "pro-life feminist," labeled her in an essay in *Politico Magazine*. Bachiochi, a keynote speaker at the 2020 March for Life antiabortion rally in Washington, wrote that "Barrett embodies a new kind of feminism, a feminism that builds upon the praiseworthy anti-discrimination work of Ginsburg but then goes further." The author's "further" consisted of a belief that "sexual equality is found not in imitating men's capacity to walk away from an unexpected pregnancy through abortion, but rather in asking men to meet women at a high standard of mutual responsibility, reciprocity and care."

Young women who embraced Barrett were fascinated by her combination of high attainment and motherhood. "This is the first time I have seen a woman in the upper echelons of the U.S. government in whom I recognize something of myself and my approach to feminism," Jane Sloan Peters wrote in the Jesuit magazine *America* after watching the confirmation hearing. "Specifically, this is a feminism which holds that a flourishing family is not an obstacle to personal success and that pro-life views are compatible with being both compassionate and educated—in this case, devastatingly intelligent."

During the spring of 2020, a well-received FX miniseries titled *Mrs. America* brought the largely forgotten figure of Phyllis Schlafly into the country's living rooms. Cate Blanchett played Schlafly, a Catholic mother of six with a law degree, who often began her speeches by thanking her husband for allowing her to come. She was a brilliant political strategist who masterminded the successful effort to defeat the Equal Rights Amendment and along the way created an important early piece of the political right's infrastructure, the Eagle

Forum. (The organization, still headquartered in Schlafly's adopted hometown of Alton, Illinois, continues to warn about the dangers of feminism and to fight sporadic efforts to revive the still unratified Equal Rights Amendment.) By attacking abortion and gay rights, Schlafly was able to draw traditional Catholics and newly energized evangelicals into what became a politically powerful "pro-family" movement. She died at age ninety-two in 2016, months after endorsing Donald Trump's presidential candidacy in her final public act.

The nine-part *Mrs. America* takes Schlafly's story through the 1980 election of Ronald Reagan, for whom she had mobilized important support. We see a deflated woman who, despite having achieved her political goal of defeating the ERA, found her personal ambition thwarted, her hope to serve in Congress or in the Reagan cabinet unfulfilled. In real life, the prospect of an appointment to the Supreme Court also crossed her mind, but Reagan's search for the first female Supreme Court justice passed Schlafly by in favor of Sandra Day O'Connor.

Forty years later, more than a few people looked at Amy Coney Barrett and saw Phyllis Schlafly. And how could they not, given the similarities in the two women's biographies? That Schlafly and Barrett, one in death and one striding toward a bright future, both filled the public screen in 2020 was just a coincidence—or was it? Seen from one perspective, it was Phyllis Schlafly who made Amy Coney Barrett possible.

During Barrett's confirmation hearing, Lindsey Graham served her a softball question: "People say that you're a female Scalia. What would you say?"

Barrett began her answer with her now familiar phrases about Scalia's approach to constitutional and statutory interpretation. Then she caught herself. "I want to be careful to say," she told Graham, "that if I'm confirmed, you would not be getting Justice Scalia. You would be getting Justice Barrett."

No one could doubt the validity of that statement. Justice Barrett, not Justice Scalia. Justice Barrett, not Justice Ginsburg. Or Justice Barrett, living Phyllis Schlafly's unrealized dream?

CHAPTER FOUR

NOVEMBER · TURNING POINT

Although Fox News had called Arizona for Biden at 11:20 on election night, the outcome of the presidential election was still uncertain the next morning when the nine justices met by telephone for the argument in the major religion case of the term. The question the case presented seemed far removed from the tumult of electoral politics: whether the Constitution's Free Exercise Clause entitled a Catholic social service agency to violate its contract with the city of Philadelphia by refusing to consider same-sex couples as potential foster parents for children in the city's custody. Yet of course *Fulton v. City of Philadelphia* had almost everything to do with politics.

It was politics that had populated the Supreme Court with Republican-appointed justices eager to elevate the presence of religion in the public square, politics that had now brought the court to the point of repudiating its modern approach to the Free Exercise Clause. Expressed most recently in a 1990 decision, *Employment Division v. Smith*, that approach required that religious claims to special treatment had to yield to a "neutral" and "generally applicable" law. There was no religious carve-out from laws intended to apply to everyone, the court held; just as the government could not single out religion for special burdens, neither could it bestow on religion special privileges.

Conservatives had once been content with the idea that what the Constitution required when it came to religion was simply neutrality.

Justice Scalia's majority opinion in the *Smith* case embodied that understanding and emphasized its historic roots. He reached back to a case from 1879, *Reynolds v. United States*, in which the court rejected the claim by the Church of Jesus Christ of Latter-day Saints to a religious-based exemption from the criminal law against polygamy. In the language Scalia quoted from the *Reynolds* opinion, "To permit this would be to make the professed doctrines of religious belief superior to the law of the land, and in effect to permit every citizen to become a law unto himself."

But a generation had passed since *Smith*. Not only had there been a complete turnover in the court's membership since 1990, but a mobilized religious right was pushing vigorously against the notion that neutrality sufficed as either government policy or constitutional interpretation. Persuading the Supreme Court to overturn *Smith*, or, failing that, at least to pay that precedent only the most minimal deference, became a goal of religious conservatives.

Along the way, the target of their solicitude underwent a significant shift. Like *Reynolds* more than a century earlier, *Smith* concerned a minority religion, the Native American Church, which makes sacramental use of the illegal hallucinogen peyote. Two members of the church in Oregon, employed by a private organization as drug counselors, had lost their jobs over their peyote use. Their dismissal for drug use made them ineligible for unemployment benefits under state law. Their claim to a religious exemption from that disqualification was a sympathetic one that made Scalia's language appear harsh, even retrograde. In a handful of cases during the years before *Smith*, the court had begun to interpret the Free Exercise Clause as requiring the government, in limited circumstances, to accommodate minority religious practices. Now the court had seemingly turned its back on adherents of minority religions, leaving government free to exact a heavy price for not playing by the majority society's rules.

The *Smith* decision alarmed both liberals and conservatives, producing an unusual pan-religious coalition that lobbied for a law to serve as a legislative correction. This was the Religious Freedom Restoration Act (RFRA), which sailed through Congress with near unanimity in 1993. Its title was catchy but tendentious; the law didn't so much "restore" religious freedom as reset the balance between the First Amendment's two religion clauses, one protecting religious exercise and the other prohibiting the official establishment of religion. Signing the bill at a White House ceremony, President Bill Clinton declared that "the power of God is such that even in the legislative process, miracles can happen." (While Congress of course cannot overturn a Supreme Court decision that interprets the Constitution, the bill's sponsors claimed to be doing something more modest: writing into law a standard that required the government to accommodate religious needs unless it could show a compelling reason to refuse.)

The new law offered a powerful tool for advancing religious interests. But the court ruled in 1997 that Congress had lacked the constitutional authority to make RFRA binding on the states. That meant that when it came to conflicts over claims to religious exemption from state and local laws, *Employment Division v. Smith* still governed. But while the law remained the same, the context in which demands for religious exemption were arising had undergone a transformation in the intervening thirty years. As in the *Smith* case itself, such claims historically had come from the fringes of the American religious spectrum, from minority religions that, lacking political influence, turned to the courts as a last resort. Now demands for special treatment were coming to the courts not from the fringes but from the heartland, from the country's two biggest religious groups, Catholics and evangelical Protestants. The *Fulton* case the court heard the day after Election Day exemplified this shift.

Fulton v. City of Philadelphia was brought to the court by the Becket Fund on behalf of the Archdiocese of Philadelphia and its affiliated foster care agency, Catholic Social Services (CSS). Along with two dozen other private agencies, CSS had a contract with the city to find foster placements for children in the city's custody who needed temporary homes. Each agency signed a contract that required adherence to Philadelphia's Fair Practices Ordinance, which barred discrimination on the basis of race, religion, sex, disability, and sexual orientation.

The city learned in 2018 that CSS was nonetheless refusing to consider same-sex couples as potential foster parents, a policy the agency said was based on its religious disapproval of same-sex marriage. When Philadelphia refused to renew the contract, CSS sued, claiming a violation of its First Amendment rights to free speech and the free exercise of religion. Citing *Employment Division v. Smith*, the lower courts ruled for the city, which the courts found was under no obligation to grant an exemption from its neutral and generally applicable ordinance. The Becket Fund's petition to the Supreme Court framed the issue bluntly: "Whether *Employment Division v. Smith* should be revisited."

Surprisingly, the November 4 argument barely touched on that all-or-nothing question. Instead, the two lawyers who argued on behalf of the archdiocese, Lori H. Windham of the Becket Fund and Hashim M. Mooppan, a lawyer in the Trump administration's solicitor general's office, both tried to persuade the justices that Philadelphia was applying the Fair Practices Ordinance in a way that undermined its claim to neutrality. They said the city permitted its contracting social service agencies to make distinctions among potential foster parents for reasons that had nothing to do with sexual orientation. "*Smith* doesn't control when the city uses a system of individualized exemptions," the Becket Fund lawyer told the court.

But as the lawyer for the city, Neal K. Katyal, explained when his turn came, this account conflated the two stages of the foster care placement process. At the first stage, identifying those qualified to serve as foster parents, there were in fact no exemptions from the ordinance's no-discrimination command. Katyal explained that it was only at the second stage, the placement of specific children in specific homes, that the best interests of the child might require a foster parent's characteristics, such as a disability, to be taken into account.

Justice Barrett, freed from the constraint of her scripted role at her Senate confirmation hearing, proved an active and probing questioner. To the Becket Fund's lawyer, she said: "You argue in your brief that *Smith* should be overruled. But you also say that you win even under *Smith* because this policy is neither generally applicable nor neutral. So, if you're right about that, why should we even entertain the question whether to overrule *Smith*?"

"Justice Barrett, you're exactly right that we can and should win this case even under *Smith*," the lawyer replied, her concession made necessary by the structure of her argument. She urged the court to reconsider *Smith* in any event. But the request fell flat, because Barrett's inquiry was indeed the question of the hour: If CSS could prevail despite *Smith*, on the specific facts of this case, what would be the court's justification for taking the giant step of overruling the precedent? The case seemed about to shrivel from the profound to the nearly trivial. But then Justice Alito's aggressive questioning of the city's lawyer shifted the argument in a new direction.

"Look," Alito said to Neal Katyal. "If we are honest about what's really going on here, it's not about ensuring that same-sex couples in Philadelphia have the opportunity to be foster parents. It's the fact that the city can't stand the message that Catholic Social Services and the archdiocese are sending by continuing to adhere to the old-fashioned view about marriage. Isn't that the case?" In other words, wasn't Philadelphia validating the very specter that Alito had evoked in his opinion dissenting from *Obergefell* five years earlier: that those with religious objections to same-sex marriage would soon themselves become the victims of discrimination?

This was not a case about discrimination, Katyal tried to explain, pointing out that Philadelphia was still paying CSS some $26 million a year for other child-related services, hardly evidence of anti-Catholic prejudice. Alito was unmoved. Brett Kavanaugh picked up the attack when his turn came to question Katyal. Kavanaugh used his time to deliver a stern lecture. "It seems like Philadelphia created a clash and was looking for a fight and has brought that serious, controversial fight all the way to the Supreme Court," he said. This was a strange accusation, given that it was the archdiocese, not the city, that had brought the case to the Supreme Court, and it was the court itself that had decided to accept it. Kavanaugh continued: "And what I fear here is that the absolutist and extreme position that you're articulating would require us to go back on the promise of respect for religious believers."

This was quite a performance in an argument that was supposed to be about whether to overrule *Employment Division v. Smith*. Clearly, these two justices had an agenda—but exactly what was it? What would they gain by portraying the city of Philadelphia as mired in anti-Catholic prejudice? If that was what the case was really about, what would the eventual decision mean for the next case, or the case after that? Even though the rules of the court's telephonic argument sessions made it harder than usual to read the court, it was evident that something else was going on.

By the time the justices hear a case, months have elapsed since the initial decision to grant the petition, and there has likely been little if any substantive discussion among them in the interim. So the real importance of the argument is its role in permitting the justices, using the advocates as something of a foil, to engage in cryptic conversation with one another, testing theories and seeing how colleagues respond.

But the telephonic arguments of the 2020–21 term made it impossible for an argument to serve this important purpose. That was so not only because of the absence of useful visual cues of facial expression and body language, but also because Chief Justice Roberts's practice of calling on each justice in turn, in order of seniority, and limiting each to a few minutes of question time ruled out spontaneous responses and interjections by colleagues whose turns had passed or not yet arrived. While it was hard to imagine how the telephonic arguments could have proceeded any differently without descending into chaos, there was no doubt that the procedure exacted an informational price.

Still, habits die hard, and it seemed that Justices Alito and Kavanaugh were seeking to use the *Fulton* argument in the old-fashioned way, to inject a new idea into the mix, a different way of approaching the case. Amy Barrett had not been on the court the previous winter when the justices discussed the *Fulton* case. (The court's website indicates that the justices considered the petition at four consecutive conferences before deciding on February 24, 2020, to grant it.) Alito and Kavanaugh could therefore not simply assume that Barrett was committed during her first term to overturning a major constitutional precedent—and in fact, her question to the Becket Fund lawyer suggested that she might well not be on board for that project. But Alito and Kavanaugh had a backup plan, a possible alternative approach that could be useful not only for deciding *Fulton* in the Catholic agency's favor but for enabling religious groups to prevail in other clashes between government regulation and religious conviction. If the court could find that the city was motivated by anti-religious hostility, the archdiocese's case would no longer be governed by *Smith*, but instead by a case the court had decided in *Smith*'s aftermath nearly thirty years before *Fulton*, a case with the unwieldy name of *Church of Lukumi Babalu Aye, Inc. v. City of Hialeah*.

The *Lukumi* case, decided in 1993 by a vote of 9 to 0 (there were several separate concurring opinions, making the decision technically not unanimous), held that the Florida city had violated the Free Exercise rights of the followers of an Afro-Cuban religion, Santeria, when it banned animal sacrifice within city limits. Hialeah had not prohibited killing animals for food or for sport, only for sacrifice, a central element of Santeria practice. Justice Anthony Kennedy's majority opinion, compiling abundant evidence of the city fathers' discomfort with Santeria practice and its practitioners, erased any doubt about the city's motive. "The pattern we have recited discloses animosity to Santeria adherents and their religious practices," Kennedy wrote, concluding: "The ordinances had as their object the suppression of religion."

Under *Lukumi*, a government policy shown to discriminate against religion would be deemed to violate the Free Exercise Clause unless the government could show both a "compelling" need for the policy and that the policy swept no broader than necessary to meet that need. That was the definition of "strict scrutiny," the standard that *Smith*'s critics maintained the court should have applied in the *Smith* case and that the Religious Freedom Restoration Act had ostensibly "restored." But the facts of the *Lukumi* case were so exotic, and the city's animosity toward a religious minority so unquestionable, that the decision's broader significance wasn't immediately apparent. Rarely cited for its first two decades, *Lukumi* all but disappeared from view. But as the court's interest in bolstering Free Exercise claims blossomed, the justices rediscovered *Lukumi*. In June 2018, in one of Justice Kennedy's last opinions before his retirement, *Lukumi* proved enormously convenient, enabling the court to avoid resolving the thorny constitutional question presented by the conflict between a same-sex couple seeking to celebrate their marriage and a baker who claimed that his Christian beliefs prohibited him from designing a cake for the occasion.

Coming so soon after the court's same-sex marriage decision, the *Masterpiece Cakeshop* case drew enormous attention. There seemed no way out of the dilemma the case posed. A victory for the baker could hand vendors of all kinds of goods and services a license to discriminate against same-sex couples. A majority on the court did not want to go that far. But on the other hand, the baker had framed his case as one of artistic freedom, arguing that as a "cake artist," he should not be forced to put his talents to a use that he found repellent.

But then *Lukumi* came to the rescue. The Colorado Civil Rights Commission, acting on the gay couple's complaint, had found the baker in violation of the state law that prohibited discrimination on the basis of sexual orientation, among other characteristics, by businesses that served the public. It turned out that two commission members had made statements during the deliberations that were decidedly not friendly toward religion, one of the commissioners remarking that "religion has been used to justify all kinds of discrimination throughout history." Citing *Lukumi*, Justice Kennedy's majority opinion held that the statements demonstrated sufficient hostility to religion to have infected the official proceedings. The baker prevailed; the titanic battle between religion and gay rights was postponed to another day; and the rediscovered *Lukumi* soon began serving broader purposes.

In the Supreme Court's early orders upholding pandemic-related restrictions on worship services, justices who dissented cited *Lukumi* with a subtle but important difference from the use Justice Kennedy had made of it. Neither in the first of the COVID cases, *South Bay United Pentecostal Church v. Newsom*, decided in May 2020 over a dissent by Justice Kavanaugh, nor in *Calvary Chapel Dayton Valley v. Siso-*

lak, decided over an Alito dissent two months later, was there smoking-gun evidence of religious hostility. But that proved no obstacle. The two justices offered an expansive reading of *Lukumi* that made such evidence unnecessary. Hostility was simply to be inferred any time the government treated religious activity less advantageously than secular activity. So in Alito's view in *Calvary Chapel*, Nevada's attendance limit of fifty people at worship services "blatantly discriminates against houses of worship" because, by contrast, the state capped attendance at sports arenas and casinos not at fifty people but at fully 50 percent of capacity. That public health experts discerned a difference in the transmissibility of the virus between people in close and prolonged contact at a religious service and spectators dispersed in a half-filled stadium was of no moment. The distinction might have been permissible as an emergency response at the beginning of the pandemic, Alito said, but four months later, "the problem is no longer one of exigency, but one of considered yet discriminatory treatment of places of worship."

Such a broad reading of *Lukumi*, if embraced by a majority of the court, promised something more: the effective neutering of *Employment Division v. Smith*. After all, if hostility was so easy to find, there would be little need to overturn *Smith* and take the institutional heat for repudiating a precedent. *Smith* could remain on the books, but with a careful selection of facts and a creative drawing of inferences, it could be rendered irrelevant in nearly any case where it might otherwise matter. *Lukumi*, rather than *Smith*, would control the outcome.

Supreme Court arguments are often more suggestive than predictive, and this was not the only way to understand the puzzling argument that failed to grapple with the question the justices had agreed to decide. Evidence of what strategy Alito and Kavanaugh had in mind would have to wait for the decision itself. Well before then, there were other cases to hear.

AMY CONEY BARRETT'S confirmation hearing had taken place in a Senate hearing room filled with poster-sized portraits of Democratic senators' constituents who, according to the Democrats who told their stories, depended on the Affordable Care Act—Obamacare— for their very lives. Now, on November 10, less than a month later, the moment had arrived for the Supreme Court to hear the latest challenge to that law's survival.

Three days earlier, the major television networks and the Associated Press had called the presidential election, declaring Biden the winner by a comfortable Electoral College margin. But Trump was refusing to concede, bolstered by a Republican leadership that circled around him. "The media can predict, but the media doesn't get to decide who the winner is," Senator Roy Blunt of Missouri, the senior Republican with oversight responsibility for the election, said on television the next day. Fox News became the platform for Republican leaders to air their unsubstantiated claims of fraud, talking points that would soon enough morph into lawsuits.

The Democrats hadn't managed to defeat Barrett's nomination, but their emphasis on the imperiled state of the Affordable Care Act made sure that anyone who paid the slightest attention to the hearing understood the stakes in the case called *California v. Texas*. The case boiled down to three questions. The first concerned the constitutionality of the Affordable Care Act's "individual mandate," the requirement for everyone to have health insurance. The statute enforced the mandate by imposing a financial penalty on those who failed to comply. The revenue-raising property of the penalty was what enabled Chief Justice Roberts, in the 2012 opinion that Professor Amy Coney Barrett had criticized in a law review article, to construe the penalty as a tax and to uphold the mandate's constitutionality as within Congress's power to impose taxes. Now, as part of the 2017 Trump tax package, Congress had reduced the penalty to zero. As a result, the mandate's penalty no longer raised revenue. So, its tax power rationale on which it had been sustained in 2012 having evaporated, was the mandate now unconstitutional?

The second question followed from the first. If the mandate was now unconstitutional, did that make the entire ACA, with its more than one thousand separate provisions, unconstitutional as well, as the federal district court had held? The ostensible rationale for that devastating ruling lay in the history of the ACA. The law's drafters and supporters had argued that the mandate was essential to the ACA's viability. Their fear was that without it, healthy people would not sign up for health insurance and the insurance market would collapse under the skyrocketing premiums necessary to insure a population heavily weighted toward the unhealthy. The fear had proved unfounded. Drawn by such popular provisions in the law as coverage for preexisting conditions, the public had embraced Obamacare and kept buying insurance even without the penalty. If the mandate was now held to be unconstitutional and was simply carved out from the rest of the nine-hundred-page statute, no one would blink.

The answer to the third question in the case was what really mattered: Was the mandate "severable"? Severability is a question of congressional intent: What would Congress have done had it known that a particular provision would be cut from a bill it was considering? Supreme Court precedents have established a presumption in favor of severability: If Congress would have preferred no law at all to a law without the provision at issue, let Congress say so.

In the case of the Affordable Care Act, the same Congress that eliminated the financial penalty failed to repeal the ACA itself. This was the basis for Chief Justice Roberts's comment to Kyle D. Hawkins, the solicitor general of Texas, the state leading the red-state attack on the law. "I think it's hard for you to argue that Congress intended the entire act to fall if the mandate were struck down, when the same Congress that lowered the penalty to zero did not even try to repeal the rest of the act," the chief justice said. "I think, frankly, that they wanted the court to do that. But that's not our job."

Roberts's comment on what he took as Congress's motive was no casual observation. It reflected his discomfort and annoyance with the repeated efforts, of which this was the third, to enlist the Supreme Court as a combatant in the guerrilla warfare over President Obama's most significant legislative accomplishment. Roberts himself had paid a price for having refused to follow the script the ACA's opponents had written for him back in 2012. Not only had the sniping from the right never stopped, but one of his critics was now his newest colleague.

Roberts was one of the justices least likely to tip his hand during oral argument. His questions to lawyers for both sides were usually equally pointed and unrevealing of his own opinion. This time it was different. He made his view perfectly clear, telling Hawkins: "Under the severability question, we ask ourselves whether Congress would want the rest of the law to survive if an unconstitutional provision were severed. And here, Congress left the rest of the law intact when it lowered the penalty to zero. That seems to be compelling evidence on the question."

Justice Kavanaugh picked up that thread when his turn came to question the Texas lawyer. "Looking at our severability precedents, it does seem fairly clear that the proper remedy would be to sever the mandate provision and leave the rest of the act in place, the provisions regarding preexisting conditions and the rest," he said, adding: "Congress knows how to write an inseverability clause, and that is not the language that they chose here."

Kavanaugh repeated the same point to Jeffrey B. Wall, the Trump administration's acting solicitor general, who argued in support of Texas. (Wall's participation was a head-spinning feature of the argument—a president whom the public had just rejected for reelection was on the side of those who sought to bring down a federal law that the man who would next occupy the White House fully supported.) "As you know," Kavanaugh told Wall, "we have a strong background presumption of severability, which reflects a longstanding understanding of how Congress works and our respect for Congress's legislative role under Article I. And it also establishes a clear default rule, or fairly clear default rule, against which Congress can legislate. Congress knows how to write an inseverability clause, but this language is different from how that usually looks. So I just want to give you an opportunity to respond to that."

Wall had no real answer. His response that "everyone agrees that there's no magic words requirement" was hardly a persuasive rebuttal. Almost two hours into the argument, this latest attack on the ACA appeared to have foundered on its own implausibility. The Affordable Care Act's supporters had anticipated the argument with dread, expecting the worst. They came away with hope bordering on confidence that Obamacare would once again survive its encounter with the Supreme Court.

The Senate Democrats had tried hard to portray Amy Coney Barrett as an enemy of the Affordable Care Act, arriving at the court with an agenda to assist in the law's destruction. During the argument, she surely knew that her every word would be carefully weighed. Her questions about the plaintiffs' standing and other issues off the main point gave nothing away. It appeared in any event that hers was unlikely to be the deciding vote. Assuming that the questions from Roberts and Kavanaugh reflected their actual intentions, and counting the votes of the court's three liberals, there were at least five votes for severability. The decision was months away, but whenever it came, the spotlight might land elsewhere than on the newest justice.

THE FEDERALIST SOCIETY'S stars and staunchest supporters gather every November in Washington for its annual National Lawyers Convention, always capped by a black-tie dinner with a speaker popular in the world of conservative lawyering. Samuel Alito was guaranteed to draw a Fed Soc crowd. He had spoken at the dinner over the years, always refusing to allow recording and never releasing the text of his remarks. This year was different. The convention was virtual. Alito addressed the convention on November 12 via Zoom, fully aware that his speech was also being picked up by YouTube and that he was speaking not only to the Federalist Society but to the world. He embraced the moment, declaring his loyalty to Fed Soc and describing it, for anyone unfamiliar with it, as a group of people brought together by a shared love of ideas. Then he moved to his theme, the threat to "religious liberty."

"It pains me to say this, but in certain quarters, religious liberty is fast becoming a disfavored right," he declared. "The question we face is whether our society will be inclusive enough to tolerate people with unpopular religious beliefs." The "unpopular belief" that most concerned him was opposition to same-sex marriage. "You can't say that marriage is the union between one man and one woman. Until very recently, that's what the vast majority of Americans thought. Now it's considered bigotry."

Alito relitigated recent cases, fuming over not only those his side had lost but, oddly, those in which he had prevailed. The Little Sisters of the Poor, an order of Catholic nuns who run nursing homes for the elderly poor, had won their Supreme Court case just months earlier when the Supreme Court upheld the Trump administration's rule that supported unlimited religious and "moral" objections to the Affordable Care Act's requirement for contraception coverage in employer-based health plans. But Alito still felt moved to deplore "the protracted campaign against the Little Sisters of the Poor," who he said had been "under unrelenting attack for the better part of a decade." He was still fighting the *Calvary Chapel* case, in which the court had upheld, over his dissent, Nevada's COVID-related limits on in-person gatherings. "So if you go to Nevada, you can gamble, drink, and attend all sorts of shows. But here's what you can't do. If you want to worship and you're the fifty-first person in line, sorry, you are out of luck, houses of worship are limited to fifty attendees."

Seen from one perspective, Alito was doing little more than quoting his own words from his published opinions, which most in his core audience had surely read. Although his speech was widely reported the next day, since it was so unusual to see Alito in action off the bench, his remarks contained no real news. But as a public performance the speech was remarkable. Alito was projecting a style of grievance conservatism, as if he were suffering a deep hurt that even numerous victories could not assuage, an anger that saw no difference between winning and losing. The "certain quarters" where religious liberty was "fast becoming a disfavored right" quite obviously included the marble temple of justice at One First Street, NE.

Who was the audience for this performance? Alito had been on the court for more than fifteen years, and certainly his colleagues knew him well. He didn't have to perform for them. Was it a pep talk to the base, lest the young conservatives who make up the society's core become discouraged by the recent losses in the COVID cases? Or was he really speaking to Amy Coney Barrett, his goal being to make sure that she grasped the full dimension of the battle he was fighting and understood that she, and she alone, was in a position to turn his defeats into victories?

As closely connected as she was to the Federalist Society, Barrett certainly appreciated Alito's starring role in the conservative firmament. While the seventy-year-old justice was little known to the general public and even in Washington could have gone about his business unrecognized, inside the conservative legal world, Alito was close to a Ruth Bader Ginsburg–style rock star, the regular subject of hagiographic treatment in right-wing journals. An article in *The American Spectator* called him "in his unspectacular way, one of the noblest men in American public life today." Michael Stokes Paulsen, a prominent conservative law professor writing in the religious journal *First Things*, described him as "the most consistent, solid, successful conservative on the court" and added: "There are louder talkers, flashier stylists, wittier wits, more-poisonous pens, but no one with a more level and solid swing than Justice Samuel Alito."

What the legal right seemed most to admire about Alito was his utter reliability. There was no chance he would drift toward the middle like John Roberts. After fifteen years, his votes on the side of a defendant in a criminal case could be counted on one hand. He had none of Clarence Thomas's libertarian tendencies, nor would he waste time and influence chasing chimerical legal theories as Thomas was wont to do. Alito was a highly effective player of the long game, deploying a dissenting opinion or a "statement respecting the denial of certiorari" to lay down a marker, letting the world know the kind of case he needed in order to advance his several projects. For a graduate of Princeton (where he joined an organization that opposed the admission of women) and Yale Law School, he embraced an odd form of populism, criticizing the American Bar Association and the American Psychological Association as elite organizations that should mind their own business and not file briefs telling the Supreme Court what to do. Applying for a job in the Reagan Justice Department in 1985, when he was thirty-five years old, he wrote that when he was growing up, "the greatest influences on my views were the writing of William F. Buckley, Jr., the *National Review*, and Barry Goldwater's 1964 campaign."

With such transparency, the only mystery about Alito was the source of his anger. To all appearances, his path to the top of the legal profession had been a smooth one, missing only a Supreme Court clerkship, which he had sought but failed to get. His background was solidly middle class. His father, born in Italy, worked for the state of New Jersey as director of the Office of Legislative Services. His mother taught school. Early in Alito's career, he was a lawyer in the U.S. solicitor general's office, one of the most prestigious government legal jobs a young lawyer can have. Later, he was the United States attorney, the top federal prosecutor, in New Jersey. When President George W. Bush named him to succeed Sandra Day O'Connor, Alito held a life-tenured job as a federal appeals court judge. Sandra O'Connor, the "swing" justice of her time, occupied the center of the court. Her replacement by Alito in 2006 bore immediate results, wrenching the court to the right on issues including abortion, race, and women's rights. In recent decades, only Thurgood Marshall's replacement by Clarence Thomas in 1991 had made such a difference.

And now there was another seismic shift. Alito's Federalist Society speech came at the end of the November argument sitting, the two-week period that marked Amy Coney Barrett's initiation into the active life of the court. The justices would meet—virtually, of course—the next morning to vote on the week's cases and go over the opinion assignments for the eight cases they had heard during the sitting. That arguments wouldn't resume until after Thanksgiving did not promise a tranquil interlude. Cases challenging the presidential election results were beginning to pile up in the lower courts. The Trump administration's last-minute federal execution spree was generating urgent appeals. Even so, a pause was at hand. And Sam Alito had delivered his message.

IN 1998, WHEN Amy Coney Barrett was a law clerk at the D.C. Circuit, she and her Notre Dame mentor, Professor John Garvey, had published a law review article titled "Catholic Judges in Capital Cases." At nearly fifty pages, this was a dense and deeply felt analysis of the moral and theological problem presented by Catholic opposition to the death penalty, sourced in the secular literature on legal ethics as well as in Catholic doctrine. (Garvey later became president of the Catholic University of America.) "We believe that Catholic judges (if they are faithful to the teaching of their church) are morally precluded from enforcing the death penalty," the authors asserted near the beginning of the article. They went on to argue that the meaning of "enforce" was not self-evident. In actually imposing a death sentence, a Catholic judge would be engaged in "formal cooperation" with evil, impermissible under Catholic doctrine and requiring conscientious Catholic judges to recuse themselves from the sentencing phase of a capital trial. A judge who presided over only the guilt phase of a capital trial, on the other hand, would be engaged only in "material" rather than "formal" cooperation, and such participation could be "morally justified." Indeed, the two wrote, "the judge has a strong reason to participate in that phase: society needs judges to enforce the criminal law."

The appellate judge, Barrett and Garvey argued, is one step further removed from the evil of capital punishment; an appellate panel "neither condemns nor saves the defendant" because "to affirm the sentence is not to approve it, but to say that the trial court did its job." Nonetheless, they conceded that the problem was not that simple. "Whatever might be the legal significance of an affirmance, it probably looks to most people like an endorsement of the sentence. This can cause scandal, leading others into sin." The authors concluded that the morality of the situation "will, it seems to us, vary from one set of circumstances to another."

Least problematic, the article argued, was the role of the judge in habeas corpus cases, which follow a full round of appeals. Habeas corpus is the route state inmates take to federal court after exhausting their state appeals. At this stage, Barrett and Garvey wrote, the "real responsibility" for a death sentence lies elsewhere, and "the conscientious judge is not under a moral obligation to save all the prisoners he can."

The prospect of functioning on a death penalty case in any capacity may well have seemed remote to the young Amy Barrett in 1998. The article was an engaging intellectual exercise that combined her interests in law and religion and raised hard questions with few precise answers. Two decades later, the question of how to be a Catholic judge with a condemned inmate's life in one's hands was no longer an abstraction, but one that required an up-or-down answer. The federal penitentiary at Terre Haute, Indiana, in the Seventh Circuit, was the designated location for federal executions. The federal government had not executed anyone since 2003, but Attorney General William Barr announced in July 2019 that the federal death penalty was back. Of the sixty inmates on federal death row, more than a dozen would be designated for execution. The announcement, seemingly out of the blue as the presidential campaign was coming into view, was a shock to the criminal justice system. The federal death penalty had been quiescent for so long that the inmates' lawyers had to scramble to get their clients back into court on any available theory.

First in line was Daniel Lewis Lee, a white supremacist convicted of a triple murder and sentenced to death by a federal jury in Arkansas in 1999. A last-minute drama, not untypical, was playing out. The relatives of Lee's three victims argued that they wanted to witness the execution but wanted it postponed so they would not have to travel during the pandemic. On July 10, 2020, with days to go before the scheduled execution, a district judge in Indiana granted an injunction and the government appealed. Barrett was a member of the three-judge appellate panel that lifted the injunction and that criticized the district judge for having granted it.

Simultaneously, in a separate proceeding, a district judge in Washington, D.C., enjoined Lee's execution and those of three others on Barr's list. Bypassing the D.C. Circuit, Barr appealed directly to the Supreme Court. By a vote of 5 to 4, with Justices Breyer, Sotomayor,

Ginsburg, and Kagan dissenting, the court lifted the injunction; both Breyer and Sotomayor wrote dissenting opinions. Lee was executed that night.

Barrett's first encounter with the death penalty as a Supreme Court justice came in mid-November, by which time the Trump administration had already carried out seven executions. The next person in the queue was Orlando Hall, convicted in 1994 for the kidnap, rape, and murder of a sixteen-year-old girl. His lawyers challenged the government's plan to use a single drug, pentobarbital sodium, for the lethal injection rather than the multidrug protocol that the states had been using until lethal injection drugs became difficult to obtain. A district judge in Washington, D.C., had granted a stay of execution, and the attorney general once again took the case directly to the Supreme Court.

The court lifted the stay on November 19 over the dissenting votes of Justices Breyer, Sotomayor, and Kagan. Neither the justices in the majority nor the three dissenters issued opinions. There were no names attached to the majority's one-sentence order. Neither was there any indication that any of the six unnamed justices had refrained from participating.

Hall was executed just before midnight. It was the first federal execution by a lame duck administration in more than a century. Five more would follow in the ensuing weeks, the thirteenth and final execution carried out a mere four days before Trump left office.

There was something deeply discordant about what Justice Sotomayor, in one of her dissenting opinions, described as an "execution spree." The country as a whole was turning away from the death penalty. Only seven nonfederal death sentences were carried out in 2020, in contrast to the modern high of ninety-eight executions in 1999. While states had collectively imposed hundreds of death sentences a year in the late 1990s, they sentenced only eighteen to death in 2020. Although that number was no doubt artificially low, given that the pandemic had led most states to close courtrooms for much of the year, there had been only a few dozen death sentences a year for the previous several years. Colorado abolished the death penalty in 2020.

Virginia, which in the modern era had executed more people than any other state except Texas, repealed its death penalty in March 2021. Louisiana, once an active death penalty state, had not carried out an execution in ten years.

As the Trump administration's march to the death chamber proceeded, the divided court was mostly silent. What had been a 5-to-4 split when Ruth Bader Ginsburg was alive and voting in dissent had become a recurrent 6 to 3. There was, evidently, nothing further to say.

Not since the first decade after the Supreme Court permitted executions to resume in 1976 had the justices been so consistently divided on the question. Justices' papers from that time reveal a court close to emotional meltdown, the justices at odds with one another over such questions as whether to permit a state to execute an inmate whose Supreme Court appeal was still pending. While no member of the Roberts court had been serving as a justice during that fraught early period, there was one who had been an eyewitness: Chief Justice Roberts himself.

William Rehnquist was an associate justice when Roberts clerked for him during the 1980–81 term. Of all the members of the Burger court, Rehnquist was the most ardent supporter of the death penalty. Five years after the court's 1976 decisions reauthorizing capital punishment, the states had carried out a mere handful of executions. As death rows filled up, death penalty lawyers were growing adept at keeping their clients alive as long as possible.

And Rehnquist grew increasingly impatient. In April 1981, he let loose with a separate opinion that placed the court's internal tensions under a bright public spotlight. The forum he chose to take his battle public was an unexpected one: a pending petition from a Georgia death row inmate, Wayne Coleman, convicted eight years earlier of murdering six members of a family. Rehnquist dissented from the court's refusal to hear Coleman's second appeal, not because he found the appeal meritorious, but precisely the opposite. Rehnquist wanted his colleagues to grant the case and use it as a vehicle for speeding up executions.

"The existence of the death penalty in this country is virtually an illusion," Rehnquist wrote. "Virtually nothing happens except endless drawn-out legal proceedings." He continued: "I do not think that the court can continue to evade some responsibility for this mockery of our criminal justice system." With the Supreme Court's acquiescence, he maintained, the federal courts "have converted the constitutional limits upon imposition of the death penalty by the states and the federal government into arcane niceties which parallel the equity court practices described in Charles Dickens's *Bleak House*."

A tirade like Rehnquist's might not seem unusual today, when justices increasingly resort to the "shadow docket"—a common name for cases the court decides without formally accepting them for argument—to air their grievances about how the court is handling its business. In its time, however, the Rehnquist opinion was startling. It also proved effective, placing delays in carrying out the death penalty on the country's agenda for discussion and debate. No mere tactician, Rehnquist was a master strategist. After becoming chief justice in 1986, he presided over a steady tightening of death row inmates' access to federal court. He eventually enlisted Congress in his project; in 1996, President Clinton, running for reelection on an anti-crime platform, signed the Antiterrorism and Effective Death Penalty Act, which codified much of what Rehnquist and his court had already accomplished through case law.

Rehnquist's performance in *Coleman v. Balkcom* was undoubtedly part of Supreme Court lore, known even to those justices who were too young to have observed it (Amy Barrett would have been a third grader at the time). Roberts had lived it. Did the memory resonate as he watched judges on the lower federal courts try to slow down the Trump execution spree, or as he saw his court divide over the same issue that had caused such a schism among colleagues during the formative year of his clerkship? Over the ensuing years, his old boss had, improbably, managed to convert outsider status into leadership. The painful challenge that faced John Roberts in the sixteenth year of his own tenure as chief justice was the reverse: how to hold on to leadership that was slipping away.

IT WAS JUST before midnight on Thanksgiving eve when the irrefutable evidence arrived that showed just how much Roberts had lost. The justices decided the latest challenge to a COVID-related limit on attendance at religious services. As in the earlier cases from California and Nevada, the vote was 5 to 4. But it was a different 5 to 4. This time, with Amy Coney Barrett by his side, Alito had won. Along with Breyer, Kagan, and Sotomayor, Roberts was in dissent.

The case was from New York City. In zones with the highest and second-highest rates of COVID, neighborhoods in Brooklyn and Queens with large populations of Catholics and Orthodox Jews, Governor Andrew Cuomo had limited attendance in churches and synagogues to ten people in the "red" zones and twenty-five in the "orange." The houses of worship in these zones were better off than other places where people gathered in close proximity for prolonged periods. Theaters, auditoriums, concert halls, and sports arenas were closed entirely under the governor's executive order. But shops, liquor stores, and other businesses were open without restriction, so the Roman Catholic Diocese of Brooklyn and the Orthodox organization Agudath Israel had each sued, seeking an injunction on the ground of anti-religious discrimination.

They lost in federal district court, Judge Nicholas G. Garaufis writing in the diocese's case that "the court is satisfied, based on the evidence submitted, that the state's policy is guided by science, not a desire to target religious practice." The plaintiffs each appealed to the Second Circuit, asking for an immediate injunction while their appeals moved forward. On November 9, the appeals court denied that request while placing the appeals on an expedited schedule with a mid-December hearing date.

The vote on the panel was 2 to 1, the majority noting that the religious groups could not show discrimination when "within each zone, the order subjects religious services to restrictions that are similar to or, indeed, *less severe than* those imposed on comparable secular gatherings." The dissenter was one of the Second Circuit's newest judges, Michael H. Park, a former Alito law clerk whom Trump had named to the appeals court. The order's "disparate treatment of religious and secular institutions is plainly not neutral," he asserted. The case therefore had to be analyzed under *Lukumi*, requiring the governor to satisfy the demands of the strict scrutiny standard of a compelling interest and narrow tailoring. This, Park concluded, the governor could not do.

The diocese and Agudath Israel appealed separately to the Supreme Court, each with briefs that relied heavily on *Lukumi*. Agudath Israel's lawyers claimed that Governor Cuomo's "statements and actions are more discriminatory" than those in the *Masterpiece Cakeshop* case or in *Lukumi* itself. The diocese told the court that the governor's order "impermissibly targets religion for disparate and adverse treatment" by imposing "a value judgment that certain secular activities, ranging from supermarket shopping to working in a nine-to-five office job, are more worthy of maintaining in times of crisis than is religious worship."

By November 25, when the justices granted the injunction with an unsigned opinion that applied to both appeals, the original "red" and "orange" designations were no longer in effect. The neighborhoods' zone was now the less restrictive "yellow," meaning that there was no longer a numerical cap on attendance but rather a limit of 50 percent of maximum occupancy, a much bigger number for the diocese given that most of its churches could hold hundreds of worshippers. In his dissenting opinion, Roberts cited this change as the main reason not to grant the injunction. "There is simply no need to do so," he wrote:

Numerical capacity limits of 10 and 25 people, depending on the applicable zone, do seem unduly restrictive. And it may well be that such restrictions violate the Free Exercise Clause. It is not necessary, however, for us to rule on that serious and difficult question at this time. The Governor might reinstate the restrictions. But he also might not. And it is a significant matter to override determinations made by public health officials concerning what is necessary for public safety in the midst of a deadly pandemic.

The majority's unsigned opinion responded to Roberts's argument. There was "no justification" for the court to refrain from ruling, the majority said. The governor had changed the zone designations after the cases had reached the Supreme Court, and the plaintiffs "remain under a constant threat" that Cuomo might change them back. Citing *Lukumi*, the opinion insisted that religious worship had been singled out for discriminatory treatment. The majority offered no acknowledgment of the lower courts' findings that worship was treated more favorably than the most directly comparable activities of moviegoing or attendance at sports events. In fact, the opinion suggested that comparisons were irrelevant. All that mattered was that the state was restricting worship attendance at all:

> Members of this Court are not public health experts, and we should respect the judgment of those with special expertise and responsibility in this area. But even in a pandemic, the Constitution cannot be put away and forgotten. The restrictions at issue here, by effectively barring many from attending religious services, strike at the very heart of the First Amendment's guarantee of religious liberty.

Both Gorsuch and Kavanaugh filed separate concurring opinions. None of the others in the majority—Alito, Thomas, and Barrett—wrote separately; presumably one of them was the unsigned opinion's author. Gorsuch devoted much of his opinion to a pointed attack on the chief justice's opinion in the first of the COVID cases, *South Bay United Pentecostal Church v. Newsom*. "That opinion was mistaken from the start," Gorsuch wrote, ascribing to Roberts "a particular judicial impulse to stay out of the way in times of crisis." He went on: "But if that impulse may be understandable or even admirable in other circumstances, we may not shelter in place when the Constitution is under attack. Things never go well when we do." This was an unusually personal attack, especially from one who had just played the winning hand. More grievance conservatism.

Kavanaugh returned in his opinion to the broad view of *Lukumi* he had previously expressed in dissent. Citing the case twice in a single paragraph, he wrote:

The State argues that it has not impermissibly discriminated against religion because some secular businesses such as movie theaters must remain closed and are thus treated less favorably than houses of worship. But under this Court's precedents, it does not suffice for a State to point out that, as compared to houses of worship, *some* secular businesses are subject to similarly severe or even more severe restrictions [emphasis in original]. . . . Rather, once a State creates a favored class of businesses, as New York has done in this case, the State must justify why houses of worship are excluded from that favored class. Here, therefore, the State must justify imposing a 10-person or 25-person limit on houses of worship but not on favored secular businesses. The State has not done so.

But of course the state did justify the distinction between in-person worship and retail shopping; so did the American Medical Association and the Medical Society of the State of New York, in an amicus brief they jointly filed on the state's behalf that explained in detail how the virus spread among people in different settings and that underscored the relative danger of congregate worship. Kavanaugh proceeded as if difference alone amounted to a constitutional violation, whether there was a good reason for the distinction or no reason at all. He extracted from *Lukumi* a kind of "most favored nation" rule: Whatever anyone gets, religion must get too. That was not, as Justice Sotomayor pointed out in dissent, the rule of *Lukumi*. Nor was it the rule of any other case the court had ever decided. But it was, quite likely, the rule now.

Thanksgiving Day marked exactly one month since Amy Coney Barrett's swearing-in on the South Lawn. The president with whom she shared the spotlight on the Truman Balcony would soon be gone. But it was already clear that he would not go quietly.

Although Trump had lost Pennsylvania by more than eighty thousand votes, his campaign went to federal court days after the election for an injunction to undo the certification of Biden's victory. The lawsuit did not explicitly claim fraud, but rather complained about a series of procedures in the handling of mail-in ballots and the treatment of poll watchers that allegedly made the election's outcome "unfair." The district court dismissed the suit, a decision that the Third Circuit upheld on November 27, the day after Thanksgiving.

The Third Circuit's treatment of this obviously frivolous lawsuit might have drawn little notice except for the identity of the judge who wrote the opinion. Judge Stephanos Bibas, formerly a law professor at the University of Pennsylvania, had been one of Trump's earliest appeals court nominees. His twenty-one-page opinion for the unanimous three-judge panel made clear his disdain for the Trump campaign's litigation strategy. Calling the lawsuit's allegations "vague and conclusory," he said: "Free, fair elections are the lifeblood of our democracy. Charges of unfairness are serious. But calling an election unfair does not make it so. Charges require specific allegations and then proof. We have neither here."

The import of Judge Bibas's words was evident. Republican politicians might be willing to do the defeated president's bidding, but Trump-appointed judges were not. At least not this one.

CHAPTER FIVE

DECEMBER · TESTING TIME

ARTICLE III OF THE CONSTITUTION gives the Supreme Court "original" jurisdiction over "controversies between two or more states," and Congress made that jurisdiction "exclusive" in one of the first laws it enacted, the Judiciary Act of 1789. In other words, when one state wants to sue another, it has only one place to go: directly to the Supreme Court.

Most "original cases" involve disputes over boundaries or water rights, locally important but not of general interest. A rare exception was New Jersey's suit against New York over which state was entitled to lay claim to Ellis Island, a mostly man-made pile of landfill in New York Harbor. In 1998, in a decision that shocked New York and would have surprised the millions of immigrants who thought they had at last arrived—indeed, who were usually told by officials that they had arrived—in New York, the justices awarded 90 percent of the island to New Jersey.

In two hundred years, there had been no original case as bizarre or potentially consequential as the one the Texas attorney general, Ken Paxton, filed at the court on December 7, more than a month after Election Day. The Electoral College was to meet in a week. Although Donald Trump had not conceded, it was clear that Joe Biden had won the election by a comfortable 74 electoral votes, 306 to 232. What-ever the Constitution's framers envisioned for the role of the Supreme Court's original jurisdiction, it seems safe to conclude that they did not view it as a vehicle for a lawsuit by one state complaining about how other states had carried out their part of a national election. But that was the essence of the ninety-two-page document that Paxton submitted under the title *State of Texas v. Commonwealth of Pennsylvania, State of Georgia, State of Michigan, and State of Wisconsin.*

Of the ninety-two pages, the first three, labeled "Motion for Leave to File Bill of Complaint," were the most important. The court's practice in handling original cases was first to decide, before moving on to the merits, whether to accept the case. Typically, a motion for leave to file describes the nature of the dispute and explains why it defies resolution at any other level of the judicial system. The actual argument would be reserved for the bill of complaint itself.

This was not the pattern the Texas attorney general followed. Although very short, his motion for leave to file was shot through with red flags, from the use of the noun "Democrat" in place of the appropriate adjective "Democratic"—as in the accusation that the defendant states had used procedures that favored voters in areas "under Democrat control" and with "higher ratios of Democrat voters"—to the concluding paragraph's shocking request to the justices. Paxton was asking the court to intervene in the counting of electoral votes by handing the four states' vote results over to their respective legislatures for "review and ratification," after which those legislatures would make their own choice of electors. The request, if granted, would have voided some 20 million votes.

The states Texas sued had three things in common: Trump had carried all four in 2016; this time Biden had won the popular vote in each; and, most significantly, each had a Republican-controlled legislature. Paxton claimed that the supposed voting irregularities "affect an outcome-determinative numbers [*sic*] of popular votes in a group of states that cast outcome-determinative numbers of electoral votes." Indeed, were Texas actually to prevail in its unprecedented quest to overturn the popular vote in all four and remove the states' total of 62 electoral votes from Biden's column, Trump would win the election.

While the Texas filing was odd, the case would soon get odder. Two days later, a lawyer representing Donald Trump filed a motion to in-tervene in support of Texas. The motion strung together a set of in-disputable facts, drawing from them a completely unsupported inference. For example: "Republican candidates for the U.S. Senate and U.S. House, down to Republican candidates and [*sic*] the state and local level, all out-performed expectations and won in much larger numbers than predicted, yet the candidate for President at the top of the ticket who provided those coattails did not himself get over his finish line in first place." Except for the assumption that these down-ballot Republican victories came on Trump's coattails, this was an accurate statement of what had occurred on November 3. But then came the inference: "These things just don't normally happen, and a large percentage of the American people know that something is deeply amiss."

Could a lawyer admitted to practice in the Supreme Court actually offer such an argument as a reason to permit the president of the United States to come before the court and claim that somewhere, somehow, in some unspecified manner, victory had been stolen from him? The lawyer was John C. Eastman, a professor and former law school dean at Chapman University in Orange County, California. He had come to public attention in August for an op-ed in *Newsweek* that questioned whether Senator Kamala Harris, the California-born daughter of immigrants, was an American citizen and therefore eli-gible to run for vice president. The essay's resonance with Trump's years of questioning Barack Obama's citizenship was hard to miss. Three days after publishing the op-ed, titled "Some Questions for Kamala Harris About Eligibility," *Newsweek*'s editors apologized for it, explaining that to their dismay, "This op-ed is being used by some as a tool to perpetuate racism and xenophobia." (In January 2021, Eastman was forced to resign from his position at Chapman following an uproar on campus over his appearance at the January 6 rally that preceded the Trump-instigated raid on the Capitol. Eastman had proclaimed to loud cheers that "We know there was fraud" and "We know that dead people voted.")

Others jumped on the Texas bandwagon with motions for leave to file on behalf of Texas: seventeen Republican state attorneys general and 126 Republican members of the House, including Kevin McCarthy of California, the minority leader. An organization called the Christian Family Coalition Florida filed, describing itself as "a human rights and social justice advocacy organization representing over 500,000 fair-minded voters." (This description differed a bit from how the organization described itself on its website: "Standing in the gap to protect our traditional family values from a culture in free-fall.")

There were also briefs on the other side, urging the justices to reject the case. Josh Shapiro, attorney general of Pennsylvania, argued that Texas lacked standing to bring such a case: "Texas has not suffered harm simply because it dislikes the result of the election, and nothing in the text, history, or structure of the Constitution supports Texas's view that it can dictate the manner in which four other states run their elections." Twenty states plus the District of Columbia and the territories of Guam and the U.S. Virgin Islands filed in opposition to Texas. A group of seventeen lawyers and legal scholars who had served in Republican administrations, including prominent Supreme Court practitioners well known to the justices, argued that the court lacked jurisdiction: "It would violate the most fundamental constitutional principles for this court to serve as the trial court for presidential election disputes."

There was every reason to assume the court would make short work of the Texas effort. WHY THE TEXAS LAWSUIT TO OVERTURN THE 2020 ELECTION MAY BE THE MOST OUTLANDISH EFFORT YET, read a headline in *The Washington Post* on December 10. The Trump campaign and its Republican allies had lost forty lawsuits by that time, a number that eventually would nearly double. Would the justices want to dirty their hands with what Attorney General Shapiro of Pennsylvania described in his brief as "a cacophony of bogus claims"? William Barr, the president's loyal attorney general, had announced a few days earlier that the Justice Department had uncovered no voting fraud "on a scale that could have effected a different outcome in the election."

And yet, and yet. Who would have imagined not three weeks earlier that the court would flip its position and choose to safeguard indoor worship services rather than public health? Who could forget Trump's public justification for moving so quickly to fill Ruth Bader Ginsburg's seat? The election would "end up at the Supreme Court," he had predicted on September 23, five days after Ginsburg's death, "and I think it's very important that we have nine justices." Now the court had its nine, with Trump responsible for putting three of them there. Who, after all, could dare take anything for granted?

The end came quickly. Early on the evening of December 11, following the justices' regular Friday conference and a mere four days after Paxton brought the case, the court announced that "the State of Texas's motion for leave to file a bill of complaint is denied for lack of standing under Article III of the Constitution." The order contained a one-sentence explanation: "Texas has not demonstrated a judicially cognizable interest in the manner in which another state conducts its elections." In other words, whatever had happened in Georgia, Michigan, Pennsylvania, or Wisconsin during the 2020 election, Texas had no business complaining about it in a federal judicial forum.

The disposition of No. 155 Original, as the court's docket identified the case, was not entirely unanimous. Justices Alito and Thomas issued a "statement"—essentially a non-dissent dissent—expressing the view that "we do not have discretion to deny the filing of a bill of complaint in a case that falls within our original jurisdiction." Their position, which they had taken in previous cases, was a plausible one: that when the Constitution's framers provided that "the Supreme Court shall have original jurisdiction" over suits between states, they intended to make the exercise of that jurisdiction mandatory. "The Court has provided scant justification for reading 'shall' to mean 'may,'" the two justices had written in dissent less than a year earlier, when the court denied Arizona's request to file a bill of complaint against California over that state's imposition of taxes on some Arizona companies. But however textually reasonable their reading of Article III, Alito and Thomas had not persuaded their colleagues to reconsider the court's long-standing position that original cases lay within its discretion. Nonetheless, the two made clear that while they would have accepted the case for filing, they "would not grant other relief." The case was over.

But the election was not, at least in the mind of the president and his partisans. That night, Trump naturally turned to Twitter: "The Supreme Court really let us down. No Wisdom, No Courage!" And later: "A rigged election! Fight on!" It emerged later, in reporting by *The Wall Street Journal*, that Trump intended at that point to "fight on" by bringing his own case in the Supreme Court, but he couldn't find a lawyer to file one. Attorney General Barr; Jeffrey Rosen, Barr's temporary successor; and Jeffrey Wall, the acting solicitor general, all refused. The senior lawyers in the White House counsel's office also opposed the idea.

Trump was left alone with his Twitter account. "The U.S. Supreme Court has been totally incompetent and weak on the massive Election Fraud that took place in the 2020 Presidential Election," he tweeted on December 26. "We have absolute PROOF, but they don't want to see it—No 'standing,' they say. If we have corrupt elections, we have no country!" He closed with an invitation: "See everyone in D.C. on January 6th."

COVID-19 WAS BACK on the court's docket. In mid-November, with deaths from the virus at record levels, Governor Andy Beshear of Kentucky imposed new limits on attendance at commercial venues and social gatherings and ordered all schools to suspend in-person instruction until early January for students in kindergarten through twelfth grade. Governor Beshear was a Democrat. The state's attorney general, Daniel Cameron, was a Republican. Cameron threw the weight of his office behind a lawsuit that a religious school, Danville Christian Academy, brought against the governor. The suit claimed that Beshear's order violated the Free Exercise rights of parents who had chosen to give their children a religious education.

What legal theory could support such a lawsuit? After all, the governor was not singling out religious schools for adverse treatment.

His executive order treated all schools in the state—public and private, religious and secular—precisely the same. This was not a case of worship services being treated differently from grocery stores. It was a case of one school being treated like all other schools.

The parents' view, although their lawyers didn't express it quite so baldly, was that equal treatment didn't suffice. What was needed—what the Free Exercise Clause demanded, in this view—was special treatment. The parents' lawyers argued that in-person instruction in the faith was an essential part of a religious school's mission and that religious schools were therefore entitled to an exemption from the governor's order.

U.S. District Judge Gregory Van Tatenhove, a George W. Bush appointee sitting in Frankfort, Kentucky, accepted that argument. On November 25, the same day the Supreme Court overturned Governor Andrew Cuomo's limitations on attendance at worship services in parts of New York City, Judge Van Tatenhove enjoined enforcement of Governor Beshear's order as it applied to religious schools, and to religious schools only. He began his twenty-one-page opinion with a lecture:

> Part of the genius of the American tradition is that right from the start we were clear about what mattered. We even made a list, the Bill of Rights. Think of it as a catalogue of values so dear that they deserved protection from future edicts or even majorities at a moment in time. Infringing these values is rare. They matter that much.
>
> This case is about one of those values—the ability we each have to follow our religious convictions without interference from the government. Religious schools across the Commonwealth have been closed by the Governor to in-person teaching along with secular schools. This prevents the corporate nature of religious education which is insinuated with worship, prayer, and mentoring.
>
> Many thoughtful people believe that the reason for the Governor's action is a good one—the Commonwealth, indeed the country and the world, is facing the worst pandemic in over one

hundred years. That may be one reason to close schools. But is it a good enough reason to keep religious schools from fully achieving their mission?

Inherent in the way the judge framed the case was an assumption that religious schools alone have a mission necessitating the judiciary's protection from "interference from the government." A different judge might have pointed out that public schools, too, have a vital mission: arming members of the next generation with the knowledge necessary to assume their role as citizens in a pluralistic society. Another judge might also have observed that the governor's purpose was to protect all Kentucky children and their families from a deadly virus, the infection rate of which had quadrupled in the state during the previous nine weeks. Judge Van Tatenhove acknowledged this point in order to dismiss it. "But in an effort to do the right thing to fight the virus, the Governor cannot do the wrong thing by infringing protected values," he wrote.

Governor Beshear filed an emergency appeal with the U.S. Court of Appeals for the Sixth Circuit, which promptly granted a stay of the injunction to preserve the status quo while a formal appeal went ahead. The district judge had made a mistake of law, the three-judge panel concluded. The governor's order, applying to all public and private elementary and secondary schools in the state, "cannot plausibly be read to contain even a hint of hostility towards religion." Because the order was "neutral and of general applicability," the court said, the governing precedent was the Supreme Court's 1990 decision, *Employment Division v. Smith*. The First Amendment's Free Exercise Clause provided no exception.

On December 1, the school and the Kentucky attorney general asked the Supreme Court to vacate the stay. By then, the order was close to expiring by its own terms; most Kentucky schools would close for the Christmas break on December 18, and all would be free to reopen with in-person instruction on January 4. But the school and its supporters didn't want to prevail by the clock. They wanted a Supreme Court win, and based on the court's sudden turn on the COVID question, they had good reason to believe that they would get just that. "It's no answer to say, as Governor Beshear did before the Sixth Circuit, that the religious schools are 'not harmed by conducting 15 days of remote instruction,'" the school's brief informed the justices. "Providing in-person schooling is a core part of Danville Christian's sincerely held religious beliefs."

Among the school's lawyers was a six-person team from First Liberty Institute, a religious litigating organization in Plano, Texas, that describes itself as "the nation's best attorneys, defending your first freedom." First Liberty was best known for its representation of Joe Kennedy, a former high school football coach from Bremerton, Washington. The Bremerton School District had fired him when he refused to stop kneeling and praying at the fifty-yard line at the conclusion of every game, surrounded by players and members of the community. The "praying coach" became a celebrity on the religious right, regarded as a martyr for having sacrificed his career for his faith. His case against the school district reached the Supreme Court late in the 2017–18 term, accompanied by supporting briefs from thirteen Republican state attorneys general, fifteen Republican members of the Senate and House of Representatives, and the Billy Graham Evangelistic Association, among other evangelical groups—heavy weaponry for a high school coach's employment dispute.

The case got the court's attention. The justices considered it at conference ten times before finally denying review in January 2019. The denial was accompanied by a statement from Justices Alito, Thomas, Gorsuch, and Kavanaugh—a sufficient number of justices to have granted the case—explaining that "important unresolved factual questions" weighed against accepting the case in the preliminary posture in which it had arrived. (The coach had sought a preliminary injunction to get his job back and to permit him to pray on the fifty-yard line while his lawsuit proceeded.) The four justices' statement read as an invitation to Kennedy to keep litigating, with a focus next time on his Free Exercise claim rather than the free speech claim on which this petition was based. First Liberty promptly accepted the invitation, returning to the lower federal courts with an eye toward a more fruitful trip to a more receptive Supreme Court. The coach lost in district court and, in March 2021, in the Ninth Circuit, which included in its opinion a photograph of the football players standing in a tight circle, heads bowed in prayer, as members of the community looked on. After failing in July to persuade the full appeals court to rehear the panel's decision, First Liberty promised a swift Supreme Court appeal.

The justices turned down the *Danville Christian* case. An unsigned opinion, issued on December 17, noted that "the Governor's school-closing order effectively expires this week or shortly thereafter, and there is no indication that it will be renewed." The denial of the request to vacate the stay came "without prejudice to the applicants or other parties seeking a new preliminary injunction if the Governor issues a school-closing order that applies in the new year."

As with the Texas challenge to the election just a week earlier, the court had dodged a bullet. The big religion case of the term, *Fulton v. City of Philadelphia*, had been argued weeks earlier; presumably, opinions were already being drafted. The justices had no need to plunge further into the religious wars. With its neutral tone and emphasis on the calendar, the unsigned opinion read like the chief justice's work, but the authorship hardly mattered. What was significant was that Justices Kavanaugh and Barrett had backed Roberts up.

Alito and Gorsuch, however, did not. Each wrote a dissenting opinion. Alito's was the shorter and more conventional, underscoring the obvious but often overlooked fact that a denial of review is not a decision on the merits. "While I do not agree with the court's denial of the applicants' request for emergency relief, no one should misinterpret that denial as signifying approval of the Sixth Circuit's decision," Alito wrote. Gorsuch was more pointed, characterizing the majority as having in effect declared that "we should let this one go because this case is old news; winter break is coming soon." That was wrong, he asserted: "The applicants are entitled to a fair assessment of their rights under accurate legal rules." A governor should not "be able to evade judicial review by issuing short-term edicts and then urging us to overlook their problems only because one edict is about to expire while the next has yet to arrive."

Alito's dissent was a message to the country at large: Don't mistake our decision not to take this case for agreement with the Sixth Circuit. Gorsuch signed Alito's opinion and might have stopped there. But he had a further message to deliver, this one to John Roberts: Don't mistake your success this time as anything other than temporary.

THE TRUMP ADMINISTRATION carried out two executions in mid-December, numbers nine and ten since July, the most civilian executions by the federal government since the nineteenth century. The court denied last-minute appeals from both men, Brandon Bernard and Alfred Bourgeois. Justice Sotomayor wrote opinions dissenting from both denials, filling a largely solitary role she had assumed since Justice Ginsburg's death.

In the *Bernard* case, she wrote alone, although Justices Breyer and Kagan noted separately that like Sotomayor, they would have both granted the stay of execution and accepted the case for full argument and decision. Bernard was eighteen when he participated with fellow gang members in the kidnapping, robbery, and murder of two people at Fort Hood in Texas. In her opinion, Sotomayor pointed out that the prosecution used Bernard's gang affiliation to persuade the jury to impose the death penalty on the ground that he would connect with prison gangs and pose a danger in prison. Instead, Sotomayor noted, "Bernard has not committed a single disciplinary infraction in his two decades in prison."

Sotomayor's main argument was a legal one. The prosecution had emphasized that all members of Bernard's violent gang were "equal," meaning that he was as dangerous as any of the others. But a police official later testified at a hearing for one of Bernard's co-defendants that Bernard was actually at the bottom of a thirteen-tier gang hierarchy. Bernard then argued that this was exculpatory testimony that the prosecution should have disclosed, entitling him to a resentencing. The U.S. Court of Appeals for the Fifth Circuit held that Bernard's claim came too late and was procedurally barred by a rule against successive petitions for habeas corpus. "Under this rule," Sotomayor wrote, "prosecutors can run out the clock and escape any responsibility for all but the most extreme violations."

Kagan joined Sotomayor's dissent in the *Bourgeois* case. Bourgeois was convicted of murdering his two-year-old daughter. Because the crime occurred on a military base—Bourgeois was a civilian truck driver delivering a shipment, and his daughter was in the truck—it was prosecuted as a federal offense. Bourgeois had an IQ of between 70 and 75. At his trial, the judge rejected his claim of intellectual disability. Over the next decade, however, IQ scores in that range became accepted as the clinical standard for intellectual disability, and the Federal Death Penalty Act prohibits the execution of intellectually disabled defendants. When Bourgeois returned to court after ten years with a new habeas corpus petition, a federal district judge found that he had made a "strong showing" of intellectual disability by then current standards. But the U.S. Court of Appeals for the Seventh Circuit rejected the petition on the ground that Bourgeois was barred from relitigating the issue.

In her dissenting opinion, Sotomayor said that Bourgeois "puts forth a strong argument that federal prisoners sentenced to death should be able to file new habeas petitions if they can show a potentially dispositive change in the diagnostic landscape." She added: "I would therefore resolve this open legal issue before sanctioning Bourgeois' execution."

Aside from Elena Kagan, the other justices, including one whose article on Catholic judges and capital punishment had helped make her academic reputation, remained silent.

MORE THAN FIVE years after the *Obergefell* decision gave same-sex couples the constitutional right to marry, there was no avoiding the fact that full equality had not yet been achieved. The *Fulton* case, stemming from a Catholic agency's refusal to consider same-sex married couples as potential foster parents, was one example. Refusal by states to list both names of a same-sex couple on a baby's birth certificate was another.

Indiana was one such state. It took the position that the only way for a birth mother's female spouse to be recognized as a legal parent was through formal adoption. Eight female same-sex married couples sued the state on behalf of themselves and their children. They noted that Indiana listed the name of a birth mother's husband on the birth certificate even if the pregnancy had resulted from donor insemination and the husband was not the biological father. (In fact, one of the plaintiffs had provided the egg for her wife's pregnancy but was still denied the right to list her name on the baby's birth certificate as a parent.) The state's refusal to list both partners as parents, the women argued, therefore violated the Supreme Court's holding in *Obergefell* that the constitutional right to marry includes "the constellation of benefits that the states have linked to marriage."

In June 2016, almost a year to the day after the court had issued *Obergefell*, the women won their case in federal district court in Indianapolis. The state appealed. While the appeal was pending, the Supreme Court decided a similar case from Arkansas, where the state's high court had upheld the state's refusal to list the names of both members of a married female couple on their baby's birth certificate. Reversing that decision with an unsigned opinion—of which Justice Kennedy, who wrote the majority opinion in *Obergefell*, was most likely the author—the justices cited the "constellation of benefits" language along with the decision's injunction that a state may not "exclude same-sex couples from civil marriage on the same terms and conditions as opposite-sex couples." The unsigned opinion, *Pavan v. Smith*, noted that Arkansas law specifically required listing a husband's name on the birth certificate even if the baby had been conceived through anonymous sperm donation.

Three justices, Gorsuch, Thomas, and Alito, dissented. "To be sure, *Obergefell* addressed the question whether a state must recognize same-sex marriages," Gorsuch said, writing for all three. "But nothing in *Obergefell* spoke (let alone clearly)" to the question at hand.

The decision led to considerable speculation when the court issued it in late June 2017. Had Chief Justice Roberts voted? The ready assumption was that because he had not signed the Gorsuch dissent, he must have provided a sixth vote for the majority. But that is not actually a safe assumption when it comes to the Supreme Court's non-transparent shadow docket. Certainly the five members of the *Obergefell* majority, who were all still serving in 2017, joined the unsigned opinion in *Pavan*. But Roberts had been a vigorous dissenter in *Obergefell*. Was he now willing to accept the decision and its logical implications? Or had he perhaps decided not to engage, withholding a vote that would not change the outcome in any event? The answer mattered, but it was not one that an outsider could deduce from the available evidence.

Indiana lost its appeal in the U.S. Court of Appeals for the Seventh Circuit, which interpreted the combination of *Obergefell* and *Pavan* to require the state to treat all married couples equally when it came to their children's birth certificates. The state was not ready to give up. It filed a Supreme Court appeal, *Box v. Henderson*, in June 2020. The state's lawyers clearly had trouble grasping that, whether Indiana cared to acknowledge it or not, the world had changed. "The apparent rationale for the decision below appears to be that, for the convenience of the adults involved, the *Constitution* [emphasis in original] requires states to respect maternal assignment of parental rights," the state wrote in one of its briefs. To anyone who recalled, as perhaps Indiana's lawyers did not, that Justice Byron White, one of the two dissenters in *Roe v. Wade*, had accused women of seeking abortions for "convenience," the word jumped off the page of Indiana's brief. White had demeaned the profound nature of a woman's decision whether to carry a pregnancy to term, and Indiana demeaned the profound reason a woman would seek official recognition as a mother of the child she and her partner intended to raise. It was not convenience. It was identity.

Although the LGBTQ community followed the case closely, it received little public attention amid the tumult of the postelection weeks as it made its way onto the list for the justices' December 11 conference. On Monday, December 14, the court denied Indiana's petition, without comment and without dissent.

A strange, fraught year was drawing to an end. It had been nine months since the justices sat together on the bench, and the end of their isolation from one another was not yet in view. December was the worst month of the pandemic, with thousands of deaths a day for a monthly total of 65,000; by the end of the year, COVID-19 had killed 337,000 Americans.

The justices had assembled on September 23 in the Great Hall, when Ruth Bader Ginsburg's coffin arrived at the court for two days of public viewing. They would meet again on January 20, when the chief justice would administer the oath of office to the president—a new president.

CHAPTER SIX

JANUARY · ACROSS THE STREET

Halfway into his hourlong speech at his "Save America" rally on the morning of January 6—the speech in which he vowed he would "never concede" the election and urged his followers to "walk up Pennsylvania Avenue" to the Capitol—Donald Trump turned to the Supreme Court. His rage and sense of betrayal drove him, in plain view of thousands of people, to perform an interior monologue, unfiltered and close to unhinged.

"Look, I'm not happy with the Supreme Court," he told the throng. "They love to rule against me. I picked three people. I fought like hell for them, one in particular, I fought." He meant Brett Kavanaugh, his second Supreme Court nominee, whose confirmation was nearly derailed two years earlier by a late-breaking accusation of teenaged sexual assault. Clearly, he felt that Kavanaugh had failed to repay a debt. "They all said, 'Sir, cut him loose. He's killing us.' The senators, very loyal senators. They're very loyal people. 'Sir, cut him loose. He's killing us, sir. Cut him loose, sir.' I must've gotten half of the senators. I said, 'No, I can't do that. It's unfair to him. And it's unfair to the family. He didn't do anything wrong. They're made-up stories.' They were all made-up stories. He didn't do anything wrong. 'Cut him loose, sir.' I said, 'No, I won't do that.' We got him through. And you know what? They couldn't give a damn. They couldn't give a damn. Let them rule the right way, but it almost seems that they're all going out of their way to hurt all of us, and to hurt our country. To hurt our country."

The crowd that had gathered to hear from the president how to "stop the steal" must have been mystified as Trump continued his off-topic musing. "And the Supreme Court, they rule against me so much. You know why? Because the story is I haven't spoken to any of them, any of them, since virtually they got in. But the story is that they're my puppets. And now the only way they can get out of that, because they hate that, it's not good on the social circuit. And the only way they get out is to rule against Trump. So let's rule against Trump, and they do that. So I want to congratulate them."

How many in the crowd realized, as they set out on their hike up Pennsylvania Avenue to Capitol Hill, that the Supreme Court sat directly across the street from the Capitol's east front? Of course the building was closed to the public, but even without the pandemic, this would have been a quiet time at the court, with the justices still on their annual four-week winter break. Even those in the "Save America" crowd who knew the court's location were most likely unaware that the building, modeled by the architect Cass Gilbert on a Greek temple, had despite its air of classical permanence stood there for less than a century. From 1860 to 1935, the Supreme Court conducted business in a small, elegant chamber, preserved and all but hidden within the Capitol's labyrinth. The insurrectionists who stormed the Capitol and roamed its corridors on January 6 never found it.

The court may have been of scant interest to the mob, but a photograph that appeared the next day in newspapers and websites around the world was a reminder that the Capitol and the court building, each a physical embodiment of one of the three branches of a tripartite federal government, were inextricably linked on a level both symbolic and concrete. The photo showed the court building as seen through a shattered Capitol window, almost close enough to touch.

The Capitol's invaders, who wore or carried a startling array of symbols including Confederate flags, Nazi insignia, and Christian nationalist banners like the one that proclaimed JESUS IS MY SAVIOR— TRUMP IS MY PRESIDENT, overwhelmed the Capitol police and forced their way inside to prevent the members of the House and Senate from certifying Biden's Electoral College victory. The president, after all, had sent them to the Capitol and told them to "fight like hell." More than five hundred would eventually be identified and arrested, charged with a variety of crimes including assault, impeding law enforcement, and entering a restricted federal building.

Just a week later, on January 13, the House voted to impeach the president for inciting a violent insurrection against the government. Ten Republicans voted with 222 Democrats to launch Trump's second Senate impeachment trial. While Chief Justice Roberts had presided over the Senate trial a year earlier, as Article I of the Constitution commands ("When the President of the United States is tried, the Chief Justice shall preside"), by the time the second trial began on February 9, Trump was no longer president. His presence no longer constitutionally required, Roberts declined the honor. The Democratic senators needed the votes of seventeen Republicans to reach the two-thirds majority necessary for conviction. They got only seven. Months later, the Senate Republicans would use the filibuster to block establishing a special bipartisan commission to investigate the full dimension of what happened on January 6. A commission established by the House Democratic leadership eventually proceeded on its own.

Trump had been defeated, but the full powers of the presidency were still his, a normal if awkward state of affairs during the country's unusually long interregnum between election and inauguration. Yet there was much about this period that was anything but normal. Most obvious, of course, was Trump's refusal to concede and his insistence against all evidence that the election had been stolen from him. Another was the administration's determination to execute as many people as possible during the time remaining.

THE TEN FEDERAL executions during the second half of 2020 were the most in any year by the federal government in more than 120 years and marked the first year that federal executions outnumbered those by all the states combined. The low state total of seven (spread among five states: Texas, Alabama, Georgia, Missouri, and Tennessee) was in part a reflection of the COVID pandemic's disruption of state court proceedings. But it also reflected growing public disenchantment with capital punishment. Colorado repealed its death penalty statute in 2020. Virginia, which for years had been second only to Texas in the number of executions, would in March 2021 become the first Southern state to abolish the death penalty. There had been no federal executions since 2003.

So there was something fundamentally discordant about Trump's sudden rush to kill. There were three federal executions in January, the last taking place just four days before Inauguration Day, bringing to thirteen the number since Attorney General Barr had opened the floodgates in July. Not since the waning weeks of Grover Cleveland's first term in 1889 (Cleveland served two nonconsecutive terms as president) had the federal government carried out executions during a presidential transition. Particularly jarring was the fact that the incoming president had run on a platform that called for the death penalty's abolition. A campaign document titled "The Biden Plan for Strengthening America's Commitment to Justice" declared: "Because we cannot ensure we get death penalty cases right every time, Biden will work to pass legislation to eliminate the death penalty at the federal level, and incentivize states to follow the federal government's example."

The court proved a full partner in enabling the administration to achieve its goal during its final months in office. When a death row inmate asked for a stay of execution, the court denied it. When a lower court granted a stay, the Supreme Court vacated it. Events came to a head with the three executions that took place in January. Lawyers for Lisa Montgomery, the only woman on the federal death row, filed a series of requests for a stay as her execution date approached. She was convicted in 2008 of strangling a pregnant woman in order to cut from her body the viable fetus, which Montgomery then attempted to pass off as her own baby. The U.S. District Court for the Southern District of Indiana granted a stay to permit the law-

yers to present evidence that their client's mental health had deteriorated so sharply as to make her ineligible for the death penalty under
Supreme Court precedents barring the execution of those so divorced
from reality as to be unable to understand what was about to be done
to them and why. After the Seventh Circuit vacated the stay, the Supreme Court denied a final appeal, with Justices Breyer, Sotomayor,
and Kagan noting their dissent. Montgomery was executed on January 13.

Another of the final three, Corey Johnson, who had been part of a
crack cocaine distribution ring, was convicted in 1993 of the drug-
related murders of eight people. His lawyers sought to show that his
intellectual disability made him ineligible for the death penalty under
Supreme Court precedent. Separately, in a case combined with that of
Dustin Higgs, the final federal inmate scheduled for execution, the
lawyers argued that the lung damage both men had suffered from
COVID-19 would make execution by lethal injection "torturous" and
"akin to waterboarding." The federal district court in Washington
granted both men a temporary stay of execution on the COVID
claim. The D.C. Circuit vacated the stay, and the Supreme Court,
with Breyer, Sotomayor, and Kagan dissenting, refused to reimpose
it. The justices also refused to consider Johnson's intellectual disability claim, over dissents by Kagan and Sotomayor. He was executed on
January 14.

Troubling as those cases were, a glaring procedural irregularity
made the final case, that of Dustin Higgs, even more disquieting.
Higgs had been convicted and sentenced to death twenty years earlier
in Maryland for his participation in a triple murder on federal property. (He was not the triggerman; the actual killer pleaded guilty and
received a life sentence, but Higgs maintained his innocence and insisted on going to trial.) Under the Federal Death Penalty Act, a
death sentence must be carried out "in the manner prescribed by the
state" that imposed it. However, Maryland had repealed its death
penalty statute in 2013, making Higgs's execution impossible if the
federal statute was to be applied as written. The Justice Department
filed a motion asking a federal district judge in Maryland to designate

Indiana, where Higgs was housed on death row in federal prison, as the appropriate state for reference under the statute. The judge refused on the ground that he had no authority to make such a change. The Fourth Circuit granted a stay of execution so that it could consider "the novel legal issues presented," scheduling oral argument for January 27.

That date, of course, fell a week after Inauguration Day, and the Trump administration couldn't wait that long. So the acting solicitor general, Jeffrey Wall, went directly to the Supreme Court, asking the justices to overrule the district court without waiting for the Fourth Circuit. Higgs should not be handed such an "absurd windfall," Wall wrote in the Petition for a Writ of Certiorari Before Judgment. The Supreme Court rarely grants such a petition, but it promptly granted this one, vacating the Fourth Circuit's stay and overturning the district court with instructions to treat Indiana as if it had been the state that imposed the death penalty all along. The unsigned order offered no explanation of the majority's reasoning.

Justice Kagan noted her dissent. Justice Breyer, who in 2015 had called for the court to reconsider the constitutionality of the death penalty, wrote a brief dissenting opinion, its tone more sorrowful than angry. "What are courts to do when faced with legal questions of this kind?" he asked. "Are they simply to ignore them? Or are they, as in this case, to 'hurry up, hurry up'?"

Sonia Sotomayor's ten-page dissenting opinion radiated fury. She began by listing the names of the twelve federal inmates already executed in what she called "this expedited spree of executions." The list was an obvious allusion to the "Say their names" mantra of the Black Lives Matter movement. She noted that with Higgs's imminent execution, "the Federal Government will have executed more than three times as many people in the last six months than it had in the previous six decades."

Sotomayor clearly knew that she was not going to change any colleague's mind. Her project was to make as precise a record as possible of the court's behavior. Noting that "this Court has consistently rejected inmates' credible claims for relief," she went on:

The Court has even intervened to lift stays of execution that lower courts put in place, thereby ensuring those prisoners' challenges would never receive a meaningful airing. The Court made these weighty decisions in response to emergency applications, with little opportunity for proper briefing and consideration, often in just a few short days or even hours. Very few of these decisions offered any public explanation for their rationale.

This is not justice.

She cited the court's rule governing requests to the justices to accept a case directly from the district court without waiting for a decision from the Court of Appeals. Under the court's Rule 11, such a request requires "a showing that the case is of such imperative public importance as to justify deviation from normal appellate practice and to require immediate determination in this Court." The government's request in the Higgs case fell "far short" of that standard, she said, explaining: "After failing to act since Higgs' sentence was imposed in 2001, the Government gives no compelling reason why it suddenly cannot wait a few weeks while courts give his claim the consideration it deserves."

"There can be no 'justice on the fly' in matters of life and death," Sotomayor wrote in her concluding paragraph. "Yet the Court has allowed the United States to execute thirteen people in six months under a statutory scheme and regulatory protocol that have received inadequate scrutiny, without resolving the serious claims the condemned individuals have raised. Those whom the Government executed during this endeavor deserved more from this Court."

Higgs was executed at 1:23 the next morning, January 16, a Saturday, four days before Donald Trump would board Air Force One for the last time in order to fly to Florida and avoid the inauguration of his duly elected successor.

"JUDGE SONIA SOTOMAYOR has lived the American dream," the Obama White House proclaimed on May 26, 2009, in the official announcement of the president's choice to fill his first Supreme Court vacancy. There was no doubt of the truth of that statement about a woman born to Puerto Rican parents and raised in public housing in the Bronx, a graduate of Princeton University and Yale Law School who was about to ascend to the ultimate position in the country's legal firmament. While there had obviously never been a Supreme Court justice like her, those bare biographical facts were not the only salient facts about Sonia Sotomayor. She had begun her legal career as a prosecutor, spending five years as an assistant district attorney in the Manhattan office of the legendary Robert Morgenthau. Appointed to the federal district court in New York by President George H. W. Bush, she spent six years as a trial judge followed by eleven years on the Second Circuit. She knew the criminal justice system.

So did the only other former prosecutor on the court, her fellow Princeton alumnus Samuel Alito. (They graduated four years apart, both summa cum laude.) Alito had been the United States attorney, the chief federal prosecutor, in New Jersey. But the lessons the two drew from their prosecutorial experience were strikingly different. The federal government's criminal jurisdiction is limited, and federal prosecutors' offices are well-oiled machines compared with the gritty realities of life in a local district attorney's office. Alito emerged from his three years as U.S. attorney to a fifteen-year tenure as a federal appellate judge with the view that the criminal justice system works pretty well most of the time. Sotomayor came away from her time as a prosecutor with an understanding of how the administration of criminal justice can go wrong, sometimes disastrously so. The Supreme Court she joined was composed entirely of former federal appeals court judges. (Elena Kagan, named to the court the next year, had never been a judge.) Sotomayor was the only one who had presided over an actual trial. All in all, she had more judicial experience than any other justice confirmed to the court in the preceding seventy years.

From the beginning of her tenure, Sotomayor made it a point to call out her colleagues when they overlooked what she regarded as an injustice or let stand a lower court decision that in her view had mangled the law. These opinions typically appeared as dissents on the court's shadow docket of cases being disposed of without having undergone full review with argument and signed opinions. In later years, Ruth Bader Ginsburg often signed Sotomayor's shadow docket dissents, but in the months following Ginsburg's death, Sotomayor was notably alone. Her tone was restrained. Her detailed expositions of the record reflected deep engagement with cases that seemed to have escaped her colleagues' notice.

One such opinion came on the opening day of the term in October 2020. A woman convicted of murder in a Maryland state court had filed a motion for a new trial on the ground that her defense lawyer had provided ineffective assistance. The trial judge ordered her to turn over her "entire defense file" to the prosecution so that the state could respond to her allegations. After a hearing, the judge granted a new trial but denied her request for a new team of prosecutors who would not have been exposed to the confidential attorney-client information that the file contained. She was convicted again and sentenced to life in prison. In her appeal, she argued that the prosecutors' exposure to confidential information about her initial defense strategy was so prejudicial as to have violated her right to counsel under the Sixth Amendment. But the state appeals court ruled that prejudice had to be demonstrated rather than presumed, and found that she had failed to make that showing. That was the basis for her Supreme Court appeal, *Kaur v. Maryland*.

"I fear that, in this case, the criminal justice system failed to live up to its highest ideals," Sotomayor wrote. She faulted the trial judge and the appeals court, but she aimed her sharpest criticism at the prosecutors:

> Finally and crucially, the decision whether to allow the original prosecution team to retry Kaur was not the court's alone to make. The prosecutors, too, had a choice. . . . Prosecutors wield an immense amount of power, and they do so in the name of the State itself. That unique privilege comes with the exceptional responsibility to ensure that the criminal justice system indeed serves the ends of justice. Prosecutors fall short of this task, and therefore do

a grave disservice to the people in whose name they litigate, when they permit themselves to enjoy unfair trial advantages at defendants' expense. Here, regardless of the reason for the acquisition of Kaur's privileged information, and regardless of whatever minimum conduct was required of them by the Sixth Amendment, the prosecutors should have recused themselves from participating in Kaur's second trial as a matter of professional conscience. Their failure to do so casts a troubling and unnecessary shadow over Kaur's conviction and sentence to life imprisonment.

Would Stephen Breyer and Elena Kagan not have agreed with these sentiments? And if so, why would they not have added their names? As in any multimember organization, many calculations go into deciding how to behave as a Supreme Court justice. A new justice quickly realizes that little can be accomplished directly without the agreement of others—three others for granting a case, four others for prevailing in one. But there are other ways aside from those strict metrics to exert influence, and other audiences to cultivate outside the court's marble walls. Clarence Thomas's solitary dissenting and concurring opinions, driven by his personal view of originalism into territory best described as idiosyncratic—as when he argued in dissent in a 2011 First Amendment case that children have no free speech rights because "the founding generation believed parents had absolute authority over their minor children"—might not attract a vote from a single colleague. But his views entered directly into a conservative legal ecosystem ready to embrace them and, if necessary, to shave off their more eccentric edges to make them fit for broader public consumption. It was a world where no credential was more prized than a Thomas clerkship. Indeed, a network of former Thomas clerks was growing rapidly in influence; twenty-two held substantial positions in the Trump administration, and a dozen attained federal judgeships.

During the final years of Justice Ginsburg's tenure, a fissure opened within the court's liberal bloc, not in every case but often enough to be noticeable. Ginsburg and Sotomayor would hold to an uncompromising position, while Breyer and Kagan made obvious efforts to work with the conservatives and perhaps blunt the force of decisions they could not control. One striking example was the *Little Sisters of the Poor* case, decided at the end of the 2019–20 term. The case challenged the exemptions from the Affordable Care Act's contraception mandate that the Trump administration had granted to any employer with a religious or unspecified "moral" objection to birth control. Roberts, Alito, Gorsuch, and Kavanaugh joined a majority opinion by Thomas that overturned a nationwide injunction against the rules that established the exemptions. The court held that the rules came within the legal authority of the executive branch agencies that had issued them. Whether the rules, although properly issued, might be invalid on some other basis was left to the lower courts to decide in the first instance.

As expected, Ginsburg vigorously dissented in an opinion that Sotomayor joined. Kagan took a different approach, in an opinion that Breyer joined. They concurred only in the decision's bottom-line "judgment" while refusing to sign Thomas's majority opinion. They agreed with the majority only that the rules came within the departments' statutory authority. "But that does not mean the departments should prevail when these cases return to the lower courts," Kagan wrote. "An agency acting within its sphere of delegated authority can of course flunk the test of 'reasoned decisionmaking.'" On that basis, she continued, the rules "give every appearance of coming up short."

Kagan's tone in this seven-page opinion was perfectly flat. She gave no indication that she was aware of the preceding years of highly politicized litigation, beginning with the *Hobby Lobby* case in 2014, that had twice before brought the issue to the court. Of course she and Breyer knew the history, just as they knew that they lacked the power to control the outcome at this moment. But the case would now be on remand to the lower courts, and there was a chance that their view of what should happen in this next phase might be influential. In their opinion, Kagan and Breyer were speaking to the U.S. Court of Appeals for the Third Circuit, where the case originated and to which it was now returning.

In dissent, Ginsburg and Sotomayor were also speaking to an audience. They could not change the majority's mind, but in this closely watched case they might at least influence how the public understood the consequences of the court's action. "More than 2.9 million Americans—including approximately 580,000 women of childbearing age—receive insurance through organizations newly eligible for this blanket exemption," Ginsburg wrote. "Of cardinal significance, the exemption contains no alternative mechanism to ensure affected women's continued access to contraceptive coverage."

To build bridges or to burn them? That choice faced the members of the court's liberal bloc over the years as their numbers shrank. Ginsburg had seen herself as a bridge builder for most of her judicial career, beginning with her warm relations with the conservatives on the D.C. Circuit. She changed when the court changed, with Sandra Day O'Connor's retirement and replacement by Samuel Alito in 2006. No longer able to influence outcomes with her vote, Ginsburg began to raise her voice in dissent. Approaching her eighties, she became the Notorious RBG.

Sotomayor's trajectory was very different. The court she joined in 2009 was already deeply conservative on the issues she cared most about. She saw little prospect of making a difference inside the conference. It wasn't a question of whether to burn bridges. She had no bridges. If she wanted to make a difference, it would have to be outside the court, using her position as leverage and her "American dream" life story as her currency. She would be a role model for children diagnosed with Type 1 diabetes, as she had been at the age of seven. She would inspire young people struggling to rise from humble beginnings like hers. She would push the button to drop the ball in Times Square on New Year's Eve, and don a Yankees jersey to toss out the first pitch in a game against the Boston Red Sox at Yankee Stadium. She would chat on *The View* with the program's female hosts, who addressed her as Sonia. She would write a bestselling memoir of her pre-judicial life, *My Beloved World*, published in English and Spanish in 2013, with an audiobook read by Rita Moreno. Later came a children's edition of the memoir along with another children's book, *Just Ask! Be Different, Be Brave, Be You.*

That is not to suggest that Sotomayor was inattentive to the work of the court—quite the opposite, as her dissections of the shadow docket cases made clear—only that she was deliberately projecting herself onto a bigger canvas than the court itself and modeling a different dimension to serving there. She would tell the truth as she saw it. She would be "the people's justice."

Within the court, her solitary voice was not without impact. One revealing incident came to light only later, in reporting by the legal journalist Joan Biskupic for her 2014 book *Breaking In: The Rise of Sonia Sotomayor and the Politics of Justice*. In 2013, the court was considering yet another challenge to affirmative action in university admissions, in a case brought by a disappointed white applicant to the University of Texas at Austin. Nine years earlier, the court had narrowly preserved affirmative action with a majority opinion by Sandra Day O'Connor in a case from the University of Michigan. With O'Connor gone, it seemed highly likely that affirmative action's time had finally run out.

The case, *Fisher v. University of Texas*, was argued at the beginning of the term in October 2012. With the end of the term approaching the following June, more than nine months had gone by and the country had heard nothing. Then came a surprise, a thirteen-page majority opinion by Justice Anthony Kennedy, minimalist in the extreme, that sent the case back to the Fifth Circuit for reconsideration. The opinion demanded no particular outcome and resolved nothing. Everyone from Alito to Sotomayor was on board, with the exception of Ginsburg, who dissented on the ground that there was no need for a "second look" because the Texas plan was indisputably constitutional.

Something unusual had clearly occurred inside the court, but what? It turned out that the original vote was 5 to 3 to overturn the Texas affirmative action plan. (Elena Kagan did not participate because she had worked on the case as solicitor general before joining the court.) The dissenters were Ginsburg, Breyer, and Sotomayor. As the senior dissenting justice, Ginsburg asked Sotomayor to write a dissenting opinion for the three. Sotomayor's proposed dissent was so forceful that the majority began to unravel, leading to months of effort—with "Sotomayor as agitator, Breyer as broker, and Kennedy as compromiser"—to "lower the temperature" and produce a decision that the court could put out to the public. The opinion that emerged gave no hint of how the justices had spent the intervening months. (On remand, the U.S. Court of Appeals for the Fifth Circuit once again upheld the Texas plan, leading to a second Supreme Court appeal known as *Fisher II*. In the spring of 2016, after Justice Scalia's death and his seat still unfilled, the court affirmed the Fifth Circuit by a vote of 4 to 3.)

Sotomayor's draft dissent did not see the light of day, at least not at the time of the first *Fisher* decision. But in another affirmative action case the next term, she published a blistering and deeply personal dissenting opinion. The case was *Schuette v. BAMN*, in which the court rejected a constitutional challenge to a voter referendum in Michigan that amended the state constitution to prohibit affirmative action in higher education. By a vote of 6 to 2, the court ruled that the prohibition did not violate the Fourteenth Amendment's guarantee of equal protection.

While Ginsburg signed Sotomayor's dissenting opinion, the story the opinion told was clearly Sotomayor's own. "Race matters," she wrote. "Race matters in part because of the long history of racial minorities' being denied access to the political process." She went on:

Race also matters because of persistent racial inequality in society—inequality that cannot be ignored and that has produced stark socioeconomic disparities. . . . And race matters for reasons that really are only skin deep, that cannot be discussed any other way, and that cannot be wished away. Race matters to a young man's view of society when he spends his teenage years watching others tense up as he passes no matter the neighborhood where he grew up. Race matters to a young woman's sense of self when she states her hometown, and then is pressed, "No, where are you *really* from?," regardless of how many generations her family has been in the country. Race matters to a young person addressed by a stranger in a foreign language, which he does not understand because only English was spoken at home. Race matters because of the slights, the snickers, the silent judgments that reinforce that most crippling of thoughts: "I do not belong here."

In my colleagues' view, examining the racial impact of legislation only perpetuates racial discrimination. This refusal to accept the stark reality that race matters is regrettable. The way to stop discrimination on the basis of race is to speak openly and candidly on the subject of race, and to apply the Constitution with eyes open to the unfortunate effects of centuries of racial discrimination. As members of the judiciary tasked with intervening to carry out the guarantees of equal protection, we ought not sit back and wish away, rather than confront, the racial inequality that exists in our society.

These last sentences were barbs aimed directly and unmistakably at Chief Justice Roberts. In the *Parents Involved* case in 2007, before Sotomayor's arrival at the court, Roberts had written the opinion that invalidated two racially conscious student assignment plans aimed at preserving integration in school districts where housing patterns were driving resegregation. Roberts had concluded his opinion with the line: "The way to stop discrimination on the basis of race is to stop discriminating on the basis of race." The line was not original with Roberts—he had borrowed it, unattributed, from an opinion in an earlier phase of the case by a conservative Ninth Circuit judge, Carlos Bea—but it received wide attention and to the ruling's many critics seemed to summarize the vacuity of the decision's rationale.

Roberts, infuriated by Sotomayor's personal reference, took the unusual step of responding directly with an opinion of his own:

The dissent states that "[t]he way to stop discrimination on the basis of race is to speak openly and candidly on the subject of race." And it urges that "[r]ace matters because of the slights, the snickers, the silent judgments that reinforce that most crippling of thoughts: 'I do not belong here.'" But it is not "out of touch with reality" to conclude that racial preferences may themselves have the debilitating effect of reinforcing precisely that doubt, and—if so—that the preferences do more harm than good. To disagree with the dissent's views on the costs and benefits of racial preferences is not to "wish away, rather than confront" racial inequality. People can disagree in good faith on this issue, but it similarly does more harm than good to question the openness and candor of those on either side of the debate.

Was Sotomayor's opinion, in whole or part, the draft opinion that she had withdrawn the previous year after it had achieved its purpose in the University of Texas case? There was reason to think so. In any event, her deepest feelings about race and about her colleagues' failure to respond adequately to its reality were now available for the world to see. Impolitic as her words may have been, she had spoken her truth.

UNFINISHED BUSINESS PRESENTED itself in the form of the Trump administration's continuing effort to restore the requirement for in-person dispensing of the medication prescribed for ending an early pregnancy. Early in the pandemic, the Food and Drug Administration had lifted in-person rules for other medications on the premise that many doctors' offices were closed or otherwise inaccessible. But the agency maintained the requirement for the abortion drug mifepristone, leading a coalition of medical organizations to go to federal district court, where they argued that the requirement was medically unnecessary and imposed an undue burden on the right to abortion. In July, a federal district judge in Maryland, Theodore D. Chuang, had agreed and issued a nationwide injunction to enable doctors to mail or otherwise deliver the drug to their patients for the duration of the pandemic health emergency. When the Fourth Circuit refused to issue a stay, the Trump administration went to the Supreme Court. In October, over an angry dissent by Alito, the court issued a one-paragraph order that kept the injunction in place while inviting the administration to go back to the district court with a more persuasive explanation for the agency's position.

The administration accepted the invitation, but Judge Chuang was unmoved. In an opinion issued on December 9, during the second-wave surge in COVID cases, he noted that "the current circumstances are uniformly dire across the nation." The FDA and the Department of Health and Human Services "have offered no evidence that their temporary inability to enforce the in-person requirements has injured them or, for that matter, harmed a patient," Judge Chuang wrote. And he added a verbatim quote from the Supreme Court's order two weeks earlier that lifted New York's limitations on worship service attendance: "Even in a pandemic, the Constitution cannot be put away and forgotten."

On December 15, the administration came back to the Supreme Court. The district court was "preventing FDA from enforcing important, longstanding safety requirements" that dated to the agency's original approval of abortion medication in 2000, the acting solicitor general's brief argued. (Since 2000, medication abortion has become the most commonly used method of terminating early pregnancies.) In an awkward cutting and pasting of phrases separated by more than forty pages in the court's leading abortion precedent, *Planned Parenthood v. Casey*, the brief asserted: "It flouts this court's admonition that a law's 'incidental effect of making it more difficult or more expensive to procure an abortion cannot be enough to invalidate' the law if the law 'serves a valid purpose, one not designed to strike at the right itself.'"

In response, the medical organizations offered statistics to show how the COVID picture had deteriorated since July, when Judge Chuang had first ruled. In mid-July, the national seven-day moving average of new cases was 44,000. By early December, it had risen to 188,504. And as of December 20, it had soared to 239,604. The central issue in the case remained unchanged, the organizations argued: "the in-person requirements make heightened risk of contracting a deadly disease a condition of obtaining a medication abortion."

The court's answer came late in the afternoon of January 12. It was another shadow docket disposition, a one-paragraph unsigned order issued over three dissenting votes. The injunction was lifted, a parting gift to the administration that had reshaped the court over the past four years.

Of the six justices in the majority in *Food and Drug Administration v. American College of Obstetricians and Gynecologists*, only Roberts explained himself. "The question before us is not whether the requirements for dispensing mifepristone impose an undue burden on a woman's right to an abortion as a general matter," he began. Rather, the question was one of judicial deference to an expert agency. He drew on his own opinion from the previous May, when he and four other justices, including Ruth Bader Ginsburg, had voted to uphold California's limitations on in-person worship, quoting a line from that opinion as if nothing had changed since then. "Here as in related contexts concerning government responses to the pandemic," he said, "my view is that courts owe significant deference to the politically accountable entities with the 'background, competence, and expertise to assess public health.' In light of those considerations, I do not see a sufficient basis here for the District Court to compel the FDA to alter the regimen for medical abortion."

Breyer noted his dissent without writing. Kagan signed Sotomayor's dissenting opinion. "Significantly, the FDA's in-person requirements for mifepristone have now been suspended for six months, yet the Government has not identified a single harm experienced by women who have obtained mifepristone by mail or delivery," Sotomayor wrote. Turning to the chief justice's call for deference, she continued:

> But the record here is bereft of any reasoning. The government has not submitted a single declaration from an FDA or HHS official explaining why the Government believes women must continue to pick up mifepristone in person, even though it has exempted many other drugs from such a requirement given the health risks of COVID-19. There simply is no reasoned decision here to which this Court can defer. . . .
>
> One can only hope that the Government will reconsider and

exhibit greater care and empathy for women seeking some measure of control over their health and reproductive lives in these
unsettling times.

Sotomayor ended her opinion by quoting from one of Ruth Bader
Ginsburg's best-known dissenting opinions, from the 2007 abortion
case *Gonzales v. Carhart:* "Women's ability to realize their full potential is intimately connected to their ability to control their reproductive lives."

Sotomayor's hope for a change in federal policy would be realized
when, three months after President Biden took office, the FDA lifted
the in-person requirement for the duration of the COVID public
health emergency. A month after that, the administration announced
that it had begun proceedings toward lifting the requirement permanently.

IT WOULD BE an Inauguration Day like no other. There would be no
forgetting, not for a second, what had happened at the Capitol a mere
two weeks earlier. Washington was shut down for blocks around the
National Mall, where two hundred thousand flags were set out to
represent the nonexistent audience for the peaceful transfer of power.
The incoming president had spoken the night before at a vigil com-
memorating the four hundred thousand American lives lost to the
pandemic. "To heal we must remember," Joe Biden said. By the Reflecting Pool at the Lincoln Memorial, four hundred lights flickered,
each representing one thousand deaths.

The day dawned bright and cold. Two members of the court had
duties to perform. The chief justice, of course, would swear in the
new president. Kamala Harris, the vice-president-elect, had invited
Sonia Sotomayor to administer her oath of office. Sotomayor had
done the same for Vice President Joe Biden in 2012. While the entire
court ordinarily attends a presidential inauguration, Breyer, Alito,
and Thomas, the three oldest members of the court, were missing
from the row of black-masked justices. The public information office

explained that they were concerned about COVID and had decided to stay away for reasons of health.

The unusual absence of one-third of the Supreme Court underscored the strangeness of the moment and of the months that had led up to it. During the four years since the justices had last gathered on the inaugural platform, the court had experienced a retirement, a death, and the end of a yearlong partisan blockade of a vacant seat. It had seen the arrival of three new colleagues who, at the end of the day, stood as a bloc against the claims of a president who mistakenly assumed that their loyalty was to him rather than to the law or to the country that they, like him, had vowed to serve. It had been a period of abrupt change and deep institutional stress. While the oddly depopulated yet resonant ceremony unfolding before the justices marked a new chapter, as a new presidential administration always does, the stress and the stakes would remain high.

THE JUSTICES' REGULAR Friday conference took place by phone two days later. On the agenda were two petitions the now ex-president had filed challenging the validity of two lawsuits brought against him under the Constitution's domestic and foreign emoluments clauses. These clauses, in Article I and Article II, prohibit the president from accepting any "emolument" or profit beyond the pay and benefits granted by Congress. A coalition of hotel and restaurant owners brought one lawsuit and the District of Columbia and the state of Maryland brought the other, suing on behalf of their residents in the hospitality industry. The theory of both cases was that Trump's ownership of the Trump International Hotel, a magnet for wealthy Americans and foreign dignitaries who wanted to please the president by giving him their patronage, amounted to unlawful competition that hurt the economic interests of would-be competitors. Trump's lawyers had tried and failed to get the lawsuits thrown out.

On January 25, the Monday after Inauguration Day, the court dismissed both cases as moot. That was no surprise; whatever the president's obligation under the emoluments clauses, it evaporated with his departure from office. The only open question was what to do about the decisions in the Second and Fourth Circuits that had kept the lawsuits alive. Usually when it dismisses a case that has become moot, the Supreme Court vacates the lower court opinion, returning the situation to whatever it was before the litigation began. The plaintiffs in the emoluments cases urged the justices not to take that step; although the cases were still in early stages, there were favorable procedural precedents that the plaintiffs wanted to remain on the books. But the court did vacate the lower court decisions. That meant that the next time a real-estate-owning president declined to put his assets in a blind trust and ran a business that drew customers away from competitors, someone with a complaint would have to start the litigation process from scratch. Such a scenario seemed unlikely indeed. But then, as a new chapter opened in the history of American democracy, so did much of what had just happened.

CHAPTER SEVEN

FEBRUARY · CHOOSING SIDES

N OT EVERY SUPREME COURT DECISION is a blockbuster. Far from it: of the fifty-eight cases the Supreme Court heard during the 2020–21 term, no more than half a dozen appeared guaranteed to capture public attention. These were the cases that brought the court to the forefront of the culture wars (religion, voting rights) or that addressed important issues of the moment (the fate of the Affordable Care Act). The remainder, even cases that might affect many thousands of people or settle long-unresolved legal questions, were destined to remain obscure from the initial grant of review to the final decision. They were either too technical or too far removed from the concerns of most Americans to rise above the din of the daily news cycle. Yet in their very ordinariness, these decisions in workaday cases, as they began to be issued in midwinter, could reveal a good deal about the court as it navigated the challenge of change during the 2020–21 term.

Salinas v. United States Railroad Retirement Board, decided on February 3, was such a case. Everything about it appeared routine. It concerned the relationship between a low-visibility federal agency, the United States Railroad Retirement Board, and the federal courts. The board was created during the Depression to administer disability and other benefits for employees of the nation's railroads. An applicant whose claim for benefits was denied could seek the board's reconsideration. As the case reached the court in an appeal by Manfredo

Salinas, a railroad worker disabled by on-the-job injuries, the question was whether the board's refusal to reopen a denied claim was a "final decision" of the sort that entitled a claimant to take the case to federal court.

The answer required an intricate parsing of two statutes that defined the board's jurisdiction, as well as regulations governing its internal appeal process. The federal courts of appeals had been divided for years over the question, meaning that workers in some federal circuits but not in others were entitled to go to court when the board refused to reopen their case. Resolving such a dispute is a core Supreme Court function. Federal law should have a uniform meaning throughout the country, and the court's rules identified just such a conflict among the circuits as a primary reason for accepting a case. Statutory questions of this sort often produced unanimous decisions, with the court reasoning that its most important duty was to give the country an answer, one way or another; Congress would be free to amend the statute if it thought the court got the answer wrong.

The solicitor general's office, while arguing that the Fifth Circuit had properly found judicial review unavailable, agreed with Mr. Salinas's lawyers that the court should take the case. The court granted certiorari promptly and held argument on November 2. It was Amy Coney Barrett's first day on the (virtual) Supreme Court bench. The argument was as routine as everything else about the case. The justices probed both sides about how the various statutes and regulations interacted. There were no red flags and no excitement. The justices ran out of questions before the government's lawyer used his allotted thirty minutes.

Perhaps they had something else on their minds. The next day was Election Day.

The surprise, when the court delivered its decision in *Salinas v. United States Railroad Retirement Board* two months later, was not that the railroad worker won; it was evident from the circuit conflict that the case could plausibly have gone either way. The surprise was the vote: 5 to 4, the term's first such vote in a fully briefed and argued case. No doubt the term would eventually produce its share of 5-to-4 cases, but *Salinas*? What could account for such an outcome? And how to explain the composition of the two sides? Joining Justice Sotomayor's majority opinion were the court's two other liberals, Breyer and Kagan, along with Roberts and Kavanaugh. Thomas's dissenting opinion was joined by Alito, Gorsuch, and the court's newest member, Justice Barrett.

In addition to her interpretation of the statutory language, Sotomayor's opinion relied on "the strong presumption favoring judicial review of administrative action." She explained: "Judicial review plays a modest, but important, role in guarding against decisions that are arbitrary, inconsistent with the standards set by the board's own regulations, or otherwise contrary to law." Thomas offered a rejoinder, accusing the majority of having devised "a new form of judicial review" to which claimants in Salinas's position were not entitled: "The presumption of judicial review is not a presumption of infinite judicial review."

So there was ideology lurking in this case after all, with the justices dividing over how much protection against administrative arbitrariness was enough and how much was too much. When did access to court matter, and when was it dispensable? The battle line dividing the two sides of the argument seemed clear enough, but was this a line that predictably would have separated Roberts and Kavanaugh on the one hand from Thomas, Alito, and Gorsuch on the other?

The explanation most likely lay outside the borders of the case itself. In 2016, as a judge on the D.C. Circuit, Kavanaugh had ruled in a similar Railroad Board case, writing the opinion for a three-judge panel in favor of access to federal court for workers in the same category as Salinas. "It makes sense to provide for judicial review of potentially arbitrary and mistaken board decisions denying requests to reopen," Kavanaugh had written in *Stovic v. Railroad Retirement Board*. "Judicial review helps ensure accuracy and fairness. Moreover, the usual presumption is *in favor of* judicial review of agency action." It was hardly surprising that Sotomayor had picked up this language nearly verbatim. Salinas's lawyers had cited the D.C. Circuit case throughout their brief.

The lawyers also cited another case, one that surely caught the chief justice's attention. It was a Railroad Retirement Board case from 1966 in which the Second Circuit, while applying a different analysis, reached the same result in favor of judicial review. The author of that opinion, *Szostak v. Railroad Retirement Board*, was Henry Friendly, the judge for whom Roberts clerked years later. Friendly, who served on the Second Circuit from 1959 until his death in 1986, was a judge of towering intellect and reputation. Winning a Friendly clerkship was the ultimate prize for any graduating law student. Roberts made clear, in comments over the years, his unbounded esteem for the judge. In his own judicial career, Roberts almost never cited law review articles in his opinions the way many other judges did. He regarded academic legal writing as lacking in authority as a source for judicial decision making. But in December 2005, he used his first majority opinion as chief justice to give his old boss a subtle tip of the hat. He cited one of Henry Friendly's articles.

If Kavanaugh and Roberts were predisposed toward what might be labeled the liberal side of the Salinas case, what accounted for Barrett's vote on the other side? Hers was not a vote that would make a difference. Had she joined Sotomayor, the majority would simply have had six justices instead of five. The country was not holding its breath for the outcome of this case. Barrett faced a choice seemingly without consequences. Yet is there any action on the Supreme Court without consequences? That she had taken a stand when it hardly mattered meant that she had taken it freely, without constraint. She had simply chosen a side. The question that lingered was what she would do in the days ahead, when her choice would matter a great deal.

IN EARLY DECEMBER, with COVID cases spreading at an accelerating rate and hospital beds in increasingly short supply, Governor Gavin Newsom of California issued one of the country's most sweeping responses to the pandemic. In parts of the state designated "Tier 1" for COVID severity—nearly the entire state at that time—people were prohibited from many activities that involved gathering indoors. The governor's order closed museums, movie theaters, and restaurants; prohibited indoor artistic performances, political assemblies, and live audiences at athletic events; and banned indoor weddings and funeral services. Hotels were even prohibited from honoring reservations from out-of-state visitors. And yes, the governor's order also prohibited indoor worship services, although it permitted unlimited attendance at services held outdoors.

South Bay United Pentecostal Church, in the city of Chula Vista, near San Diego, was soon back in court. In May 2020, the church had lost a challenge to California's initial pandemic order that had placed a one-hundred-person cap on indoor worship services. The justices had voted then to deny the injunction the church wanted. Roberts, in control of a 5-to-4 majority that included Ruth Bader Ginsburg, explained that government efforts to contain the pandemic were evolving rapidly and "should not be subject to second-guessing by an unelected federal judiciary, which lacks the background, competence, and expertise to assess public health and is not accountable to the people."

Seven months had passed since then. It took no special insight on the part of South Bay's lawyers from the Thomas More Society, a Chicago-based Christian right litigating group with an agenda that focused on abortion, to suppose that things might turn out differently this time.

After losing in the lower courts, South Bay filed a Supreme Court petition along with a request for an emergency injunction to block the new restriction. "This Court is the last resort for restoring religious freedom to its proper place as a 'first class right,'" the church's lawyers told the court. "It is during the most difficult times of our country, including a nationwide pandemic, that we cannot afford to let tyranny against religion rise in the guise of well-meaning police power of the State."

In an unsigned order issued late on the night of February 5, the court gave the church incomplete but significant relief. Under the terms of the court's injunction, California could not impose the zero-capacity limit in Tier 1 locations, but it could opt for a 25 percent cap on indoor worship services if it chose. The governor had also banned "singing and chanting" in indoor Tier 1 locations, and that restriction remained. The 6-to-3 majority was fractured in interesting ways. Justice Alito would have lifted all capacity limits along with the ban on singing, although he noted that he would have preferred to defer the injunction for thirty days, with the deferral to expire unless the state during that time could demonstrate the need for any limits on indoor worship. Gorsuch and Thomas agreed that the church could now reopen and would have also lifted the ban on singing, but they did not address what fallback position was now available to the state. They noted that "nothing in our order precludes future challenges" to whatever limits the state imposed next.

Amy Barrett's one-paragraph concurrence was her first opinion in any case since arriving at the court. The court was properly keeping the singing ban in place, she said, because the church had not met its burden of showing why the ban should be lifted. In this respect, Barrett, whose opinion was joined by Kavanaugh, distanced herself from Alito. While she placed the burden on the church to show why the ban was unnecessary, Alito would have required the state to justify the ban's retention.

Barrett also took issue with Gorsuch, whose separate opinion accused the state of "playing favorites" by permitting singing in the recently reopened film and television studios but not in the church. "Of course," Barrett wrote, "if a chorister can sing in a Hollywood studio but not in her church, California's regulations cannot be viewed as neutral." However, she added, the record on this point was "uncertain, and the decisions below unfortunately shed little light on the issue." Her single cryptic paragraph left unclear what weight she was attaching to the word "neutral." The requirement of neutral treatment between religion and non-religion was settled constitutional law—the very settlement that was now buckling under the weight of the cases granting special religious exemptions. Was Barrett choosing this moment to weigh in on the side of neutrality as opposed to special treatment? It was a tantalizing thought, but one seemingly refuted by the very structure of the injunction the court had just issued in an order that Barrett had supported. California's Tier 1 regulations were in fact neutral, treating indoor worship no better or worse than other indoor gatherings that presented a similar risk of contagion. Wasn't it the court, not the state, that was "playing favorites" now?

Barrett was not alone in skirting that issue. Roberts wrote separately to explain why he was now casting his vote for the church after having supported the state seven months earlier. While he stood by his earlier opinion upholding capacity limits, he said that the state had gone too far this time: "The state's present determination—that the maximum number of adherents who can safely worship in the most cavernous cathedral is zero—appears to reflect not expertise or discretion, but instead insufficient appreciation or consideration of the interests at stake."

What "interests" were those, exactly? Religious interests, obviously. But to name religion would have required Roberts to acknowledge the profound doctrinal shift the court was making, from equal treatment to special treatment. Better to leave it vague for now. "Deference, though broad, has its limits," he concluded.

In dissent, Justice Kagan, joined by Breyer and Sotomayor, had no trouble naming what had just occurred:

> The Court orders California to weaken its restrictions on public gatherings by making a special exception for worship services. The majority does so even though the State's policies treat worship just as favorably as secular activities (including political assemblies) that, according to medical evidence, pose the same risk of COVID transmission. Under the Court's injunction, the State must instead treat worship services like secular activities that pose a much lesser danger. That mandate defies our caselaw, exceeds our judicial role, and risks worsening the pandemic.

In a footnote, Kagan observed that during the previous week, the pandemic had killed more than thirty-five hundred Californians.

THERE SEEMED NO limit to the variety of religious claims reaching the court. An Alabama death row inmate who had become a born-again Christian during his two decades in prison went to court as the date for his execution approached seeking the attendance of his pastor in the execution chamber. The inmate, Willie B. Smith III, lost in federal district court. But on February 10, the day before the scheduled execution, the Eleventh Circuit granted Smith a stay of execution and ordered the state to comply with the inmate's request. With the execution hours away, Alabama asked the justices to vacate the stay.

The case touched a nerve at the court. It was not the first such case. Two years earlier, the justices had voted 5 to 4 to grant Alabama's request to vacate a stay of execution obtained by a Muslim inmate who wanted an imam by his side instead of the Holman Correctional Facility's sole chaplain, a Protestant, whom the state required to attend every execution. The Eleventh Circuit found a strong likelihood that the prison's policy violated the First Amendment's establishment clause by preferring one religion above all others.

Rather than confront that problem directly, the five justices in the majority (Roberts, Thomas, Alito, Gorsuch, and Kavanaugh) had issued a one-paragraph order lifting the injunction on the ground that the inmate, Domineque Ray, had waited too long to bring his religious claim. Justice Kagan, in a dissenting opinion joined by Ginsburg, Breyer, and Sotomayor, called the court's action "profoundly wrong." There was nothing untimely about the inmate's claim, she said; the state had informed Ray just two weeks before his execution date that only the Protestant chaplain would be present. "Ray has put forward a powerful claim that his religious rights will be violated at the moment the State puts him to death," Kagan wrote. "The Eleventh Circuit wanted to hear that claim in full. Instead, this Court short-circuits that ordinary process—and itself rejects the claim with little briefing and no argument—just so the State can meet its preferred execution date." Ray, convicted in 1995 of murdering a fifteen-year-old girl, was executed less than two hours after the court lifted the stay.

The court's 2019 ruling, *Dunn v. Ray*, drew strongly negative reaction both domestically and around the world. DOMINIQUE RAY DIED ALONE ON DEATH ROW—IF HE HADN'T BEEN A MUSLIM, IT WOULD NEVER HAVE HAPPENED read the headline on a commentary piece in a British newspaper (using a different spelling of the inmate's first name). The sub-headline elaborated: "America is busy turning religion into a 'super right,' but such efforts didn't extend to one man who wanted an imam in his execution chamber a few days ago."

A few weeks later, another case gave the court an opportunity to present a better face to the world. In March 2019 the justices received a request for a stay of execution from a Buddhist inmate on death row in Texas. Texas had refused to permit Patrick Murphy's Buddhist spiritual adviser, or any other Buddhist, to accompany him in his final moments. The state explained that for security reasons it permitted only state-employed chaplains to be present in the execution chamber, and there happened to be no Buddhists on the payroll, only Christians and a Muslim.

Murphy was one of the notorious "Texas 7," a group of inmates who in 2000 escaped from a high-security prison and went on a rampage, killing a police officer among other crimes. He came to the Supreme Court after failing to get a stay of execution from the federal district court and the Fifth Circuit. As in Ray's case, his scheduled execution was just hours away by the time the application reached the justices. But this time, the outcome was different. In an unsigned one-paragraph order, the court barred the execution "unless the State permits Murphy's Buddhist spiritual advisor or another Buddhist reverend of the State's choosing to accompany Murphy in the execution chamber during the execution." The dissenters were Thomas, Gorsuch, and Alito. Alito waited six weeks to file a lengthy dissent complaining about the late-day nature of Murphy's application. The inmate "egregiously delayed in raising his claims," Alito wrote in an opinion that Thomas and Gorsuch joined. "By countenancing such tactics, the Court invites abuse."

For their part, Kavanaugh and Roberts might have been expected to offer some explanation for their abrupt change in position from the *Ray* case only a few weeks earlier. Roberts initially wrote nothing.

Kavanaugh wrote a brief opinion, concurring in the grant of the stay of execution without mentioning the *Ray* case. "The Government may not discriminate against religion generally or against particular religious denominations," Kavanaugh wrote. The state had a choice: Either allow religious advisers of all denominations into the execution room, or allow none. "The choice of remedy going forward is up to the State," he concluded. Five days later, Texas accepted Kavanaugh's invitation and barred all chaplains from the execution chamber. Alabama did the same. Problem solved? Not quite.

After Alito filed his delayed dissenting opinion in *Murphy v. Collier,* Kavanaugh and Roberts offered an explanation for their votes in an additional statement, written by Kavanaugh and joined by Roberts. Murphy's case differed from Ray's, they wrote, in that Murphy's lawyers had directly raised a claim of unequal treatment while Ray's lawyers, basing their argument on the Establishment Clause, had not. That was an observation rather than an explanation for the drastically different outcomes in the two cases. But it would be the last word on the subject until Alabama came to the court in February 2021 seeking to vacate Willie Smith's stay of execution.

The court, ruling in *Dunn v. Smith*, kept the stay in place. Smith was already in the execution chamber when the order arrived a few minutes past 11:00 P.M. on February 5. Smith was convicted of killing a woman he abducted from in front of an ATM in 1991. His execution had been set for 6:00 P.M. but was delayed while Alabama prison officials waited to hear from the court. Now it turned out that he would not die that night, and perhaps not for many months.

Although the court offered no explanation, it was clear from Justice Kagan's concurring opinion that a majority had rejected the view of the state's options that Kavanaugh had expressed in the *Murphy* case. It was not sufficient, Kagan wrote, simply to bar all clergy members from the execution chamber. Formalistic nondiscrimination of that sort failed to meet the requirements of the Religious Land Use and Institutionalized Persons Act, which Congress enacted in 2000 to protect the religious rights of prisoners. The law placed a heavy burden on the government to justify policies that imposed a "substantial burden" on an inmate's "religious exercise." Excluding all chaplains from the execution chamber was such a burden, Kagan concluded, and it was one that Alabama had not shown to be necessary. "The Eleventh Circuit was right to bar Alabama from executing Smith without his pastor by his side," Kagan wrote. "The law guarantees Smith the right to practice his faith free from unnecessary interference, including at the moment the State puts him to death."

Justices Breyer, Sotomayor, and Barrett joined Kagan's opinion. There were three dissenters: Thomas, Kavanaugh, and Roberts. Thomas did not write. Kavanaugh, in a dissenting opinion that Roberts joined, repeated his view from the *Murphy* case that barring all chaplains was all the answer that was necessary. "Because the State's policy is non-discriminatory and, in my view, serves the State's compelling interests in ensuring the safety, security, and solemnity of the execution room, I would have granted the State's application to vacate the injunction," Kavanaugh wrote. Almost as an afterthought, he added that "States that want to avoid months or years of litigation delays" would be well advised to "figure out a way to allow spiritual advisors into the execution room, as other States and the Federal Government have done." Four days later, the Alabama Department of Corrections announced that it was amending its rules accordingly.

Where were Gorsuch and Alito? Seven justices were accounted for in the pages of the order, but those two were not. Did they not vote? They couldn't both have dissented; had they done so, the state would have prevailed. Were they both persuaded by Kagan's opinion but, given their past positions, did not want to have to explain or even identify themselves? When the court decides a case that it has accepted for full briefing and argument, a court officer whose title is reporter of decisions attaches to the decision a summary known as a headnote, which includes a list of the justices who participated in the case and the position each took. But cases that emerge, as this one had, from the shadow docket have no headnotes. That two such outspoken members of the court as Alito and Gorsuch would simply go missing hardly seemed likely.

It was a mystery, to be sure, but not as intriguing as what the face of the order did reveal: that Amy Coney Barrett had voted with the court's liberals. The newest justice was the only one of the nine who had no record on the question of chaplains in the execution chamber, no prior vote to defend or explain away. Unencumbered by the past, she had chosen freely.

IN OCTOBER, WHEN the court refused to expedite consideration of the Pennsylvania Republicans' challenge to the state's relaxed mail-in ballot deadline, Justice Alito had made clear his belief that they had a good case. "The question presented by the Pennsylvania Supreme Court's decision calls for review by this court," he had written in the October 26 order. "But I reluctantly conclude that there is simply not enough time at this late date to decide the question before the election."

The Republicans' petition argued that the state supreme court had exceeded its authority under the U.S. Constitution by ordering that ballots received within three days after Election Day should be counted. The theory behind this argument was what political scientists call the "independent state legislature doctrine," based on a minority view of the meaning of the Constitution's two "elections clauses." Article I, clause 4, provides that the "Times, Places and Manner of holding Elections for Senators and Representatives, shall be prescribed in each State by the Legislature thereof." Article II, clause 2, provides that "Each State shall appoint, in such Manner as the Legislature thereof may direct, a Number of Electors . . ."

The word "legislature" in the two clauses had generally been assumed to stand in for the state government as a whole, simply distinguishing the state's authority over elections from that of the federal government. But a concurring opinion in *Bush v. Gore* by Chief Justice Rehnquist put in play a different view: that the power to set the terms for federal elections resided solely and specifically in the state legislatures, as opposed to state courts. That was the reason his opinion gave for overturning the Florida supreme court's order for a recount of the state's presidential ballots. Although Thomas and Scalia signed the Rehnquist opinion, it did not control the outcome of the 2000 election case and was subsequently never adopted by the court. But the notion of the independent state legislature sprang to life during the 2020 election cycle as state courts responded both to the COVID pandemic and to the apparent collapse of the country's postal system by relaxing deadlines and making other accommodations to make sure that as many votes would be counted as possible. Pennsylvania election law provided that in order to be counted, ballots had to be received by the end of Election Day. To the fury of the state's Republican Party and the Trump campaign, the state supreme court added three days to the deadline based on its interpretation of the state constitution's requirement that "Elections shall be free and equal."

After the justices' refusal to expedite the Pennsylvania Republicans' petition, the case was placed on the normal calendar and disappeared from view. On November 4, on the morning after the election, Trump filed a motion to intervene in the case as a petitioner   in effect, to take it over from the state party, which quickly acquiesced. The president was "the real party in interest," Trump's lawyer, Jay Alan Sekulow, told the court, explaining: "Given last night's results, the vote in Pennsylvania may well determine the next president of the United States. And this court, not the Pennsylvania Supreme Court, should have the final say on the relevant and dispositive legal questions."

In other words, the Trump legal team was making it perfectly clear that the Supreme Court was being asked to decide not an abstract question of constitutional interpretation, but quite plausibly the 2020 presidential election itself. On the date of Trump's filing everything was still in flux. The election had not been called. Would Pennsylvania's twenty electoral votes prove critical? No one knew.

To anyone who had lived through the presidential election crisis of twenty years earlier, the filing was an eerie reminder of the Saturday afternoon in early December 2000 when, with the election still undecided and everything turning on the outcome in Florida, the justices voted 5 to 4 to stop the recount there that had just begun. The Florida supreme court had ordered the recount at the request of Vice President Al Gore, the Democratic candidate. George W. Bush was claiming victory and had appealed the state court's decision, seeking an immediate stay of the recount in the meantime. Justice Scalia, one of the five who voted for the stay, explained in a short opinion that in his view, the recount threatened "irreparable harm" to the Republican nominee "by casting a cloud upon what he claims to be the legitimacy of his election."

Of the nine justices to whom Trump's motion to intervene was addressed, only two—Thomas and Breyer—had been serving on the court at the time of *Bush v. Gore*. But no justice could have been unaware that Scalia's rationale for interrupting the recount was at least open to interpretation as an acknowledgment that the court was putting a thumb on the scale for Bush. As the weeks passed, the court let Trump's motion simmer on the docket.

The Pennsylvania Republicans' petition finally went to conference on January 8, the justices' first meeting following their four-week winter recess. Only in the early morning hours the day before had Congress certified Biden's electoral victory, the vote delayed for hours by the violent insurrection that had overrun the Capitol and left the Capitol grounds across the street from the court littered with debris. The heart of the nation's capital remained locked down, National Guard troops patrolling the streets. Of course, the justices were meeting remotely rather than at the court building, where they would have witnessed these shocking sights.

It was not until February 22 that the court finally disposed of the Republicans' case. In the interval, the Senate had conducted an unprecedented and highly abbreviated second trial of the former president, impeached by the House for inciting the January 6 insurrection. The Senate proceeding lasted only four days, in contrast with Trump's three-week impeachment trial a year earlier on charges growing out of his covert effort to induce Ukraine to produce damaging information about Biden's son Hunter. Roberts had presided over that trial, as the Constitution's Article I requires. His role then was a passive one.

He steered away from any possible controversy, making clear in advance that he would not vote to break a tie if the closely divided Senate were to split 50–50 on whether to issue a subpoena for a witness or a document. Such a role for "an unelected official from a different branch of government" would be inappropriate, he explained. After the trial ended with Trump's acquittal, Roberts thanked the senators and Senate staff for helping him to carry out his "ill-defined responsibilities." Choosing this time to stay on his side of First Street, the chief justice was presiding over Trump's fate in a different way.

The justices unanimously dismissed as moot Trump's motion to intervene in the Pennsylvania Republicans' case. What to do about the Republicans' petition was a more contentious issue. The vote to deny review was 6 to 3, with Alito, Gorsuch, and Thomas dissenting. Alito was still angry about the court's failure in October to block the three-day extension. Now that the election was over, he wrote, there was no reason for the court not to take up a question that predictably would arise in the future. The Pennsylvania supreme court "claims that a state constitutional provision guaranteeing 'free and equal' elections gives the Pennsylvania courts the authority to override even very specific and unambiguous rules adopted by the legislature for the conduct of future elections," Alito wrote. "It would be surprising if parties who are unhappy with the legislature's rules do not invoke this decision and ask the state courts to substitute rules that they find more advantageous."

Gorsuch joined Alito's opinion. Thomas wrote separately. The court's refusal to take the case was "inexplicable," he wrote. "If state officials have the authority they have claimed, we need to make it clear. If not, we need to put an end to this practice now before the consequences become catastrophic." The court should resolve the question now, two years before the next federal election, rather than waiting for more state courts to "justify intervening in elections and changing the rules.

"One wonders what this Court waits for," Thomas went on. "We failed to settle this dispute before the election, and thus provide clear rules. Now we again fail to provide clear rules for future elections. The decision to leave election law hidden beneath a shroud of doubt is baffling."

Brett Kavanaugh had been one of the four justices who voted in October to grant the stay and block the three-day extension. While it takes five votes to grant a stay, only four votes are needed to accept a case for argument and decision. But this time, in what was arguably a less freighted postelection context, Kavanaugh withheld his vote. He offered no explanation. Amy Barrett, who was not yet on the court at the time of the stay application and did not vote on the motion to expedite, also said nothing.

The next voice to be heard, a week later, was that of Donald Trump. In his first public speech since leaving office, he addressed the Conservative Political Action Committee, which was meeting in Orlando. Rambling on for a grievance-filled ninety minutes, he tossed out attacks on the court to keep the crowd fired up. "They should be ashamed of themselves for what they've done to the country," he said at one point. And at another: "They didn't have the guts or courage to make the right decision." His reference appeared to be to all his recent losses, from the failure of the Texas original case in December to the justices' refusal to hear the Pennsylvania Republicans' case. And then, for all his self-pitying lies about the "rigged election," Trump said something about the Supreme Court that was quite likely true: "They didn't want to talk about it," he said.

CHAPTER EIGHT

MARCH · PRESSURES

I T BEGAN WITH A FEW BLOG POSTS and op-eds, random drops in the stream of commentary about the Supreme Court. Soon it became a flood of progressive voices raised in near unison: Justice Stephen Breyer, retire!

Not that progressives disliked Breyer, although in fact many on the left had never warmed to his coolly analytic style; his increasingly frequent dissenting opinions rarely displayed passion or even contained a quotable line. The reason for the demand that he make his twenty-seventh year on the court his last was obvious: Joe Biden was in the White House, the Democrats had a tenuous and perhaps evanescent hold on the Senate, and Ruth Bader Ginsburg had placed a spectacularly bad bet in not giving Barack Obama a vacancy to fill. The message to the eighty-two-year-old Breyer was simple: Don't make RBG's mistake. Go now.

Erwin Chemerinsky, dean of the law school at Berkeley, who in 2014 had published an essay under the headline LOVE YA RUTH, BUT IT'S TIME TO GO, struck a more somber tone in a *New York Times* op-ed urging the Democratic Party to "grab its opportunity and focus on nominating and confirming judges" across the federal judiciary. "To that end, Justice Stephen Breyer should seriously consider stepping down from the Supreme Court in July 2021, at the end of the court's current term."

Others took to reasoning publicly with Breyer in the kind of pragmatic terms they hoped the justice might find persuasive. Paul Waldman, a *Washington Post* opinion writer, observed that given the rightward shift on the court, "most of the time, all he can do is watch while the conservatives carry out an assault on everything he believes in." Waldman urged Breyer to "make an investment in the future, allowing President Biden to secure his seat for the next few decades."

But a liberal academic who actually knew Breyer, Noah Feldman of Harvard Law School, warned that a shrill retirement campaign would backfire if it led a justice who clung to the notion of law as an apolitical art to fear that his retirement would be taken as the ultimate political act. "So it is absolutely essential for liberals to stop lecturing the man about it being his time to go," Feldman wrote. "Every column or television comment—the more prominent, the worse—traps Breyer into having to stay so as not to appear to be acting as a partisan."

In December, before the retirement frenzy began in earnest, Breyer had given an interview to Dahlia Lithwick, *Slate*'s Supreme Court writer. "I mean, eventually I'll retire, sure I will," Breyer told the reporter, adding: "And it's hard to know exactly when." As the calls mounted, he said nothing more.

In mid-March, the National Judicial College held a virtual meeting to mark what would have been Ruth Bader Ginsburg's eighty-eighth birthday. One speaker was Deborah Jones Merritt, a law professor at Ohio State University who in 1980 had been one of Ginsburg's first law clerks on the D.C. Circuit. The two remained close for the next forty years. Merritt recounted that in 2015, the justice came to her with a question: "People are saying that maybe I should resign just in case the next president is not a Democrat. What do you think?" Merritt replied: "Who the next president is is our job, not your job. I think you should stay on the court as long as you can feel capable to do your job. The rest of us will do our job."

There were some eight hundred judges in virtual attendance, most from state courts. Only one Supreme Court justice was on the call: Stephen Breyer.

WHILE LIBERALS WERE obsessing over whether Breyer would stay or go, some on the right were quietly beginning to wonder what to make of Amy Coney Barrett's performance so far. Of course, there was almost no evidence to go on—but that was precisely the concern for those searching for proof that the new justice was fulfilling conservatives' hopes. Having missed the cases heard in October, Barrett had taken part in only seven of the argued cases the court decided by the end of March, none of major consequence. The real action of the term so far, as everyone knew, was not in the argued cases but the ones on the shadow docket.

Barrett had not joined the Alito group in voting to grant the Pennsylvania Republicans' case against the mail-in ballot extension. In the most recent COVID case from California, she had even pushed back against Neil Gorsuch, rejecting his view that because singing might be taking place in Hollywood studios, it should also be permitted in houses of worship. "You have a lot of people in the conservative movement who are so far disappointed and a little despondent about those votes," Kelly Shackelford, president of the Christian right First Liberty Institute, told Ariane de Vogue of CNN.

Barrett issued her first majority opinion in early March. It was in the first case she had heard after joining the court, *United States Fish and Wildlife Service v. Sierra Club, Inc.* The subject was the Freedom of Information Act, which requires federal agencies to make their records available to those who request them unless any of the statute's nine exemptions apply. One exemption is for documents that were part of the agency's internal "deliberative process," such as preliminary drafts of memos that might have pointed the way to a final decision but do not themselves reflect the agency's final policy choice. The line between deliberative and final, the first shielded from disclosure and the second requiring it, can be a fine one, and it was that distinction that was at issue in the case.

Barrett's opinion accepted the federal agency's position that it was not required to disclose the "draft biological opinions" that its staff had prepared on the likelihood of harm to fish from a particular industrial process. "A document is not final solely because nothing else follows it," Barrett wrote. What mattered, she explained, was "not whether a document is last in line, but whether it communicates a policy on which the agency has settled." In this instance, the staff's opinion was indeed "last," but only because it "died on the vine" when the agency took its proposed rule in a different direction. "The staff recommendations were part of a deliberative process that worked as it should have," Barrett concluded. The vote was 7 to 2.

Often a new justice's first opinion comes in a case that the court decides unanimously. Perhaps in this case there had been an initial unanimous vote in conference that led Chief Justice Roberts to hand his new colleague what looked like an easy assignment. Or perhaps the chief justice made the assignment because this was one of the least controversial cases from the blockbuster-loaded November argument sitting. In any event, administrative law cases can be more complicated than they first appear, often involving a hornet's nest of formal rules, congressional delegation, and agency practice.

If there was an administrative law expert on the court, it was Stephen Breyer. Earlier in his career, he taught administrative law at Harvard and wrote or co-authored four books on the subject. He reveled in the field's intricacies, in its combination of law and policy. In Barrett's first case, Breyer was a dissenter. His objection was not to the distinction she drew between deliberative and final documents, but rather to how she applied it to the documents at issue. Some of the documents might have moved from the first category to the second, "complete but for a final signature," and might be subject to disclosure, Breyer wrote. But he found sufficient ambiguity in the record to recommend that the lower court take a more fine-grained look at the documents and their context in the agency's decisional process. "I would remand to allow the Court of Appeals to determine just how much work was left to be done," he concluded.

His dissenting opinion, which Sonia Sotomayor joined, was gentle, a meticulous dissection of the problem the case presented, without a hint of personal critique. This was a beginning, a time to build connections, or at least not to forgo the chance to build them. In his nearly fourteen-year tenure on the First Circuit, where he was serving as chief judge when President Bill Clinton named him to the Supreme Court in 1994, Breyer was known as a consensus builder. He brought that reputation from the Senate, where he worked with Senator Edward Kennedy as chief counsel to the Senate Judiciary Committee. He was so well regarded across the aisle that in December 1980 he won bipartisan confirmation to the First Circuit in a lame duck session after Jimmy Carter, the president who nominated him, had been defeated for reelection. It was to be the last Democratic judicial confirmation for more than twelve years. Breyer always called himself an optimist, even as consensus on the Supreme Court proved ever more elusive and optimism was growing hard to sustain.

THE COURT HAD one last piece of business left over from the 2020 election. At the end of December, a team of lawyers from Indianapolis representing the defeated president had filed a petition challenging more than 221,000 votes cast in Wisconsin, which a statewide recount showed Biden won by 20,600 votes. The petition's complaint was that voters should not have been permitted to deposit their ballots in drop boxes. Asking the justices to take up the petition on an expedited basis, the lawyers had described the case as urgent because "large swaths of the population believe the election was tainted by fraud and irregularities." In early January, without comment, the court had denied the motion to expedite.

The dozen Wisconsin entities and individuals Trump had sued, including the governor and the state elections commission, all waived their right to respond to the petition. In such a situation, permitted by the court's rules and not uncommon, any justice can call for a response. None did. On March 8, without a word, the court denied the petition.

The court's silence was not matched by the former president. "The Supreme Court should be ashamed of itself," he complained a week later, not for the first time; the shame theme was becoming a fixture in his attacks on the court. In a Fox News interview with Maria Bartiromo, he elaborated: "The Democrats used COVID to do things they can't believe they got away with, that they didn't get their legislatures to approve, and our courts and the Supreme Court didn't have the courage to overturn elections that should have been overturned because you're talking about decisive amounts, hundreds of thousands and even millions of votes."

AT ANY TIME in recent years, the Voting Rights Act case from Arizona that the court accepted at the start of the term would have been deemed significant. But few would have predicted how important it would become during the five months of electoral turmoil that took place between the early October grant and the March 2 argument. The opening months of state legislative sessions in the new year found Republican majorities waving the banner of election integrity and echoing the defeated president's cry of a stolen election. With breathtaking speed, they rushed to reverse the steps that had made voting easier during the COVID pandemic. It was also a moment to achieve the long-held goal of making it harder for people who were unlikely to vote Republican to cast their ballots.

The new measures limited early voting, even placing caps on the number of drop boxes where voters could securely deposit their ballots; imposed onerous new authentication requirements on mail-in ballots; tightened existing voter ID requirements or imposed new ones; and curbed the discretion election officials had traditionally been granted to carry out their nonpartisan duties. Nothing would be left to chance, or to a rogue election administrator who had not received the Republican message.

Many of the new measures would predictably place a disparate burden on Black and other minority voters. (In one particularly flagrant move, the Georgia legislature even made it a crime to offer water to people waiting in line to vote; many in Georgia had observed that during the 2020 election cycle, the lines were much longer in Black neighborhoods due to the unequal distribution of polling places.) Under Section 5 of the Voting Rights Act, "covered jurisdictions" like

Georgia, those states with a history of racial discrimination in access to the polls, would have had to obtain federal permission before making changes like these. The states would have had to persuade either the Justice Department or the federal district court in Washington that the changes would have "neither the purpose nor effect of denying or abridging the right to vote on account of race or color."

But Chief Justice Roberts's opinion in the *Shelby County* case in 2013 had disabled Section 5 by declaring unconstitutional the formula for identifying the states to which it applied. That left the other main provision of the Voting Rights Act, the quite different Section 2, standing alone. Section 2 applied to all states and prohibited any practice that "results in a denial or abridgment of the right of any citizen of the United States to vote on account of race or color." That was the section now at issue in the Arizona case. The national implications were obvious. By the time of the March argument, the question of how to interpret and apply Section 2 had become not only important, but urgent.

The two Arizona measures before the court in *Brnovich v. Democratic National Committee* predated the new push to suppress the vote. One required discarding the entire ballot cast by someone who turned out to have voted in the wrong precinct. Such votes could not be counted even for statewide offices that were not dependent on precinct lines and for which the errant voter was clearly eligible to cast a vote. The other provision made it a crime to collect and deliver someone else's completed mail-in ballot. The U.S. Court of Appeals for the Ninth Circuit held that both restrictions violated Section 2 by making it more difficult for Black, Latino, and Native American voters to exercise their franchise. The court explained that precinct lines in Arizona changed more frequently in minority communities, often unpredictably and with little notice, and that the practice of "ballot collection" was common on Indian reservations and in other rural parts of the state where distances were great and post offices were few.

The real issue before the Supreme Court wasn't whether the Ninth Circuit had reached the right result on the two policies so much as the fundamental question of whether it had applied the right standard for finding Section 2 liability. That was clear from the two-hour argument, during which the actual details of the case seemed of only minor interest to the court. Instead, the justices peppered the lawyers with questions about how Section 2 would apply in a variety of other settings. Hypothetical questions are common at oral argument. But unlike typical "hypos," there was not much about many of these that was hypothetical.

For example, although the question of Sunday voting was not before the court, limiting Sunday voting was a prominent part of the Republicans' drive to deter Black voters, for whom voting on the way home after church was a popular tradition in parts of the South. Georgia's new voting law, enacted in March amid great controversy, while not imposing a statewide ban on Sunday voting, gave local jurisdictions the option of keeping polling places closed on Sunday if they chose.

Justice Kagan addressed a barely hypothetical question to Michael Carvin, the lawyer representing the Arizona Republican Party in the appeal from the Ninth Circuit's ruling. Carvin was a familiar figure to the justices, a prominent Republican lawyer with an active Supreme Court practice. Along with many victories, he bore a few battle scars, including having led unsuccessful cases against the Affordable Care Act in 2012 and again in 2015. The core of Carvin's argument now was that as long as access to the vote was equally open to all, courts could not find a Section 2 violation.

Kagan posed her question: "A state has long had two weeks of early voting, and then the state decides that it's going to get rid of Sunday voting on those two weeks, leave everything else in place. Black voters vote on Sunday ten times more than white voters. Is that system equally open?"

"I would think it would be," Carvin replied. "Let's think about it. Sunday is the day we traditionally close government offices. It would be the exception rather than the rule to have government workers come in on a Sunday." As his answer implied, Carvin's view was that formal equality, devoid of all consideration of context, was sufficient to insulate a practice from Section 2 liability. As he made the point in answer to a question from Justice Breyer, "equally open" meant that "everyone has a complete opportunity to vote" and that "the state has not erected any barrier."

But might the "barrier" not also derive from culture, history, or economic circumstance? This was what Jessica Amunson, the lawyer arguing for Katie Hobbs, Arizona's secretary of state, explained in a colloquy with Justice Thomas. Hobbs, a Democrat, was the state's top election administrator. Having successfully run for the office in 2019 on a platform of expanding voting rights, she had refused to appeal the Ninth Circuit's ruling, and instead threw the weight of her office in with the Democrats who had brought the original lawsuit. Arizona's Republican attorney general, Mark Brnovich, filed the appeal on behalf of the state.

Explaining why the Ninth Circuit was correct to find that the ballot collection ban violated Section 2, the secretary of state's lawyer told the court: "With respect to Native American voters who rely on ballot collection to vote, simply saying that those voters can go ahead and vote in person or go ahead and vote by mail when they don't actually have home mail service or access to postal facilities, that's exactly the contrast that we draw with Mr. Carvin's position that it's all just about opportunity." Amunson continued: "Instead, you have to actually look at the reality of how the burden is affecting voters on the ground under the totality of circumstances inquiry."

How could the basic question of how Section 2 actually worked still be unanswered decades after the law's enactment? The answer lay in the convoluted history of the Voting Rights Act and the relationship between its two principal provisions. Much of that history involved the Supreme Court, and a good deal of it, in fact, involved John Roberts.

While it was operative, Section 5 was the preferred tool of the voting rights community because it operated prospectively. Under the preclearance regime, the covered states bore the burden of showing that a proposed change would be nondiscriminatory. If the states failed to prove their case, the challenged provision never took effect. Section 2, by contrast, operated retrospectively. The burden was on those challenging a particular provision to show that it was discriminatory in operation, not just in contemplation. If a provision was serving to discourage or exclude minority voters, it might be necessary to go through one or more election cycles in order to make the case that it was the provision and not some other factor that was causing the harm.

In a 1980 decision, *City of Mobile v. Bolden,* the court had interpreted Section 2 as applying only to intentional discrimination, not additionally to measures with a discriminatory effect. To ascribe intention to an entire legislative body is notoriously difficult. A requirement to show intentional discrimination threatened to render this part of the Voting Rights Act all but useless. Intense controversy surrounded the congressional effort to overcome the decision by amending Section 2 to make clear that it applied to discriminatory outcomes regardless of the legislature's intent.

By 1982, when the issue came to a head, the twenty-six-year-old Roberts had completed his clerkship for William Rehnquist and was working in the Reagan Justice Department as a special assistant to Attorney General William French Smith. He received the voting rights portfolio. The Democratic-controlled House had voted to add a results test to Section 2. Conservatives in the administration were determined to stop the bill in the Senate or, if that failed, to persuade President Reagan to veto it. Documents released in connection with Roberts's nomination to the court in 2005 showed his active participation in a battle that raged for months. He drafted speeches and op-eds for the attorney general and friendly senators and wrote many internal memos in his own name, including one to the attorney general titled "Why Section 2 of the Voting Rights Act Should Be Retained Unchanged." In that memo, he wrote: "Violations of Section 2 should not be made too easy to prove, since they provide a basis for the most intrusive interference imaginable by federal courts into state and local processes." (Michael Carvin was also a young lawyer in the Reagan Justice Department at the time, working for William Bradford Reynolds, the assistant attorney general in charge of the department's Civil Rights Division and the administration's point man in the Voting Rights Act fight.)

The effort to block the House bill failed, due in large measure to the intervention of Senator Bob Dole, the Kansas Republican who headed the Finance Committee. Dole was a widely respected figure who fourteen years later would be his party's presidential nominee, losing to Bill Clinton. Urging his fellow Republicans to support the amendment, he said Republicans needed to make "the extra effort to erase the lingering image of our party as the cadre of the elite, the wealthy, the insensitive." Reagan signed the bill into law.

In the intervening years, Section 2 was invoked often to challenge redistricting plans. A robust body of law grew up for these "vote dilution" cases that typically involved the claim that a redrawn district deprived members of minority groups of the opportunity to elect a candidate of their choice. But for "vote denial" cases, the term for challenges to provisions that placed obstacles in the path of minority voters, the go-to provision for many years remained Section 5. In the years since the *Shelby County* decision took Section 5 off the table, the court had not had a chance to develop a Section 2 jurisprudence for vote denial cases. Now, nearly forty years after the law's passage in its current form, the moment had finally arrived.

With the court's telephonic arguments, questioning proceeded in order of seniority. As the junior justice, Amy Barrett was the last to question Michael Carvin. As her final question, she asked what the Arizona Republican Party's motivation was "in keeping, say, the out-of-precinct voter ballot disqualification rules on the books." Her question seemed to spring from simple curiosity, or perhaps from puzzlement; Carvin's position, after all, was that the provision didn't help or hurt anyone in particular, and that voters who wanted to be sure their votes would count should simply vote in the right precinct. Why fight all the way to the Supreme Court to preserve something so meaningless?

That was not quite the question Carvin answered. Instead, he seemed to take Barrett as asking why the Arizona Republicans were in

the case at this point at all, rather than letting the Ninth Circuit opinion stand. "Because it puts us at a competitive disadvantage relative to
Democrats," he said. "Politics is a zero sum game, and every extra
vote they get through unlawful interpretations of Section 2 hurts us."
It was, Carvin went on, "the difference between winning an election
50 to 49 and losing 51 to 50."

In two hours of intense argument, this might have been the most
revealing moment, an acknowledgment that keeping some people's
votes from being counted actually had a purpose, and the purpose was
to help Republicans. This was no political science seminar, no abstract exercise in statutory interpretation. It was a street fight for
votes, and the meaning the Supreme Court would give to Section 2 of
the Voting Rights Act of 1965 would determine the winner.

JOHN ROBERTS'S ISOLATION on the court that bore his name was becoming ever more apparent. A decision in early March offered a startling piece of evidence. A low-visibility case posed the question
whether once the opposing parties in a lawsuit resolve their differences, the suit's dismissal for mootness can be avoided as long as the
plaintiffs are still seeking one dollar in nominal damages. By a vote of
8 to 1, the court answered yes, that the request for one dollar was
enough to keep the case alive. The lone dissenter was Roberts.

It was his first solitary dissent in more than fifteen years on the
court, years during which he had filed very few dissenting opinions
and rarely even voted in dissent. His position in this case, *Uzuegbunam v. Preczewski*, was consistent with his long-expressed view that
the Constitution places strict limits on people's ability to bring cases
to federal court and concomitantly on the courts' jurisdiction to decide the cases they receive. This was nothing new for Roberts. What
required explanation was the unity of the other eight members of the
Roberts court, justices whose views on jurisdictional questions had
often diverged.

The case began as a lawsuit brought by an evangelical Christian
student at a public college in Georgia after officials told him that his

open-air preaching on campus was disturbing the peace and violating school policy. The student sued for an injunction and "nominal damages" for a violation of his First Amendment right to free speech. The college quickly yielded, then moved to dismiss the lawsuit as moot. Dismissal would save the college from a possibly adverse federal court judgment. It would also deprive the student of the chance for a formal vindication of what he saw as his constitutional right. That was the conflict. The federal district court dismissed the case as moot, a decision that the Eleventh Circuit affirmed.

In the Supreme Court, the student was represented by Alliance Defending Freedom, a Christian right litigating group increasingly active at the court. (The Christian baker in the *Masterpiece Cakeshop* case was one of its clients.) The Alliance lawyers argued that nominal damages played an "indispensable role" in litigation over constitutional rights, especially in campus speech cases where students typically suffer no financial damages and college policies change quickly in response to complaints.

Under the doctrine of standing, plaintiffs must show not only that they were injured by the defendant, but that the injury was one that a court can redress, typically by ordering a change in the defendant's behavior or by awarding damages to the plaintiff. Is an award of one dollar in nominal damages merely symbolic, or does it count as sufficient under the "redress" prong of the standing doctrine?

"Despite being small, nominal damages are certainly concrete," Justice Thomas wrote for the majority in an opinion that delved into English common law and early Supreme Court cases. "Early courts routinely awarded nominal damages alone," he wrote. "Certainly, no one seems to think that those judgments were without legal effect. Those nominal damages necessarily must have provided redress."

In his dissenting opinion, Roberts argued that the prospect for redress had to be "meaningful" for a case to present the live controversy that the Constitution's Article III requires for federal court jurisdiction. "To satisfy Article III, redress must alleviate the plaintiff's alleged injury in some way," he wrote, "either by compensating the plaintiff for a past loss or by preventing an ongoing or future harm.

Nominal damages do not serve these ends where a plaintiff alleges only a completed violation of his rights."

Roberts offered his view of history to counter Thomas's, noting that the justices in the country's earliest years refused to offer advisory opinions not anchored in concrete cases. But now, he wrote, "the Court sees no problem with turning judges into advice columnists." He continued: "Today's decision risks a major expansion of the judicial role. Until now, we have said that federal courts can review the legality of policies and actions only as a necessary incident to resolving real disputes. Going forward, the Judiciary will be required to perform this function whenever a plaintiff asks for a dollar."

This was a standard conservative view, albeit expressed more colorfully than in a typical judicial opinion. Why was Roberts alone? For his fellow conservatives, the answer perhaps lay in specific aspects of the case: the conflict over religious speech that prompted the lawsuit; the involvement of Alliance Defending Freedom, underscoring the implications of the case for religious interests; and conservative unease about the state of open discourse on the nation's campuses. A brief from the Foundation for Individual Rights in Education (FIRE), a prominent critic of campus speech codes, described nominal damages as often the only way for students to vindicate their free speech rights.

For their part, liberal justices have long resisted limitations on access to federal court. This case was an opportunity for a modest change of course in what for years has been a losing battle against tightening the requirements for standing. The American Civil Liberties Union filed a brief that was unusual in being joined by two conservative organizations, the Institute for Justice and the Americans for Prosperity Foundation, as well as by Americans United for Separation of Church and State, an organization usually on the opposite side from Alliance Defending Freedom. These groups "disagree about many issues," the brief said, "but share the belief—informed by their experiences—that nominal damages play a critical role in preserving plaintiffs' ability to vindicate their constitutional rights and to challenge unconstitutional government policies." This brief made clear that more was at stake than the rights of student preachers.

Members of each wing of the court had reason, in other words, for not going over to the chief justice's side. *Uzuegbunam v. Preczewski* was far from the most notable case of the term, but neither was it trivial. The decision would enter the casebooks on civil procedure and federal court jurisdiction. It would determine litigation strategy and set the course for innumerable lawsuits. Whether it would also mark a turning point in the career of one particular chief justice remained to be seen.

THE FISSURE BETWEEN Roberts and the justices to his right only seemed to grow, as shown by a decision later in the month. It may be hard to believe that any unanswered questions remain about the meaning of the Fourth Amendment's prohibition of "unreasonable searches and seizures," but this case, *Torres v. Madrid*, presented one. The question was whether a "seizure" occurred when a police officer shot and wounded a fleeing suspect who, rather than submit, continued to flee and evaded capture. The suspect was arrested at a hospital the next day. She later sued the police officer for having used excessive force, characterizing the shooting as an unreasonable seizure. The federal district court in New Mexico ruled for the officer in a decision affirmed by the Tenth Circuit on the ground that no seizure had occurred.

Roberts wrote the majority opinion reversing the Tenth Circuit. He said the suspect's continued flight did not negate the fact that the police officer had applied "force with the intent to restrain." That was the common law definition of a seizure as the Constitution's framers understood it, Roberts continued; that the effort to restrain was unsuccessful was irrelevant. He said that a rule limiting "seizure" to actual physical control "would be difficult to apply" because "it will often be unclear when an officer succeeds in gaining control over a struggling suspect. Courts will puzzle whether an officer exercises control when he grabs a suspect, when he tackles him, or only when he slaps on the cuffs."

The vote was 5 to 3. (Amy Barrett was not on the court in mid-October when the case was argued, and did not vote.) The dissenters were Gorsuch, Thomas, and Alito. Gorsuch's dissent was scathing. "The majority holds that a criminal suspect can be simultaneously seized and roaming at large," he began. "It's a seizure even if the suspect refuses to stop, evades capture, and rides off into the sunset never to be seen again. That view is as mistaken as it is novel."

Gorsuch was just getting warmed up. "Really, the majority's answer to the Constitution's text is to ignore it," he wrote. "The common law offers a vast legal library. Like any other, it must be used thoughtfully. We have no business wandering about and randomly grabbing volumes off the shelf, plucking out passages we like, scratching out bits we don't, all before pasting our own new pastiche into the U. S. Reports." And to Roberts's observation that it would be hard for courts to apply a rule that fixed the moment of seizure at the achievement of physical control, Gorsuch had this to say: "Surely our role as interpreters of the Constitution isn't to make life easier for ourselves."

This was Gorsuch as he had appeared during his first months on the court, even his first weeks, when he flung barbs with abandon at colleagues with decades of seniority. Dissenting from a majority opinion by Ruth Bader Ginsburg in a complicated administrative law case that had been argued on his first day on the bench, April 17, 2017, Gorsuch delivered a condescending lecture. "If a statute needs repair, there's a constitutionally prescribed way to do it," he wrote. "It's called legislation." Reports from inside the court in the late spring and summer of 2017 suggested that the justices found their new colleague anywhere from annoying to insufferable. In subsequent terms, he seemed to have dialed back his rhetorical instincts. But now here was the original Gorsuch again.

Roberts's response to Gorsuch's opinion was restrained. "There is no call for such surmise," he wrote of Gorsuch's remark about wanting "to make life easier for ourselves." "At the end of the day," Roberts continued, "we simply agree with the analysis of the common law of arrest and its relation to the Fourth Amendment set forth thirty years ago by Justice Scalia, joined by six of his colleagues, rather than the competing view urged by the dissent today."

THE PANDEMIC WAS finally relaxing its grip. On Friday, March 19, the court's public information office announced that the justices, at least most of them, had convened in person for their weekly conference. All had been vaccinated. The court would remain closed to the public, and the term's final round of arguments in April would take place by telephone, but for the first time since March 2020, the justices would be meeting face-to-face to conduct their communal business.

The closed-door conference is where the justices' most intimate interactions take place. No one else is admitted, not even law clerks or secretaries. With the unexpected announcement, it was left to outsiders to wonder whether the members of the Roberts court would greet each other like long-lost friends, or whether they would have trouble looking one another in the eye.

CHAPTER NINE

APRIL · AGENDAS

IT WAS ONLY A MATTER OF TIME before the court accepted another Second Amendment case, and in April that time arrived. That the country had just experienced a third deadly mass shooting incident in as many months was no deterrent to justices impatient with the court's failure to widen the Second Amendment opening it had created with its *Heller* decision nearly thirteen years earlier. That 5-to-4 decision, with a majority opinion by Justice Scalia, was the court's first interpretation of the Second Amendment's "right to bear arms" to protect not only the collective right suggested by the amendment's reference to "a well regulated Militia" but an individual right—specifically, the right to keep a handgun at home for personal protection. *Heller* was a stunning constitutional departure; in 1991, Warren Burger, the conservative chief justice, then retired, had declared in a television interview that the notion that the Second Amendment protected an individual right to own a gun "has been the subject of one of the greatest pieces of fraud, I repeat the word 'fraud,' on the American public."

Although it changed the long-accepted meaning of the Second Amendment, *Heller* actually changed little for the great majority of American gun owners. Only two jurisdictions—the District of Columbia, where the case originated, and the city of Chicago—prohibited owning a gun in the limited circumstance that the decision addressed. Questions about carrying a weapon outside the home, and to where one might carry it, whether open or concealed, were left to future cases.

The cases came, but the court refused to accept them, avoiding every opportunity to address the questions *Heller* left unanswered. A mobilized social movement had succeeded in propelling *Heller* to the Supreme Court, but just as its appetite was whetted for more, the court seemed to turn away. Justices Thomas, Alito, and Scalia—and Gorsuch, who took Scalia's place—were eager to build on *Heller*. But Roberts and Kennedy, having joined the *Heller* majority, were now wary about pushing the new individual right any further. By 2015, Thomas was publicly complaining, in a series of opinions dissenting from successive denials of review, that the court was turning the Second Amendment into a "second-class right" and a "constitutional orphan."

Brett Kavanaugh's arrival in the fall of 2018 to replace Justice Kennedy changed the dynamic. On the D.C. Circuit, Kavanaugh had been an aggressive advocate of expanded gun rights. In 2011, he dissented from a decision that upheld the District of Columbia's ban on certain assault weapons. "A ban on a class of arms is not an 'incidental regulation,'" Kavanaugh wrote then. "It is equivalent to a ban on a category of speech."

Finally, in January 2019, the court accepted a case brought by a New York State affiliate of the National Rifle Association and three individual gun owners. The petitioners were challenging an unusually strict New York City rule that prevented licensed gun owners from taking their guns outside the city to a second home or a shooting range. While the Second Circuit had upheld the rule, the chance for a successful defense before the Supreme Court was slim at best, and the city didn't try. Instead, with the cooperation of the state legislature, which amended the underlying statute, the city repealed its rule and informed the court that the case was moot.

But was it? The justices who had grabbed this promising case were determined not to let it slip away. Instead of the immediate dismissal the city asked for, the court scheduled oral argument for December 2019 with this unusual notation: "The question of mootness will be subject to further consideration at oral argument, and the parties should be prepared to discuss it." At the argument, the plaintiffs maintained that their Second Amendment rights were still impaired despite the rule's repeal: that even though they could now take their guns outside the city to a second home, they might face legal trouble if they stopped for coffee along the way. Not so, the city responded; routine stops were permissible. The city insisted that the plaintiffs had received everything their lawsuit had asked for, the very definition of mootness.

The battle inside the court that began with the rule's repeal went on for months. It was not until April 2020 that the court finally dismissed the case as moot with a two-page unsigned opinion. Alito, joined by Thomas and Gorsuch, dissented with a thirty-one-page opinion. "By incorrectly dismissing this case as moot," Alito began, "the court permits our docket to be manipulated in a way that should not be countenanced." He concluded: "The city violated petitioners' Second Amendment right, and we should so hold."

It did not take long for the same organizational plaintiff, the New York State Rifle & Pistol Association, to come back with a new case. Filed in December 2020, the case was an appeal of another Second Circuit ruling, this one concerning licenses to carry handguns outside the home. New York law made such licenses available only to applicants who could show that "proper cause exists." The statute itself did not define "proper cause." Judicial interpretations over the years had interpreted the phrase narrowly to require that applicants demonstrate some special need that set them apart from the general public. While the two members of the NRA affiliate who joined in the lawsuit had both received limited licenses that permitted them to use their guns for hunting, they wanted the unlimited ability to carry their guns as a routine matter for self-defense. Their applications were denied, and their constitutional challenge to the law foundered on a Second Circuit precedent from a few years earlier that had upheld the law against a similar challenge. (The Supreme Court had denied review of that earlier decision in 2013.)

Unlike the first New York case, this one, *New York State Rifle &*
Pistol Association, Inc. v. Corlett, was in no danger of becoming moot.
Its implications were obvious. At stake, finally, was the shape of the
post-*Heller* world. Not that the justices needed much prompting, but
twenty-two states filed a brief urging the court to accept the case. The
states' brief pointed to New York's status as an outlier with its open-
ended "proper cause" standard. Most states have what are known as
"shall-issue" or "objective-issue" gun licensing laws, under which the
license is granted if the applicant passes a background check and
meets other stated criteria. The administrative discretion inherent in
"proper cause" was a point of obvious vulnerability for New York.

As presented by Paul Clement, a prominent Supreme Court practitioner who served as solicitor general in the George W. Bush administration, the petition asked one question: "Whether the Second
Amendment allows the government to prohibit ordinary law-abiding
citizens from carrying handguns outside the home for self-defense."
In granting the petition, the court tweaked the question to make it
more fact-specific and less rhetorical: "Whether the state's denial of
petitioners' applications for concealed carry licenses for self-defense
violated the Second Amendment." Whether these were "ordinary
law-abiding citizens" was not something the court would assume.
That was a case for the petitioners' lawyer to make.

Among Donald Trump's appointees to the Supreme Court, Kavanaugh's Second Amendment views were well known, and Gorsuch
soon made his abundantly clear. Within weeks of taking his seat in
April 2017, he joined Thomas's dissent from the court's denial of review in a case that challenged California's ban on carrying concealed
weapons. The dissenting opinion concluded with a remarkable passage:

> For those of us who work in marbled halls, guarded constantly by a
> vigilant and dedicated police force, the guarantees of the Second
> Amendment might seem antiquated and superfluous. But the Fram-
> ers made a clear choice. They reserved to all Americans the right to

bear arms for self-defense. I do not think we should stand by idly while a state denies its citizens that right, particularly when their very lives may depend on it.

The unknown of the three was Amy Barrett. In her brief time on the Seventh Circuit, she had participated in one Second Amendment case. The case concerned the federal law that prohibits those convicted of a felony from subsequently possessing a firearm. Could that prohibition be constitutionally applied to a person whose conviction, while for a felony, was for nonviolent white-collar crime? In this case, *Kanter v. Barr*, the individual was a first-time offender convicted of Medicare fraud. Second Amendment challenges to the "felon-in-possession" bar were coming up in courts around the country. The felons almost always lost, with courts citing a combination of deference to Congress and historical evidence that at the time of the Constitution's framing, the right to own a gun was limited to "virtuous citizens." The Seventh Circuit decision in the *Kanter* case was in line with those of the other courts.

Barrett dissented. She concluded that the law could not constitutionally be applied to a person whose gun ownership, despite a felony conviction, would pose no risk to public safety. Her thirty-seven-page opinion, half again as long as the panel's majority opinion, was a meticulous exploration of the historical evidence for stripping felons of the right to bear arms. She wrote as an originalist, her opinion replete with references to the views of the founding-era generation and of the policies of the state legislatures that ratified the Constitution.

But it was a subtle originalism. "History does not support the proposition that felons lose their Second Amendment rights solely because of their status as felons," she wrote. "But it does support the proposition that a state can take the right to bear arms away from a category of people that it deems dangerous." Legislatures were entitled to make such decisions "based on present-day judgments about categories of people whose possession of guns would endanger the public safety," she continued, adding that "'exclusions need not mirror limits that were on the books in 1791.'" That last phrase was a quotation from an earlier Seventh Circuit opinion on the scope of the felon-in-possession law. Authorizing "present-day judgments" not limited to the precise public understanding at the moment of the Constitution's framing? This was an originalism different in degree, although most likely not in kind, from that of Barrett's mentor, Antonin Scalia.

Even so, where would that distinction, if it was one, place Barrett in the post-*Heller* moment that was now at hand? Her one opinion sent mixed signals. At its conclusion, she wrote that rejecting a non-dangerous individual's right to own a gun simply by virtue of a felony conviction "treats the Second Amendment as a 'second-class right, subject to an entirely different body of rules than the other Bill of Rights guarantees.'" This quotation was from a 2010 opinion by Justice Alito. By 2019, when Barrett issued her opinion, she had to know that the "second-class right" phrase was a familiar dog whistle that signified sympathy with the gun rights cause. Although the new case would not be argued until the fall and would most likely not be decided until the spring of 2022, there was not the slightest doubt about where Alito would be. The question was how many justices would join him, and how far they would be willing to go.

By April, with vaccinations increasingly available and the pandemic easing its fierce grip, it might have seemed that the Supreme Court had said all it needed to say about the validity of COVID-related limits on communal worship. But the majority's work was not yet done.

On April 2, an "emergency application" arrived at the court. It was another case from California, this time challenging the state's limit on in-home and private backyard gatherings to three "households" at a time. Although the limitation was set to expire in two weeks, the applicants, who included a pastor and a woman who held Bible study sessions in her home, described the matter as "urgent." In fact, they requested action by the next day, "Holy Saturday," the day before Easter.

Although the outlines of this case, *Tandon v. Newsom*, were familiar, it was not typical of the COVID cases that had reached the court earlier. By this time, in response to the Supreme Court's most recent decision, California was permitting church attendance at 50 percent of the building's capacity up to two hundred people, with no numerical limit on a church's outdoor worship services. Church-focused limits were no longer at issue. The applicants, Jeremy Wong and Karen Busch, who referred dismissively to church worship as "traditional, ritualistic faith practices," maintained that because their version of Christian worship was centered in the home, it was the home-based limits that violated their right to the free exercise of religion.

In federal district court in San Francisco, Judge Lucy Koh made short work of the plaintiffs' claim. "The State's private gatherings restrictions treat religious and secular gatherings alike and make no reference to religion," she wrote. A panel of the Ninth Circuit rejected the applicants' request for an emergency injunction to keep the restriction from taking effect while the appeal was pending. The vote was 2 to 1. The majority opinion echoed the district court, noting that "the gatherings restrictions apply equally to private religious and private secular gatherings, and there is no indication, or claim, of animus toward religious gatherings."

The dissenting opinion by Judge Patrick Bumatay expressed a completely different understanding of the case. To deny the injunction, he wrote, was to "turn a blind eye to discrimination against religious practice." How could this be? Wherein did the discrimination lie? The proper comparison, he claimed, was not the one Judge Koh and the panel majority had made between religious and secular activities in the home. Rather, it was to "analogous secular activities" outside the home such as hair salons, barbershops, and tattoo parlors, where "hours-long physical proximity and touching is [*sic*] required." By allowing such venues to operate with fewer limitations than those on in-home gatherings, California was engaging in a "religious gerrymander."

Two of the three judges on the Ninth Circuit panel were Trump appointees. One was Bumatay and the other was Bridget S. Bade, who voted in the majority with Judge Milan D. Smith, an appointee of

President George W. Bush. Bumatay and Bade had both started their careers as law clerks to well-known conservative federal judges, and both worked as assistant federal prosecutors. But their careers diverged. When she was nominated to an Arizona seat on the Ninth Circuit, Bade was serving as a federal magistrate judge, a workaday judicial position of low visibility and political salience. Her nomination was uncontroversial, and she attracted little attention even when her name briefly appeared in the news as a possible replacement for Ruth Bader Ginsburg.

Bumatay, by contrast, had served in several positions in the Trump Justice Department, including as a special assistant to Attorney General William Barr. The son of immigrants from the Philippines, he was a favorite of the Federalist Society, which he joined during his first year at Harvard Law School. Along with leading civil rights organizations, both California senators opposed his nomination to a California seat on the appeals court, and Senate Democrats succeeded in derailing the nomination during the 2018 congressional session. The partisan struggle over Bumatay's nomination took place well below the public radar. But it was followed intensely by those who were mapping the future of the Trump judiciary. By the time he was narrowly confirmed in late 2019 at the age of forty-one, his youth, unblemished conservative credentials, and persistence in seeking a life-tenured federal judgeship had earned him a kind of stardom. With his dissent in the *Tandon* case, he did not disappoint.

The tone of the emergency application to the Supreme Court that followed was bold to the point of impudence. "This court undoubtedly has better things to do than sheepdog California and the Ninth Circuit," the plaintiffs' lawyer, Ryan J. Walsh, told the justices. "Yet until state leaders and lower court judges respect the boundaries established by the Constitution, the task of protecting religious believers from overzealous government officials remains this court's cross to bear." As Walsh, a former Scalia law clerk, surely knew, only a lawyer who felt certain of holding a winning hand would risk addressing the court in such terms.

Walsh judged his audience correctly. While the court did not give him absolutely everything he asked for—instead of the twenty-four-hour turnaround he requested, a week went by and Easter had passed by the time the justices granted the injunction shortly before midnight on April 9—he, his clients, and the country got something of great importance. The unsigned four-page opinion took the suggestion in the earlier COVID cases and made it explicit: Government regulations were subject to the strictest judicial scrutiny "whenever they treat *any* comparable secular activity more favorably than religious exercise" (italics in the original). The opinion continued: "It is no answer that a State treats some comparable secular businesses or other activities as poorly as or even less favorably than the religious exercise at issue."

While the opinion at first appeared to leave the meaning of "comparable" undefined, it was clear by the third page that the majority embraced Judge Bumatay's analysis:

> First, California treats some comparable secular activities more favorably than at-home religious exercise, permitting hair salons, retail stores, person care services, movie theaters, private suites at sporting events and concerts, and indoor restaurants to bring together more than three households at a time.

The vote was 5 to 4. In dissent, Roberts said nothing beyond "The Chief Justice would deny the application." Kagan, Breyer, and Sotomayor had more to say. "The majority continues to disregard law and facts alike," Kagan wrote in an opinion the other two joined. She explained:

> The First Amendment requires that a State treat religious conduct as well as the State treats comparable secular conduct. Sometimes finding the right secular analogue may raise hard questions. But not today. California limits religious gatherings in homes to three households. If the State also limits all secular gatherings in homes to three households, it has complied with the First Amendment. And the State does exactly that: It has adopted a blanket restriction on at-home gatherings of all kinds, religious and secular alike.

Kagan went on to assert that the First Amendment did not require the state to treat religious gatherings the same as hardware stores and hair salons. She noted the evidence the state had put forward, and that the lower courts had accepted, for why in-home gatherings posed a greater risk of COVID transmission than commercial settings, adding, "the law does not require that the State equally treat apples and watermelons."

The justices had reason to expect that *Tandon v. Newsom* would be the last of the COVID cases. Restrictions were being lifted all over the country. In less than a week, the three-household California limit was due to expire and to be replaced by a twenty-five-person cap, more than enough to accommodate the dozen people who had gathered regularly for the plaintiffs' Bible study. To the objection that the court's intervention was simply unnecessary, the majority had an answer: California had "a track record of 'moving the goalposts,'" and in any event, the applicants were being "irreparably harmed by the loss of free exercise rights for even minimal periods of time." Or perhaps it was that had the court stayed its hand, the case would soon have evaporated and the justices in the majority would have forfeited the opportunity to shape the law of religion to their liking as, thanks to Amy Coney Barrett, they finally had the votes to do.

ONE OF ANTONIN Scalia's final dissenting opinions, one of two issued on January 25, 2016, nineteen days before his death, came in a case about life sentences for juvenile murderers. The case, *Montgomery v. Louisiana*, was one in a line of decisions insisting that the criminal justice system take into account the particular characteristics and vulnerabilities of juvenile defendants. In *Roper v. Simmons*, in 2005, the court had barred the death penalty for those who committed a capital crime before age eighteen. In response, many states had enacted new laws to impose a mandatory sentence of life without parole on those convicted of capital crimes committed as juveniles. In *Miller v. Alabama* in 2012, the court ruled that these mandatory sentences also violated the Eighth Amendment's prohibition on cruel and unusual punishment and were not an acceptable alternative to a death sentence. Rather, judges needed the discretion to take into account a young defendant's specific characteristics, including whether evidence of "irreparable corruption" or "irretrievable depravity" was present or absent. The court's suggestion was that it would be the rare juvenile who was utterly irredeemable. Only after a process that considered such issues could a judge sentence a juvenile murderer to what would be, in effect, an eventual death behind bars.

The question in *Montgomery v. Louisiana*, the case from 2016 that provoked Scalia's dissent, was whether to give the *Miller* decision retroactive application to the twenty-one hundred juvenile murderers then serving mandatory life sentences. Scalia had dissented from the prior decisions that required taking youth into account, regarding them as unacceptable departures from the original meaning of the Eighth Amendment. This time, he objected that by making the *Miller* decision retroactive, the majority was imposing "utterly impossible nonsense" on courts that would lack the means to evaluate whether an inmate would have been judged "incorrigible" at the time of sentencing years or decades earlier. Scalia lost the argument by a vote of 6 to 3. The *Montgomery* majority included Roberts, Ginsburg, and Kennedy, who wrote the opinion.

A Mississippi prisoner named Brett Jones was serving a sentence of life without the possibility of parole for a murder committed at age fifteen; he had stabbed his grandfather to death with a kitchen knife during an argument. He was originally sentenced under Mississippi's mandatory sentencing law. After the *Miller* decision, he received a new sentencing hearing. Although the judge who reimposed the life sentence did not make a specific finding on incorrigibility, the state courts held that Jones's youth and personal characteristics had received adequate consideration.

The question for the Supreme Court was whether more was necessary under the *Miller* and *Montgomery* cases. There was in fact considerable confusion among state and federal courts about whether those decisions, properly interpreted, required the sentencing judge to make a specific oral or written finding or whether it was enough for the judge to have the discretion to take the defendant's personal qualities into account in some fashion. Jones's lawyers argued vigorously that the Supreme Court's emphasis on the "rare children whose crimes reflect irreparable corruption"—a phrase from the *Montgomery* case—made clear that a specific finding on the point was constitutionally required. "Whether the Eighth Amendment requires the sentencing authority to make a finding that a juvenile is permanently incorrigible before imposing a sentence of life without parole" was the question the lawyers presented in *Jones v. Mississippi*.

Had Ginsburg and Kennedy still been on the court, the answer to that question would most likely have been yes. But Kavanaugh was now in Kennedy's place, and of course Ginsburg had been succeeded by Amy Barrett. As much as any case of the term, *Jones v. Mississippi* showed what those changes meant. The vote was 6 to 3 and the answer was no.

Writing for the majority, Kavanaugh said that "the key assumption of both *Miller* and *Montgomery* was that discretionary sentencing allows the sentencer to consider the defendant's youth, and thereby ensures that life-without-parole sentences are imposed only in cases where that sentence is appropriate in light of the defendant's age." That was all that was required. "If the *Miller* and *Montgomery* Court wanted to require sentencers to also make a factual finding of incorrigibility, the Court certainly could have said so—and surely would have said so."

In dissent, Sotomayor, joined by Breyer and Kagan, accused the majority of having gutted the two precedents and of reaching a conclusion that "would come as a shock to the Courts in *Miller* and *Montgomery*." She said the court in those decisions "expressly rejected the notion that sentencing discretion, alone, suffices." Sotomayor quoted from the *Montgomery* case: "Even if a court considers a child's age before sentencing him or her to a lifetime in prison, that sentence still violates the Eighth Amendment for a child whose crime reflects unfortunate yet transient immaturity." She went on: "The Court is fooling no one. Because I cannot countenance the Court's abandonment of *Miller* and *Montgomery*, I dissent."

Did the *Jones* decision represent a gratuitous gutting of the two precedents, or a necessary clarification of their ambiguity? The answer would remain in the eye of the beholder. A headline in an account of the decision in the *National Review* may have come closest to the heart of the matter: VINDICATING SCALIA'S LAST OPINION. And hadn't Amy Barrett, speaking of her late mentor as she stood with the president in the Rose Garden eight days after Ruth Ginsburg's death, declared "His judicial philosophy is mine, too"?

EVER SINCE SENATOR Mitch McConnell's successful ten-month blockade kept President Obama from filling the Scalia vacancy, progressives had wanted to do something to reclaim the "stolen" seat—the seat Trump filled with Neil Gorsuch. The cry went up: Add a seat. Add two seats. After Amy Barrett's election eve confirmation, the number most often heard was four.

On April 15, Rep. Jerrold Nadler of New York, the chairman of the House Judiciary Committee, and three other Democrats introduced the Judiciary Act of 2021 to create a thirteen-member Supreme Court. In his own remarks, Nadler adopted a nonpartisan tone. In the nineteenth century, when there were only nine federal appellate circuits, it made sense to have nine justices, he explained, but now that there were thirteen circuits, the number of justices should grow accordingly: "Thirteen justices for thirteen circuits is a sensible progression."

The Judiciary Committee's press release offered a more pointed—and accurate—explanation: "This bill will restore balance to the nation's highest court after four years of norm-breaking actions by Republicans led to its current composition and greatly damaged the court's standing in the eyes of the American people."

The ink on the proposed Judiciary Act, a mere six lines long, was barely dry before Rep. Nancy Pelosi, the House speaker, made her own view clear. "I have no intention to bring it to the floor," she said just hours after the bill was introduced. Pelosi did not elaborate, nor did she have to. The fact was that even if the bill could clear the

House, it stood no chance of surviving a Republican filibuster in the Senate. Why spend the narrow Democratic majority's limited time and political capital on an effort that was doomed to fail?

Nor was there general agreement, even among progressives, that expanding the court at this politically freighted moment was a good idea. The "court-packing" epithet that Republicans were quick to affix to the plan was a reminder of one of the best-known episodes in twentieth-century American political history, President Franklin D. Roosevelt's unsuccessful effort to add as many as six seats to a conservative court that stood in the way of the New Deal's major initiatives. Shortly after his overwhelming reelection to a second term in 1936, Roosevelt proposed the Judicial Procedures Reform Bill of 1937, under which a new seat, up to a total of fifteen, would be added to the court for every justice who had served at least ten years and had reached the age of seventy. The president explained that the court needed "new blood" and the aging justices needed help with their workload. The proposal was widely denounced as a threat to judicial independence. It failed, but Roosevelt won the long game. Within the next few years, three justices retired and two died. Roosevelt got to choose eight justices, one of whom, William O. Douglas, was still sitting on the court in 1975, thirty years after Roosevelt's death.

Proponents of the modern court expansion plan were dismayed when Justice Breyer, in a lecture at Harvard Law School, warned that Americans should "think long and hard" before making structural changes to the Supreme Court. Changes understood to be politically motivated would only further undermine trust in the institution, he said. Some progressives seethed with frustration. Not only was Breyer not taking their hints that it was time to retire, he was publicly undermining their effort to reclaim what had been lost during the Trump years. "I wish that he would just stop talking about that and stick to actually adjudicating cases," said Rep. Mondaire Jones, a New York Democrat who was a co-sponsor of the Nadler bill.

There were other proposals for making the Supreme Court more responsive to the public. Replacing life tenure with fixed eighteen-year terms was one widely discussed idea that would guarantee each president two Supreme Court vacancies during a four-year term. Life tenure was an anomaly not only among the world's constitutional democracies but also among the fifty state judicial systems. Only Rhode Island provided life tenure for the judges of its highest court, with all the others imposing a cutoff of either years of service or age.

Polls showed public support for ending life tenure. In September 2020, three House Democrats had introduced the Supreme Court Term Limits and Regular Appointments Act, setting eighteen-year terms of active service for future justices. The bill provided that after the first eighteen years, a justice would be placed on senior status, available to serve on the lower courts—as some justices have done during retirement—or to fill a temporary vacancy on the Supreme Court. Even the proposal's supporters did not argue that it could be applied to impose term limits on incumbent justices. So from a political standpoint, its deficiency was obvious: It couldn't fix the current problem.

As a presidential candidate, Joe Biden had expressed no interest in adding seats or making other changes to the court. "The last thing we need to do is turn the Supreme Court into a political football," he said on *60 Minutes* during the campaign. But as president, he could not ignore an issue that would continue to fester on the Democratic Party's left. On April 9, he signed an executive order setting up a commission to study the entire range of proposals for changing the court. The commission's thirty-six members were drawn largely from academia. The president gave them 180 days to complete their work.

CHAPTER TEN

MAY · THE QUESTION

IT WAS ALWAYS ABOUT ABORTION.

Ever since Ronald Reagan won the presidency in 1980 on a Republican Party platform that called for "the appointment of judges at all levels of the judiciary who respect traditional family values and the sanctity of innocent human life," the future of the right to abortion has hung over every Supreme Court vacancy. The titanic battle over Reagan's nomination of Robert Bork in 1987 turned in large measure on the nominee's disdain for the court's recognition of a constitutional right to privacy. While Bork's adversaries deployed "privacy" as a euphemism for the right to abortion, everyone knew the real subject was the future of *Roe v. Wade*, the decision's original 7-to-2 majority having shrunk by then to 5 to 4. Bork's nomination was defeated by a coalition of Democratic and moderate Republican senators.

Subsequent nominees, lacking Bork's paper trail on the issue, were able to take refuge in simply acknowledging that there was a precedent called *Roe v. Wade* and then claiming that the canons of judicial ethics prevented them from expressing a view on an issue likely to be back before the court. The only Supreme Court nominee after Bork to speak forthrightly on the subject was Ruth Bader Ginsburg. The right to abortion was "essential to women's equality," she told the Senate Judiciary Committee at her confirmation hearing in 1993. The Senate, evidently not unduly alarmed by this declaration, confirmed her nomination by a vote of 96 to 3.

More typical was John Roberts, who during his 2005 confirmation hearing identified *Roe* as "settled as a precedent of the Supreme Court" and declined senators' invitation to say more. "I think I should stay away from discussions of particular issues that are likely to come before the court again," he repeated several times. In similar fashion, Neil Gorsuch answered a senator's *Roe* question during his 2017 hearing by saying "I would tell you that *Roe v. Wade*, decided in 1973, was a precedent of the United States Supreme Court." He then offered an additional observation: "So a good judge will consider it as precedent of the United States Supreme Court, worthy of treatment as precedent like any other."

"Precedent" and "settled law" are comforting words from Supreme Court nominees if one doesn't probe too deeply—as Senator Susan Collins of Maine evidently had not when she emerged from a two-hour meeting with Brett Kavanaugh in August 2018 to announce, as if this were a revelation rather than a truism, that the nominee had confided to her that he regarded *Roe v. Wade* as "settled law." Collins, a Republican who eventually voted to confirm Kavanaugh, told reporters: "He said that he agreed with what Justice Roberts said at his nomination hearing in which he said that it was settled law."

Unlike Gorsuch, who as a judge had not handled an abortion case, Kavanaugh actually had a judicial record on abortion. In 2017, the year before his Supreme Court nomination, a troubling case reached the D.C. Circuit. The Trump administration had tried to stop a pregnant teenager, an undocumented immigrant who was in federal custody as an "unaccompanied minor," from getting an abortion. The seventeen-year-old had managed to find a lawyer and had taken all necessary legal steps to exercise her right to terminate her pregnancy. This included persuading a judge in Texas, where she was being held in a private shelter under contract with the government, that she was mature enough to make the decision. Volunteers had agreed to make all arrangements and pay the cost. But the political appointee in charge of handling unaccompanied minors would not allow the plan to proceed, on the ground that the federal government could not be in a position to "facilitate" an abortion. There was, of course, nothing for the government to facilitate; without federal intervention, the abortion would have taken place through the actions of private parties.

By the time a federal district judge in Washington ordered the government to stop blocking the abortion, the teenager's pregnancy was well into the second trimester. She would "suffer irreparable injury" with further delay, the judge ruled, including the prospect that she would reach the point at which abortion in Texas was no longer legally available. A panel of the D.C. Circuit voted 2 to 1 to vacate the district court's order. Although the majority opinion was unsigned, it was presumed to be Kavanaugh's because the other judge in the majority wrote and signed a separate concurring opinion. The Office of Refugee Resettlement had been trying for weeks to find the teenager a sponsor, who presumably could arrange for the abortion while freeing the government from its facilitation problem. No sponsor had come forward. Nonetheless, the D.C. Circuit panel's majority gave the government eleven more days to find one. The dissenting judge, Patricia Millett, accused the government of exercising a unilateral veto over a young woman's exercise of the constitutional right to an abortion.

A sad personal drama that had begun in private now played out in the full glare of a public spotlight. The full D.C. Circuit, voting 6 to 3, vacated the panel opinion and permitted the abortion to proceed. Kavanaugh dissented, complaining that the majority had created "a new right for unlawful immigrant minors in U.S. government detention to obtain immediate abortion on demand." He said the decision marked "a radical extension of the Supreme Court's abortion jurisprudence." The phrase "abortion on demand" is well known as an antiabortion dog whistle, brutal-sounding words not used to describe a patient's request for any other medical procedure. Judge Millett, in a concurring opinion, picked up on Kavanaugh's use of the phrase. Recounting the facts of the case, she wrote: "That sure does not sound like 'on demand' to me. Unless Judge Kavanaugh's dissenting opinion means the demands of the Constitution and Texas law. With that I would agree." At Kavanaugh's Supreme Court confirmation hearing,

Senator Richard Durbin, an Illinois Democrat, pressed him at length on his handling of the case. After sparring with the senator for some minutes about how best to protect the interests of a pregnant teen-aged girl, the nominee finally said: "I did my level best in an emergency posture."

Amy Coney Barrett also had a track record on abortion, although not in a judicial capacity. Statements attesting to her opposition to abortion surfaced during the lightning-fast run-up to her confirmation hearing. One was a statement placed in the Notre Dame student newspaper by Notre Dame's University Faculty for Life, of which Barrett was a member, to mark the fortieth anniversary of the *Roe* decision in 2013. "In the 40 years since the Supreme Court's infamous *Roe v. Wade* decision, over 55 million unborn children have been killed by abortion," the statement read. Barrett was one of six law professors among the 106 signatories from across the university calling for "the unborn to be protected in law and welcomed in life."

In "Catholic Judges in Capital Cases," her best-known academic article, co-written with one of her law school professors, Barrett wrestled with how Catholics on the bench should incorporate the church's "fairly complicated" teaching on capital punishment into their judicial obligation to civil law. The early pages of the article noted the "evident differences" in Catholic doctrine between, on the one hand, war and capital punishment, and on the other, abortion and euthanasia. "The prohibitions against abortion and euthanasia (properly defined) are absolute; those against war and capital punishment are not," Barrett and her co-author, John H. Garvey, wrote. The two added: "We might distinguish between executing criminals and killing the aged and the unborn in this way: criminals deserve punishment for their crimes; aged and unborn victims are innocent."

With its focus on the death penalty, the forty-seven-page article said little more about abortion. Its suggestion was that while Catholic judges could participate in many phases of a capital punishment case, including the trial itself and the appeals that follow a conviction, they should not participate in the sentencing phase, the actual handing down of a death sentence. The proper course was recusal. The implications for abortion cases were left unstated in the authors' conclusion: "Judges cannot—nor should they try to—align our legal system with the Church's moral teaching whenever the two diverge. They should, however, conform their own behavior to the Church's standard. Perhaps their good example will have some effect."

During her confirmation hearing, Barrett got the questions she no doubt anticipated, and she gave the answers the senators no doubt expected. Senator Feinstein asked whether she shared Justice Scalia's view that *Roe v. Wade* was wrongly decided. "Senator, I completely understand why you are asking the question," Barrett replied. "But again, I can't pre-commit or say, 'Yes, I'm going in with some agenda,' because I'm not."

The Supreme Court's most recent abortion decision, barely four months old at the time of Barrett's confirmation, underscored the extreme fragility of the status quo. *June Medical Services v. Russo* was a case from Louisiana on the constitutionality of a law requiring doctors who performed abortions to have admitting privileges at nearby hospitals. The Fifth Circuit upheld the law despite the fact that it was identical to a Texas law the Supreme Court had struck down in 2016, in *Whole Woman's Health v. Hellerstedt*. Texas's defense of its law as a protection for women's health was an obvious fiction. Abortion complications requiring hospital admission in Texas and elsewhere were extremely rare, and in any event federal law requires hospitals to treat emergencies regardless of whether the patient has a doctor with admitting privileges. What the law was intended to do, and what it in fact accomplished before the Supreme Court's ruling, was shut down abortion clinics. Hospitals often refuse privileges to doctors who perform abortions, either because of the procedure's stigma or because the doctors are unable to guarantee a minimum number of admissions—or any admissions at all.

Breyer wrote the majority opinion in *Whole Woman's Health*. To apply the "undue burden" standard the court had set in *Planned Parenthood of Southeastern Pennsylvania v. Casey* in 1992, Breyer weighed the benefits the admitting privileges requirement conveyed against the obstacle it posed to women seeking abortions. On the one hand, he found no benefit to women's health, noting that "there was no significant health-related problem that the new law helped to cure." On the other hand, he found that by closing half the abortion clinics in the state, the law placed a substantial obstacle on access to abortion in Texas, as measured by the resulting longer wait times and greater travel distances. Consequently, the burden was "undue" and the law was unconstitutional.

The balancing test that Breyer employed—weighing benefits against burdens—was an important clarification of the *Casey* decision's undue burden test. Under *Casey*, an abortion regulation was an undue burden if it had "the purpose or effect of placing a substantial obstacle in the path of a woman seeking an abortion of a non-viable fetus." That sounded clear enough, but how was a court to measure whether an obstacle was "substantial" in its effect? In evaluating an antiabortion law from Pennsylvania, the *Casey* majority had proceeded largely by example, upholding a twenty-four-hour waiting period and a mandatory counseling provision while striking down as an undue burden a requirement that a married woman inform her husband in advance of terminating a pregnancy. On this last provision, the court observed that while most married women do include their husband in the decision, for those who feel unable or afraid to do so the burden of mandatory notice was clearly substantial. (Samuel Alito, a judge on the Third Circuit at the time, had voted to uphold the spousal notice requirement when the case was before the appeals court.)

The balanced-weighing approach of *Whole Woman's Health* promised a new consistency in courts' application of the undue burden test, especially when states acted to single out abortion providers for onerous regulations that were not imposed on doctors who performed procedures of equal or even greater risk. Such regulations were known as TRAP laws, for "targeted regulation of abortion providers." Justice Ginsburg, in a concurring opinion in *Whole Woman's Health*, observed that "So long as this Court adheres to *Roe v. Wade* and *Planned Parenthood of Southeastern Pennsylvania v. Casey*, Targeted Regulation of Abortion Providers laws like H. B. 2 [the Texas law] that 'do little or nothing for health, but rather strew impediments to abortion,' cannot survive judicial inspection."

The vote to strike down the Texas law was 5 to 3. Scalia had died nearly five months earlier, and his seat remained unfilled; had he lived, he surely would have provided a fourth dissenting vote. The key vote was that of Anthony Kennedy. He had written a major portion of the controlling opinion in *Casey* but had seemed more recently to drift back to the unease with abortion he exhibited during his first years on the court. Kennedy signed Breyer's opinion. In fact, as the senior justice in the majority, he was presumably the one who gave Breyer the assignment. The dissenters were Roberts, Thomas, and Alito.

By the time the Louisiana case reached the court four years later, Gorsuch was sitting in Scalia's seat and Kavanaugh had replaced Kennedy. The outcome in *June Medical* would turn on Roberts. Covering Texas, Louisiana, and Mississippi, the Fifth Circuit was the most conservative of the thirteen federal appeals courts. It had decided the Texas case in favor of the state on the ground that the state's claim that the law's purpose was to protect women's health was owed nearly complete judicial deference. The Supreme Court had just rejected not only the appeals court's conclusion but its entire approach. The Fifth Circuit's decision to uphold the identical Louisiana law now was a brazen act of judicial defiance, a transgression against the hierarchy by which the federal judicial system is organized. It hardly seemed possible that the chief justice, any chief justice, could countenance such behavior, and Roberts did not.

The vote in *June Medical* to strike down the Louisiana law was 5 to 4. While Roberts parted company from the dissenters—Thomas, Alito, Gorsuch, and Kavanaugh—he did not join Breyer either, agreeing only with the result. His refusal to sign Breyer's opinion meant that Breyer wrote only for a plurality of four justices, not for a majority. Roberts gave only the most minimal of reasons for agreeing with the judgment. "*Stare decisis* instructs us to treat like cases alike," he wrote. "The result in this case is controlled by our decision four years ago invalidating a nearly identical Texas law."

What kept Roberts from signing Breyer's opinion? He had not written a separate dissenting opinion in *Whole Woman's Health*, instead joining a dissent by Alito that focused primarily on what Alito claimed was a failure of proof that the Texas law had actually imposed an undue burden. That dissenting opinion reflected a dispute about facts more than over constitutional analysis. Roberts's own problem with *Whole Woman's Health* was obscure. Now, in his separate opinion in *June Medical*, Roberts made his objection clear: It was to Breyer's balancing test. "Nothing about *Casey* suggested that a weighing of costs and benefits of an abortion regulation was a job for the courts," Roberts wrote. "Pretending that we could pull that off would require us to act as legislators, not judges, and would result in nothing other than an 'unanalyzed exercise of judicial will' in the guise of a 'neutral utilitarian calculus.'" (His quotations were from an opinion by Justice William Brennan in an unrelated context.) By contrast, Roberts continued, "*Casey* instead focuses on the existence of a substantial obstacle, the sort of inquiry familiar to judges across a variety of contexts." Whether a regulation actually conferred the benefit the state claimed for it, and how the benefit stacked up against the burden, were not for judges to say.

The *June Medical* decision, released on June 29, 2020, sowed instant confusion. What was the law of abortion now? How were courts to apply the undue burden test? Was *Whole Woman's Health* still good law? Almost immediately, lower courts that were in the midst of handling the constant flow of TRAP laws began to diverge. Some judges interpreted Roberts's controlling vote in *June Medical* as meaning that the Supreme Court had repudiated *Whole Woman's Health*. Others insisted that *Whole Woman's Health* remained binding law unless and until the Supreme Court formally overturned it. Americans United for Life, the antiabortion organization that had generated many of the TRAP laws now being enacted by state legislatures, claimed a sort of victory despite the fact that its side had lost this round. In its annual report on "life-affirming law and policy," the organization advised its supporters that "After the *June Medical* decision, state lawmakers should feel empowered to pass and enact life-affirming laws with less concern that they will be immediately challenged and struck down by district judges making subjective judgments about the benefits or burdens of the law."

Clearly, and sooner rather than later, the Supreme Court would have to intervene—but with what outcome? Forty-seven years after *Roe v. Wade* and twenty-eight years after *Casey*, the court was as divided on abortion as it had ever been. There were four justices on one side, four on the other, and in the middle a chief justice who felt himself bound by the rule of stare decisis to adhere to a precedent he did not accept and had just managed to undermine.

Then Ruth Bader Ginsburg died.

GINSBURG WAS STILL on the bench when on June 15, 2020, a petition titled *Dobbs v. Jackson Women's Health Organization* reached the court. Dobbs was Thomas E. Dobbs, M.D., an official in the Mississippi Department of Health. The Jackson Women's Health Organization was the only abortion clinic in the state of Mississippi.

The state was appealing a decision of the Fifth Circuit that declared unconstitutional a ban on abortion after fifteen weeks of pregnancy. Mississippi defended the law, enacted by the legislature in 2018, as a regulation of abortion rather than a ban. But as U.S. District Judge Carlton W. Reeves observed in his opinion striking down the law—the opinion the Fifth Circuit affirmed—"The Act's full title is 'An Act to be Known As the Gestational Age Act; To Prohibit Abortions After 15 Weeks' Gestation.' 'Ban' and 'prohibit' are synonyms. This Act is a ban. It is not a regulation."

Mississippi's law, which offered limited exceptions for medical emergencies and cases of "severe fetal abnormality," was one of a growing number of state bans on abortion at a particular point in pregnancy. Some states were banning abortion as early as six weeks of pregnancy. The reason for this shift in antiabortion strategy was a growing impatience within the antiabortion movement with the efficacy of TRAP laws. These laws were clearly making abortion more expensive by imposing unnecessary physical requirements on clinics and by requiring women to make two trips to comply with counseling and waiting period rules. But it wasn't clear whether they were actually stopping many abortions. "There are few additional babies to be saved by laws that do not simply prohibit some abortions," as Gerard V. Bradley, a Notre Dame law professor, described the situation in the conservative Christian journal *First Things* after the Dobbs petition was filed. "*Roe* and *Casey* stand athwart the pro-life path forward."

And that was Mississippi's problem. The Supreme Court's precedents gave women an absolute right to terminate a pregnancy before fetal viability, considered to occur at roughly twenty-three or twenty-four weeks into the normal forty-week pregnancy. (Some 90 percent of abortions take place before the end of the first trimester, at thirteen weeks.) The *Casey* decision made the scope of the abortion right unmistakably clear: "A state may not prohibit any woman from making the ultimate decision to terminate her pregnancy before viability." The court explained that under the undue burden standard, "the means chosen by the state to further the interest in potential life must be calculated to inform the woman's free choice, not hinder it."

Consequently, by the time the Fifth Circuit ruled in the Mississippi case in December 2019, every gestational-age abortion prohibition had been struck down in the lower courts: bans at twenty weeks in Arizona and North Carolina, six and twelve weeks in North Dakota, twelve and eighteen weeks in Arkansas, six weeks in Ohio and Kentucky. More to the point, in each of the cases that had reached the Supreme Court, the justices had refused to hear the states' appeals.

In his opinion for the Fifth Circuit, Judge Patrick E. Higginbotham wrote:

The central question before us is whether this law is an unconstitutional ban on pre-viability abortions. In an unbroken line dating to *Roe v. Wade*, the Supreme Court's abortion cases have established (and affirmed, and re-affirmed) a woman's right to choose an abortion before viability. States may *regulate* abortion procedures prior to viability so long as they do not impose an undue burden on the woman's right, but they may not ban abortions. The law at issue is a ban. Thus, we affirm the District Court's invalidation of the law.

Judge Higginbotham was very familiar with the antiabortion activism in the states. A year earlier, in *June Medical*, he had dissented from the Fifth Circuit's opinion that upheld the Louisiana admitting privileges law. Named first to the federal district court in Dallas by President Gerald Ford and then in 1982 to the Fifth Circuit by Ronald Reagan, Higginbotham was in his forty-fourth year of federal judicial service by the time he wrote the opinion in *Dobbs*. The circuit was now dominated by judges who likewise were named by Republican presidents, but Higginbotham was often out of step with his new colleagues. These more recent arrivals were the products of a different, more ideologically driven appointment process than the one he had experienced, none more so than another judge on the Dobbs panel, James Ho. One of six judges named by Trump to the Fifth Circuit, which has a full complement of seventeen judges, Ho quickly earned a reputation after his arrival in 2018 for writing separate opinions laced with flamboyantly conservative rhetoric on culture war issues.

Dobbs was no exception. Ho concurred separately with the panel majority, noting that the Supreme Court's abortion precedents left no choice but to affirm the district court decision and strike down the Mississippi law. But he made clear his contempt for the court's abortion jurisprudence. "Nothing in the text or original understanding of the Constitution establishes a right to abortion," his opinion began. "Rather, what distinguishes abortion from other matters of health care policy in America—and uniquely removes abortion policy from the democratic process established by our Founders—is Supreme Court precedent." Ho spent much of his opinion, in which he referred to fetuses as "babies," criticizing the district judge, Carlton Reeves. Reeves, an appointee of President Barack Obama and the second African American ever to serve as a federal judge in Mississippi, had employed some strong rhetoric of his own. The state legislature's "professed interest in 'women's health' is pure gaslighting," Reeves had written. "The state chose to pass a law it knew was unconstitutional to endorse a decades-long campaign, fueled by national interest groups, to ask the Supreme Court to overturn *Roe v. Wade*. With the recent changes in the membership of the Supreme Court, it may be that the state believes divine providence covered the Capitol when it passed this legislation. Time will tell."

Ho, who had clerked on the Supreme Court for Clarence Thomas, accused Reeves of disparaging "the millions of Americans who believe in the sanctity of life." He was "duty bound to affirm the judgment of the district court," Ho wrote. "But I cannot affirm the opinion of the district court."

IN ITS SUPREME Court petition, Mississippi did not ask the justices directly to overturn *Roe* and *Casey*. The first of three questions the state attorney general's office posed asked "whether all pre-viability prohibitions on elective abortions are unconstitutional." There were two other questions, one challenging the "balancing of benefits and burdens" in *Whole Woman's Health* (*June Medical* was pending but not yet decided when Mississippi filed its petition), and the other questioning whether abortion providers have standing to sue to invalidate "a law that protects women's health from the dangers of late-term abortions." The state assured the court: "To be clear, the questions presented in this petition do not require the court to overturn *Roe* or *Casey*. They merely ask the court to reconcile a conflict in its own precedents." This was puzzling. While there was certainly a conflict among the justices over abortion, the court's precedents were not in conflict. All pointed in the same direction: toward viability as a firewall protecting the right to abortion, one the states could not breach. If that wall failed to hold, there was no obvious safety zone for women's reproductive autonomy. The six-week bans, for example, would outlaw abortion before many women realized they were pregnant.

The petition urged the court to "reject 'viability' as the bright line for determining when a state may legislate to advance its substantial interests in health, safety, and dignity." Acknowledging in a footnote that such an outcome would require no small leap of reinterpretation, the state advised: "If the court determines that it cannot reconcile *Roe* and *Casey* with other precedents or scientific advancements showing a compelling state interest in fetal life far earlier in pregnancy than those cases contemplate, the court should not retain erroneous precedent." (In its brief on the merits, filed on July 22, the state changed course and asked the court directly to overturn *Roe* and *Casey*.)

The justices' handling of the Mississippi petition was highly unusual. On September 2, the court scheduled it for consideration at the September 29 conference, the so-called "long conference" immediately before the new term begins on the first Monday in October, at which the justices review petitions that have accumulated over the summer recess. Perhaps because of Ruth Ginsburg's death on September 18, the petition was rescheduled, then rescheduled again— nine times during the remainder of the calendar year. Finally, on January 8, their first conference of the new year, the justices took up the petition. They considered it again the next week, and the week after that, and on into the spring even as the term's final argument sessions concluded. No one could recall such a prolonged consideration of a petition, especially one that differed only in detail from those the court had denied with regularity over the past few terms. Certainly this case was receiving something more than routine treatment—but what?

The justices' conference is a black box. Only the justices attend— although during January and February and into March 2021, attendance was of course virtual. The outside world learns that a case is under active consideration via the electronic docket that accompanies every petition posted on the court's website. Anyone checking under docket number 19-1392 could follow this petition's lack of progress: "DISTRIBUTED for conference of 1/8/2021," "DISTRIBUTED for conference of 1/15/2021," and on as the weeks and months passed.

On the right, this strange state of affairs was met with growing alarm. The fear was that the justices would deny the petition, leaving the Fifth Circuit's decision as the last word. "I hope I am proved wrong," Ed Whelan wrote on his *National Review* blog in March, "but it is difficult to be optimistic about this long delay." He offered one common theory: "One dispiriting possibility is that the petition was unable to garner the four votes needed for a grant of certiorari and that one or more justices are in the process of writing a dissent from the court's failure to grant." Speaking directly to his friends on the court, Whelan warned that the right would be keeping score: "If the court ends up failing to grant certiorari, there will be ample cause for deep disappointment with any conservative justices who failed to provide the needed votes." In his article in *First Things*, published in April, Gerard Bradley also raised this theory and then discounted it. "I suspect that the justices cannot decide what to do, and that they will kick the can down the road," he predicted.

And then, after thirteen conferences and more than seven months of silence, the court granted *Dobbs v. Jackson Women's Health Organization*. The May 17 order limited the grant to the petition's first question, the question of whether the viability line would hold. Maybe inside the conference there had been a fight over whether to grant either of the other two, the question of whether the clinic had standing to litigate on behalf of its patients and/or the state's challenge to *Whole Woman's Health*'s balancing of an abortion law's burdens and benefits. In October, before its petition went to conference for the first time, Mississippi had filed a supplemental brief to argue that the rapidly diverging lower court interpretations of the chief justice's opinion in *June Medical* required the Supreme Court's attention.

In the end, the justices decided that the other questions in the Mississippi petition could wait. If *Roe* and *Casey* proved to be no longer good law, the answers would be irrelevant.

IT WAS AS if the death penalty held the Supreme Court in its grip. Omnipresent on the court's docket term after term, death penalty cases eluded any search for common ground. The term that began with the Trump administration's "execution spree" was approaching its final weeks with a ragged internal dispute over lethal injection.

The court's first encounter with lethal injection came in *Baze v.*

Rees, a case in 2008 that rejected a challenge to the procedure while splitting the court and failing to produce a majority opinion. By then, the federal government and every death penalty state had adopted lethal injection as the method of execution, in preference to electrocution or the firing squad. The claim was that although lethal injection promised a humane way of carrying out a death sentence, there was a substantial chance that the three-drug protocol then in use would be administered improperly, causing a prolonged and agonizing death in violation of the Eighth Amendment's prohibition of cruel and unusual punishment.

Seven years later, in *Glossip v. Gross*, the court rejected a similar challenge to a variant of the lethal injection protocol that some states had adopted when one of the original drugs became hard to obtain. The vote was 5 to 4. Alito explained in the majority opinion that the death row inmates who brought the case "failed to identify a known and available alternative method of execution that entails a lesser risk of pain." In other words, a death-sentenced prisoner should not be able to avoid execution simply by identifying a flaw in the state's chosen method. Offering the state an alternative, Alito said, was "a requirement of all Eighth Amendment method-of-execution claims."

In another 5-to-4 decision in 2019, the court rejected a Missouri inmate's claim that because he had a medical condition likely to make lethal injection extremely painful, the state should execute him by using nitrogen gas. In the majority opinion, Gorsuch said that Missouri had never used gas for an execution. The method lacked "a track record of successful use," he wrote, and the court should not require the state to use it now. Gorsuch expressed the majority's impatience with death penalty appeals. "The proper role of courts is to ensure that method-of-execution challenges to lawfully issued sentences are resolved fairly and expeditiously," he wrote. "Courts should police carefully against attempts to use such challenges as tools to interpose unjustified delay."

In a concurring opinion, Kavanaugh noted that during the argument, the state's lawyer had suggested that if the inmate had requested execution by firing squad, the state might have accommodated him.

"An inmate who contends that a particular method of execution is very likely to cause him severe pain should ordinarily be able to plead some alternative method of execution that would significantly reduce the risk of severe pain," Kavanaugh wrote.

In August 2020, another Missouri death row inmate, Ernest Johnson, convicted of murdering three gas station attendants during an armed robbery in 1994, filed a petition seeking an alternative means of execution. Surgery for a brain tumor had left him with a neurological disorder that put him at risk of a violent and painful seizure in response to a lethal injection. The Supreme Court's decision the previous year, *Bucklew v. Precythe*, preempted his effort to have the state use nitrogen gas. The Eighth Circuit refused to permit him to amend his complaint to ask for a firing squad. Based on Brett Kavanaugh's concurring opinion, he brought that request to the Supreme Court.

The justices took the inmate's petition, *Johnson v. Precythe*, to conference eight times during the winter and spring of 2021. After the eighth conference, the court issued an order requesting both sides to brief the question of whether Johnson should be permitted to file a new complaint in federal district court seeking death by firing squad. The state told the justices that Johnson had no entitlement to his preferred method of execution and that any new complaint would inevitably be dismissed on any of a variety of procedural grounds. On May 24, after two more conferences, the court denied the petition.

Sotomayor dissented, joined by Breyer and Kagan. "Although not authorized in Missouri, the firing squad has a long history of successful use," she wrote, noting that "Indeed, during oral arguments in *Bucklew*, Missouri itself suggested the firing squad as an available alternative." Sotomayor said there was "no reason to think Johnson sought leave to amend as a delay tactic," given that the court the previous year had held out the firing squad as an option. "Johnson seeks only to take *Bucklew* up on that promise," she wrote. "Denying him leave to amend his complaint under these circumstances renders this Court's words an empty gesture." Sotomayor wrote "this Court's words," but she meant Kavanaugh's. He might have provided the necessary fourth vote, had he meant what he said.

MISSOURI SCHEDULED ERNEST Johnson's execution, by lethal injection, for October 5, 2021. A new Supreme Court term would have begun by then. The term would include a high-profile death penalty case, the federal government's appeal of a decision that overturned the death sentence for Dzokhar Tsarnaev, one of the two brothers who set off powerful bombs near the finish line of the Boston Marathon in April 2013, killing three people and injuring 260. The First Circuit, while upholding the jury's guilty verdict, invalidated the death sentence on the ground that the trial judge, who had denied a defense request for a change of venue, should have asked specific questions of all prospective jurors about their exposure to the extensive publicity about the crime.

But before the justices could turn to the next term, they faced the challenge of finishing this one. Opinions in the term's most important cases were still circulating inside the court. Outcomes for the most part were set, but dissenting opinions—as well as the concurrences that read like dissents—still had to be responded to, with the dissenters then responding in turn. While the final weeks of any Supreme Court term are never easy, the weeks ahead looked more daunting than usual, on numbers alone. By the end of May, the court had issued twenty-nine opinions in argued cases. That left twenty-nine to go, the equivalent of the entire term and the work the term would be known for, crammed into a single month: June.

CHAPTER ELEVEN

JUNE–JULY · RELIGION, ESTABLISHED

A LTHOUGH JUSTICE STEPHEN BREYER'S OPINION made the Obama-care case look easy, it clearly wasn't. By June 17, when the court issued its decision, *California v. Texas* was one of the two oldest argued cases on the docket. The November 10 argument had gone well for the statute's supporters. Beginning with Chief Justice Roberts's opening questions, a majority of the justices appeared skeptical of the notion that intentionally or not, Congress had somehow invalidated the entire Affordable Care Act when it zeroed out the tax penalty for not complying with the requirement—the "individual mandate"—to buy health insurance. Texas and other anti-Obamacare red states insisted that since the court had previously upheld the mandate's penalty as a tax, removal of the tax made the mandate unconstitutional and, like a house of cards, the whole thousand-page statute now had to fall.

That chain of reasoning had appeared to gain so little traction with the justices that the court was widely expected to make short work of this latest effort to kill the Affordable Care Act. So what was taking so long? Senate Democrats had tried to turn Amy Coney Barrett's confirmation hearing into a kind of passion play built around their warning that if confirmed, she would vote to kill the law's guarantee of insurance coverage for preexisting conditions. As spring turned to early summer, there was growing concern that the Democrats' dire prediction might come to pass.

In a succinct sixteen pages, Breyer's majority opinion swept the worry aside along with all the intricate arguments about whether the mandate, if found to be unconstitutional, was "severable" from the hundreds of other provisions in the statute. The court never got around to discussing the constitutionality of the mandate. Rather, Breyer's opinion held that Texas, along with the seventeen other Republican-governed states and the two individuals who had brought the case, had no business being in court. Having suffered no harm from the reduction of the penalty to zero, they had nothing to complain about. They had no standing.

Standing is an essential prerequisite to a federal court's exercise of jurisdiction. It requires a plaintiff with an actual injury that was caused by the defendant and that can be redressed by a court's judgment. The court sent the case of *California v. Texas* back to the Fifth Circuit "with instructions to dismiss." The vote was 7 to 2. Even Clarence Thomas, a dissenter from the two previous decisions that saved Obamacare, joined Breyer's opinion. "Although this court has erred twice before in cases involving the Affordable Care Act, it does not err today," he wrote in a concurring opinion.

It was Roberts who assigned the case to Breyer, and he no doubt joined the opinion with a special sense of satisfaction—and not only because his court had once again freed itself of the onus of invalidating an increasingly popular statute. Roberts had paid special attention to the rules of standing throughout his career. His interest mirrored that of his mentor William Rehnquist, who set a high bar for standing and was well known for deploying jurisdictional rules to keep cases out of court. During his long tenure, Rehnquist pushed back successfully against the relaxation of standing rules that a more liberal Supreme Court had applied during the 1960s and '70s, and Roberts learned that lesson well. His first major dissenting opinion after becoming chief justice came in a 2007 case, *Massachusetts v. Environmental Protection Agency*, in which the majority accorded Massachusetts standing to challenge the agency's refusal to exercise its authority under the Clean Air Act to regulate motor vehicle emissions that contribute to climate change. The court held that the state's "quasi-sovereign interests"—in this instance, protecting its coastline from rising waters caused by global warming—entitled it to "special solici-tude" in the court's standing analysis. Roberts objected that there was "no basis in our jurisprudence" for relaxing the rules of standing just "because asserted injuries are pressed by a state."

And now Texas and a coalition of other Republican-governed states were claiming injury from a law that Congress had rendered unen-forceable by erasing the penalty for noncompliance. The states' cyni-cal objection to the Obamacare mandate was that if more people obtained health insurance, then more people would gain access to medical care, causing states to incur various administrative expenses and giving them a dollars-and-cents claim to standing. Breyer wrote that the penalty-free mandate having become unenforceable, no state injury could be traced to it, and a judicial opinion on the law's consti-tutionality would thus be no more than "advisory." To find standing for plaintiffs in these circumstances "would threaten to grant un-elected judges a general authority to conduct oversight of decisions of the elected branches of government."

Although it was a narrow way to dispose of the case and avoid ad-dressing the merits of the dispute, the decision actually had broader implications. Suits brought by states—blue states against a Republi-can president's policies and red states against a Democratic White House—had become increasingly common. During the Trump years, Democratic state attorneys general filed more than one hundred law-suits against the administration, seeking to block new policies or pre-vent the rollback of existing ones. Even before the November election, the Republican Attorneys General Association began planning for the prospect of litigating against a Biden administration. (In March, Trump's former adviser Stephen Miller, along with other former ad-ministration officials, established an organization called America First Legal to advise Republican attorneys general on litigation strategy and to file suits on its own against the Biden administration.) Now that the justices had made it clear that states needed to show at least a semblance of a concrete injury, the future for these politically fueled suits had become cloudy.

It was Alito's dissenting opinion that most likely accounted for the delay in issuing the decision. (Although it's often said that the Supreme Court "saves" its most important decisions for the end of the term, that is not the case. Difficult cases with high stakes simply take longer, and no decision is issued until every justice has agreed that the moment of finality has arrived.) Joined by Gorsuch, Alito's dissenting opinion was twice the length of Breyer's majority opinion. Alito called the majority's conclusion "a fundamental distortion of our standing jurisprudence." He listed recent cases in which the court had been "selectively generous in allowing states to sue." These included the *Massachusetts* case, in which both he and Roberts dissented, and *Department of Commerce v. New York*, a 2019 case in which New York successfully challenged the Trump administration's plan to add a citizenship question to the 2020 census. Alito had dissented from Roberts's majority opinion in that case. His point now was that if states in those cases were entitled to standing, then so were the Texas plaintiffs in this case. The states had offered "plenty of evidence" that the Affordable Care Act saddled them with financial burdens. Although not in so many words, Alito was accusing the majority of hypocrisy. Yet his own record on standing and on related jurisdictional questions was hardly a model of consistency. In his dissenting opinion in the *June Medical* abortion case just a year earlier, he had argued for overturning a 1976 precedent that recognized doctors' standing to challenge abortion restrictions on behalf of their patients.

Alito's real target, in any event, was the Affordable Care Act itself, and the court's role in sustaining it during a decade of scorched-earth litigation. "No one can fail to be impressed by the lengths to which this Court has been willing to go to defend the ACA against all threats," he complained. He was still fighting the outcome of the first Obamacare case in 2012. The fight then was over the constitutionality of the individual mandate, which had been challenged as exceeding the power of Congress to regulate interstate commerce. Although Roberts had agreed with Alito on the Commerce Clause challenge, he went on to get the four liberal justices to join him in upholding the mandate as an exercise of Congress's power to impose taxes. It was surprising to find Alito writing now, "The relevant provisions were passed as a comprehensive exercise of Congress's Commerce Clause and (arguably) Taxing Clause powers. Those powers cannot justify the individual mandate." Evidently the mandate remained indefensible in Alito's mind even though a majority of the court, in *National Federation of Independent Business v. Sebelius*, had concluded otherwise.

Alito's opinion even invited further attacks against the Affordable Care Act. In a footnote, he wrote that dismissal of a case for lack of jurisdiction did not preclude the same plaintiffs from reframing their argument and trying again. "Many other parties" could claim a burden from the mandate and could bring their own suits, he wrote. "Our Affordable Care Act epic may go on."

With only Gorsuch as an ally, Alito may have labored over his opinion in an effort to find additional support from among the conservatives. Such an effort presented obvious challenges: Kavanaugh was carving out a less flamboyantly conservative role for himself and was voting most often with Roberts, and Barrett, so soon after her Obamacare-inflected confirmation process, was unlikely to enlist in so public an effort to relitigate the case against the law. Clarence Thomas, however, would have seemed a likely partner. Had he been tempted to vote with Alito but then pulled back in the face of what looked like an overreach? That was one way to interpret the stern lesson in judicial restraint that he administered to Alito when he wrote in a brief concurring opinion that "whatever the Act's dubious history in this Court, we must assess the current suit on its own terms." He continued:

> And, here, there is a fundamental problem with the arguments advanced by the plaintiffs in attacking the Act—they have not identified any unlawful action that has injured them. Today's result is thus not the consequence of the Court once again rescuing the Act, but rather of us adjudicating the particular claims the plaintiffs chose to bring.

Thomas and Alito—and, more recently, Gorsuch—had become such reliable allies on the court's far right that few would have predicted the position Thomas took or the words he chose. It would have been easy for him simply to sign Breyer's opinion without elaboration, as Kavanaugh and Barrett did. While surprises from Clarence Thomas were nothing new, they almost invariably came from the opposite direction: not from his agreement with others, but from staking out a fringe position that no one had thought of, or at least no one had thought to articulate, for many decades.

In 2019, for example, he used a woman's unsuccessful defamation case against Bill Cosby, in which the court had denied review, as the occasion to denounce *New York Times v. Sullivan*, the foundational 1964 decision that interpreted the First Amendment to shield the press from many libel suits by public figures. (The lower courts had dismissed the woman's lawsuit, deeming her a "limited-purpose public figure" as defined by subsequent Supreme Court decisions.) "*New York Times* and the Court's decisions extending it were policy-driven decisions masquerading as constitutional law," Thomas wrote. "We should not continue to reflexively apply this policy-driven approach to the Constitution. Instead, we should carefully examine the original meaning of the First and Fourteenth Amendments." His call was soon taken up by a prominent senior judge on the D.C. Circuit and, at the end of the 2020–21 term, by Justice Gorsuch.

Thomas's sudden attack on one of the court's most famous First Amendment precedents was at once startling and typical. He chose his targets for maximum impact—not necessarily with his colleagues in the case at hand, but with other judges and an attentive conservative echo chamber. And his critiques were always anchored in a particular version of history that flew under the label of originalism.

IF ALITO OVERREACHED with Thomas in the Affordable Care Act case, he may have done the same with Amy Barrett in the term's big religion case, *Fulton v. City of Philadelphia*. This was a Free Exercise Clause challenge to the city's termination of a contract with a Catholic social service agency that refused for reasons of religious doctrine to consider same-sex married couples as potential foster parents for children in the city's care who needed homes.

Fulton was the oldest argued case on the docket when the court decided it on June 17, the same day it issued the Affordable Care Act decision. The case had been argued on November 4, the day after Election Day, during Amy Barrett's first week on the (virtual) bench. The argument strongly suggested that while the court was looking for a way to rule for Catholic Social Services, it was not going to accept the invitation of the Becket Fund, representing the Catholic agency, to use the case to overrule *Employment Division v. Smith*. That was the 1990 precedent, intensely disliked on the religious right, that had interpreted the Free Exercise Clause to withhold a constitutional basis for claiming a religious exemption from a law that was "generally applicable" and "neutral" with respect to religion.

Indeed, although all nine justices agreed that Philadelphia had violated the Free Exercise Clause by refusing to exempt the Catholic agency from the city's nondiscrimination requirement, *Employment Division v. Smith* remained on the books. Along with the court's seeming unanimity—none of the liberal justices wrote a separate opinion to express an objection—the failure to overturn *Smith* produced a muted public response to the decision. Here was a case on subjects at the heart of the Trump-era culture wars: religion and LGBTQ rights. *Fulton* appeared to put the two in direct conflict, just as Alito had predicted years earlier in his dissent from the same-sex marriage decision. *Fulton* was unlike the shadow docket cases that had struck down COVID-related limitations on attendance at houses of worship. Those were decided summarily, often late at night, without full briefing or argument. This was a fully briefed and argued religion case, the first the court had heard since Amy Barrett's arrival. Yet, to many, it appeared that nothing much had happened after all. A prominent theme in the post-decision commentary was that a major constitutional clash had ended with a whimper, without clear guidance on how courts should handle future disputes between religion and government over the principle of nondiscrimination.

That widespread interpretation of the decision appealed to those looking to the Supreme Court for signs of comity in a polarized world. But it was seriously misleading. Behind the unanimous judgment lay an angry "concurring" opinion by Alito, joined by Thomas and Gorsuch, that excoriated the other six justices. "*Smith* was wrongly decided," Alito wrote in his seventy-seven-page opinion. "As long as it remains on the books, it threatens a fundamental freedom." Clearly, there had been a ferocious battle inside the court and, as in the Affordable Care Act case, Alito had lost and was venting his anger at his conservative colleagues in public.

The winner in *Fulton* was Roberts. Both he and Alito shared the goal of enabling the Catholic agency to retain its public foster care contract without forfeiting its objection to same-sex marriage. Yet the difference between the two justices, named by President George W. Bush to the court within five months of each other from a Republican Party short list on which both had been prominent for years, was glaring, and it was growing. While Alito specialized in verbal blunt force, Roberts deployed a surgeon's subtle dexterity, his skill nowhere so apparent as in this case. His opinion was a mere fifteen pages long. There was no need to revisit *Smith*, he wrote, because the agency could win its case under a different precedent. This was *Church of Lukumi Babalu Aye, Inc. v. City of Hialeah*, a once obscure 1993 decision that had made its reappearance in the shadow docket COVID cases. Roberts had dissented from the more recent of the COVID cases, which he viewed as unwarranted judicial interventions into matters best left to public health experts. But this was different. The expertise the *Fulton* case required was the conventional expertise of judges, not doctors, and the *Lukumi* case proved a very useful tool.

The court in *Lukumi* had invalidated several ordinances in the city of Hialeah, Florida, that prohibited animal sacrifice as practiced by followers of the Afro-Caribbean religion Santeria, who at the time were moving into South Florida from Cuba in substantial numbers. While prohibiting sacrificial animal slaughter, the ordinances exempted the killing of animals by hunters and by butchers. Therefore, Justice Kennedy said in his opinion for a unanimous court, the ordinances failed the test of neutrality. "The record in this case compels the conclusion that suppression of the central element of the Santeria worship service was the object of the ordinances," he wrote. Because its laws were not neutral, Hialeah could not claim protection under the *Smith* decision. The lack of neutrality and general applicability, the court held, meant that the ordinances were subject to the strictest judicial scrutiny and the city had to demonstrate a "compelling interest" in targeting a religious practice. This was a test the city could not meet.

For Roberts to fit Philadelphia's antidiscrimination policy, which applied equally to every city contract, into *Lukumi*'s framework required an interpretive leap of substantial dimension. While Hialeah's treatment of Santeria was baldly discriminatory, Philadelphia applied the same contract language to all two dozen of the social service agencies on which it relied for foster care placements. In what way did the city fail the twin tests of neutrality and general applicability?

Roberts fastened on a provision of the standard contract labeled "Rejection of Referral." It provided that no foster child or foster family could be rejected based on race, religion, or sexual orientation, "unless an exception is granted by the Commissioner or the Commissioner's designee, in his/her sole discretion." Citing that language, the chief justice wrote that "the creation of a formal mechanism for granting exceptions renders a policy not generally applicable." So the deferential standard of *Smith* did not apply, and the strict scrutiny of *Lukumi* did. The difference was crucial. Under *Smith*, the government defendant nearly always won; a neutral, generally applicable law required no exemptions. *Lukumi* gave the religious plaintiff the upper hand, putting the burden on the government to meet the compelling interest test.

As Philadelphia's lawyer, Neal Katyal, had tried to explain during the argument, the provision that Roberts focused on applied only to the actual placement of a child with a foster family. This was the stage of "referral." The language offering a potential exemption did not apply to the initial stage of creating a pool of potential foster parents, and it was that stage that was at issue in the case. At that initial stage, Katyal insisted, the city permitted no discrimination and there were no exceptions. Asked for an example of when an exception might be granted at the later placement stage, he said there had been a case of a foster child who had used a racial slur and consequently was not placed with a foster family of that race. No exception had ever been made at the initial certification stage, Katyal told the court.

It was an important distinction, but an inconvenient one, and Roberts glossed over it. "The creation of a system of exceptions under the contract undermines the City's contention that its non-discrimination policy can brook no departures," he wrote, adding a reference: "See *Lukumi*." He continued: "The City offers no compelling reason why it has a particular interest in denying an exception to CSS while making them available to others."

Gorsuch, in a separate opinion that Thomas and Alito joined, called Roberts out for a "dizzying series of maneuvers." The case, he said, "has nothing to do with the referral—or placement—stage of the foster process," but only with the "recruitment and certification stages—where foster agencies like CSS screen and enroll adults who wish to serve as foster parents." And at that stage, Gorsuch emphasized, the contract "seems to prohibit discrimination entirely." He went on: "Given all the maneuvering, it's hard not to wonder if the majority is so anxious to say nothing about *Smith*'s fate that it is willing to say pretty much anything about municipal law and the parties' briefs."

Gorsuch, it appeared, was developing a specialty in taunting the chief justice. But his opinion did raise the question of why Roberts had gone to such lengths to avoid a direct confrontation with *Smith*. After all, when the court granted the case in February 2020, it was presumably to decide the questions the petition presented, one of which was "Whether *Employment Division v. Smith* should be revisited." There was no conflict among the lower courts on that question, nor could there have been, so the purpose of the grant was not to restore uniformity within the judicial system. It was a grant in service of an agenda.

Perhaps it was never Roberts's agenda. Perhaps his was not one of the four votes needed to grant the petition. Or perhaps something changed after Ruth Ginsburg died and the country watched the president push ahead, with just weeks to go before Election Day, with the selection of a nominee strongly identified with conservative Catholicism. As the justices were working out their positions in *Fulton* during the winter and spring, they had also been debating whether to accept the Mississippi abortion case. With that case now added to the docket, they had to know that the court would be under a harsh public spotlight the moment the next term opened, even more intense than in the aftermath of the presidential election. The court, after all, had ultimately not accepted any of the election cases. But the future of the right to abortion, it was obvious to all, was now once again in the court's hands. There would be time enough to take another look at *Smith*. This was not the time, nor the term.

In effect, Amy Barrett said as much in a concurring opinion that Breyer and Kavanaugh joined. Although only two pages long, it was her most important writing to that point. She said that while she was inclined to agree with *Smith*'s critics, there was more to the question than simply whether to overrule the precedent. Overruling was one thing, "yet what should replace *Smith*?" she asked:

> The prevailing assumption seems to be that strict scrutiny would apply whenever a neutral and generally applicable law burdens religious exercise. But I am skeptical about swapping *Smith*'s categorical antidiscrimination approach for an equally categorical strict scrutiny regime, particularly when this Court's resolution of conflicts between generally applicable laws and other First Amendment rights—like speech and assembly—has been much more nuanced.

This was a fascinating if cryptic passage. "Nuance" was not a word often seen in recent years in opinions by conservative justices. Taken at face value, Barrett's expression of skepticism seemed to suggest that the free exercise of religion was neither more nor less special than other rights protected by the First Amendment. Was this what she meant? Yet she had joined the majority in the COVID cases; indeed, her vote to strike down pandemic-related restrictions in place of Ruth Ginsburg's vote to uphold them had made all the difference in those cases. In taking the term's measure, where did those cases fit? Shadow docket or not, the rulings that invalidated capacity limits on in-person worship services cases made an important doctrinal innovation. They established a "most favored nation" status for religion, meaning that government had to treat religious activity at least as well as the best-treated comparable secular activity. The debate on the court had been over the meaning of "comparable" in the face of a readily transmissible disease. Was a trip to a supermarket really comparable to attendance at a worship service in the midst of a pandemic? The majority, with Barrett providing a fifth vote, thought so. Roberts and the liberal justices deferred to the experts who thought not.

In any event, *Fulton* occupied a different part of the Free Exercise landscape. The question was how readily the government could justify refusing a requested religious exemption. In *Fulton*, the entire court had agreed that Philadelphia could not justify its treatment of Catholic Social Services. "I therefore see no reason to decide in this case whether *Smith* should be overruled, much less what should replace it," Barrett concluded. For anyone waiting for the newest justice to reveal herself, this was not much more than a glimpse, but it was at least that. A fuller picture would have to wait.

CLEARLY, *Fulton v. City of Philadelphia* was something other than the display of judicial minimalism and collegiality that many commentators perceived. It provided a window on the court near the end of an extraordinary term: on the fracturing of alliances and the potential birth of new ones; on a profound debate over how aggressively to advance a shared goal; on what priority to place, if any, on the court's institutional interests. Gorsuch and Kavanaugh, named to the court by the same president within eighteen months of each other, were now in very different places: Gorsuch the unrestrained firebrand who poured rhetorical gasoline on Alito's smoldering anger, Kavanaugh seemingly intent on persuading the world that he really had looked at all sides of every question before embracing the conservative position he had started out with. That the court's three liberals joined an opinion in *Fulton* that they most likely found unpersuasive, even troubling, spoke to their strategic judgment; better to provide a working majority to save the ultimate question for another day than to leave Roberts and Alito with competing plurality opinions that would mean only disarray for First Amendment doctrine. And what of Amy Barrett? Was it possible that her call for nuance was meant to send Alito a message that her style was not going to be his and that her vote was not to be taken for granted?

Nor was *Fulton* inconsequential as legal doctrine. While not overruling *Smith*, the decision went far toward making *Smith* and its fate irrelevant. Roberts knew the *Lukumi* decision well, and he had made creative use of the 1993 precedent in two recent opinions on state expenditures on behalf of religious schools. Now he invested *Lukumi* with even greater significance, elevating it to a status as one of the last several decades' most important religion decisions instead of, as it had been for most of that time, one of the most obscure. The court had decided *Lukumi* just three years after *Smith*, when the public controversy over the earlier decision was at a peak and Congress was debating the pointedly named Religious Freedom Restoration Act, a highly unusual rebuke to the court by which Congress sought to blunt *Smith*'s impact. By unanimously overturning a city's openly discriminatory attack on a disfavored religious sect, the court aimed in *Lukumi* to reassure the public that it had not left vulnerable religious minorities unprotected.

Now, three decades later, *Lukumi* was placed in service to the country's largest religious denomination, and in a context that required the court to strain to extract even an inference of discrimination from language that under no plausible interpretation discriminated against anyone. Was there any law that couldn't similarly be found, either in text or practice, to fall short of "general applicability"? Would there be a religious claim in the future that could not be tailored to *Lukumi*'s protean dimensions, so that strict judicial scrutiny would apply and any burden on religion, however slight, would have to meet *Lukumi*'s compelling interest test? As the universe of laws deemed "neutral" and "generally applicable" shrank, so too would the footprint of

Employment Division v. Smith. That was the accomplishment of *Fulton v. City of Philadelphia* and of the chief justice whose handiwork it was.

OTHER RELIGION CASES awaited the court's attention, including two petitions the justices had placed on hold for eventual disposition in light of *Fulton*. One was another case from the politically savvy Becket Fund, the prominent religious right litigating group that had its hand in many of the court's recent Free Exercise decisions. The petitioner, an Idaho building contractor named George Ricks, asserted a religious objection to having to submit his Social Security number to the government as part of Idaho's registration process for contractors. The Idaho Court of Appeals, finding the Idaho Contractor Registration Act to be a neutral law of general applicability, invoked *Smith* and denied Ricks's claim for an exemption. The Becket Fund's petition asked the Supreme Court to overturn *Smith*. Within hours of the *Fulton* decision, the Becket lawyers filed a supplemental petition asserting that "*Fulton* only underscores the need for this court to revisit *Smith*, and this case presents an ideal vehicle to do so." The court denied the petition without comment on June 28.

The other petition sought review of a case long familiar to the justices. *Arlene's Flowers v. State of Washington* had made a previous trip to the court. The petitioner was a florist in Richland, Washington, who refused on religious grounds to provide a custom floral arrangement for a client's same-sex wedding. Both the couple and the Washington attorney general sued under the state's Consumer Protection Act, invoking Washington's Law Against Discrimination, which applied to sexual orientation. In 2017, after the Washington supreme court had ruled against the florist, the Christian right litigating organization Alliance Defending Freedom took the case to the U.S. Supreme Court. The justices then held the petition for *Masterpiece Cakeshop*, a similar case the court had already agreed to decide, brought by a Colorado baker who refused to design a cake to celebrate a same-sex marriage. The justices eventually ruled for the baker on the barely plausible case-specific ground that two of the several

Colorado officials who had handled the case at the administrative level had spoken disparagingly about the role of religion. The court then vacated the Washington supreme court's ruling in *Arlene's Flowers* and told the court to reconsider the case.

The Washington court reinstated nearly all of its original decision, noting that "we have painstakingly reviewed the record for any sign of intolerance on behalf of this court or the Benton County Superior Court, the two adjudicatory bodies to consider this case." The court added: "After this review, we are confident that the two courts gave full and fair consideration to this dispute and avoided animus toward religion. We therefore find no reason to change our original decision in light of *Masterpiece Cakeshop*."

Not surprisingly, Alliance Defending Freedom promptly returned to the U.S. Supreme Court, filing a new petition in September 2019. It did not ask the court to overturn *Employment Division v. Smith*, but with *Smith* clearly implicated, the justices held the petition for *Fulton*. The justices took up the case at their final conference of the term. The division on the court mirrored that in *Fulton* itself. Alito, Gorsuch, and Thomas voted to grant, leaving *Arlene's Flowers* one vote short.

Clearly, the *Smith* question had run its course for the time being. But there was another unfinished religion project for which the justices' appetite for completion remained undimmed. The subject was a recurring one: the channeling of public resources to religious education. Unfolding now was the flip side of this issue as it had arisen in a series of cases during the 1960s and '70s. The court's focus in that earlier era was on the constraint that the Establishment Clause placed on public aid to religious schools. Now the question was not what the Constitution prohibited but what it demanded: whether the government could make a benefit available to parents with children in secular schools without offering the same benefit to parents who sent their children to religious schools. That the answer might be yes was a socially and politically explosive proposition toward which the Roberts court had proceeded in deliberately measured steps. The case the court granted on the term's final day, *Carson v. Makin*, offered a chance to complete the project.

The first decision in the series leading up to the new case was *Trinity Lutheran Church of Columbia, Inc. v. Comer* in 2017. The question was whether a preschool operated by a Missouri church was entitled to participate in a state program that provided grants for upgrading school playgrounds. Because the Missouri constitution provided that "no money shall ever be taken from the public treasury, directly or indirectly, in aid of any church, sect, or denomination of religion," the state deemed the church ineligible for the grant. The federal district court and the Eighth Circuit upheld the denial. Both relied on Chief Justice Rehnquist's 2004 opinion in *Locke v. Davey*, which held that even if the Establishment Clause would permit a state to subsidize religious education, the Free Exercise Clause did not require it. The playground case was "nearly indistinguishable from *Locke*," the district court concluded.

The Supreme Court ruled for the church by a vote of 7 to 2; only Sotomayor and Ginsburg dissented. In his majority opinion, Roberts framed the question as one of unvarnished discrimination. The policy "expressly discriminates against otherwise eligible recipients by disqualifying them from a public benefit solely because of their religious character," he wrote. In a crucial move, Roberts declared that *Locke v. Davey* did not control the case. He explained that in *Locke*, a student was denied a state-funded scholarship because he planned to use the money to study for the ministry. "Davey was not denied a scholarship because of who he *was*," Roberts said of the student. "He was denied a scholarship because of what he proposed *to do*—use the funds to prepare for the ministry. Here there is no question that Trinity Lutheran was denied a grant simply because of what it is—a church."

Although Roberts stressed that the case involved only a religious school's playground and not the school itself, his concluding paragraph was a summons to a broad application of the decision in future cases. Perhaps only "a few extra scraped knees" might result if children fell on the preschool's unimproved playground, he wrote. "But the exclusion of Trinity Lutheran from a public benefit for which it is otherwise qualified, solely because it is a church, is odious to our Constitution all the same, and cannot stand."

"Odious" is not a word often seen in a Supreme Court opinion. *Trinity Lutheran* galvanized the religious right. Less than two years later, in March 2019, the Institute for Justice filed a petition challenging Montana's exclusion of religious schools from the state's program of tax credits for private school tuition. Montana's constitution, like Missouri's, prohibited state aid to "any church, sect, or denomination." Long a leader in the "school choice" movement, the Institute for Justice was interested in fostering nonpublic education in general rather than religious education in particular. But in Montana, as in most parts of the country, the great majority of private schools were sectarian; in 2018, 94 percent of the tuition money generated by Montana's program went to religious schools. So for the Institute for Justice, the Free Exercise Clause was an indispensable tool for achieving its distinct agenda.

Roberts wrote the majority opinion in *Espinoza v. Montana Department of Revenue*, issued on June 30, 2020. Not surprisingly, the underlying principle of the *Trinity Lutheran* decision controlled the outcome, while *Trinity Lutheran*'s limitation to school playgrounds silently fell away. There was no denying the fact that these were schools. What Roberts retained was *Trinity Lutheran*'s distinction between religious status and religious use. "This case also turns expressly on religious status and not religious use," he wrote. "The Montana Constitution discriminates based on religious status just like the Missouri policy in *Trinity Lutheran*." Holding to that distinction enabled Roberts to insist that the court was being faithful to its precedents and making no new law.

Whatever the validity of the "religious status" label in *Trinity Lutheran* when limited to a playground, it was remarkable in the context of classroom education. Just how remarkable became clear a week later, when the court ruled that federal antidiscrimination laws could not apply to the employment relationship between a religious school and many of its classroom teachers. The reason was the pervasively religious nature of religious education. "The religious education and formation of students is the very reason for the existence of most private religious schools," Alito wrote for the majority in *Our Lady of*

Guadalupe School v. Morrissey-Berru, "and therefore the selection and supervision of the teachers upon whom the schools rely to do this work lie at the core of their mission." That decision, issued on July 8, 2020, greatly expanded an opinion Roberts had written for a unanimous court eight years earlier. In that case, the court had for the first time recognized a "ministerial exception" to antidiscrimination laws for employees of religious organizations who performed religious functions. The new decision extended the exemption to ordinary elementary school teachers in church-run schools. Even they played a role in carrying out the school's religious mission, the court held.

The vote in the Montana tuition case was 5 to 4. Roberts lost the votes of Breyer and Kagan and was again subjected to Gorsuch's scorn. The status-versus-use distinction made little sense, Gorsuch wrote in a concurring opinion. "In the first place, discussion of religious activity, uses, and conduct—not just status—pervades this record." He added: "Maybe it's possible to describe what happened here as status-based discrimination. But it seems equally, and maybe more, natural to say that the State's discrimination focused on what religious parents and schools *do*—teach religion."

Of course, John Roberts, product of an elite school for Catholic boys, did not need Neil Gorsuch, product of the same, to inform him of the nature of religious education. Gorsuch presumably had his reasons for tweaking the chief justice persistently and in public; Justice Scalia had done the same thing for years, famously once accusing Roberts of "faux judicial modesty" for not acknowledging the implications of one of his seemingly narrow opinions. But Roberts had his own reasons for incrementalism—or for what looked like incrementalism. As he had seen William Rehnquist do with great effectiveness, Roberts saw utility in planting seeds that could germinate and grow when the climate—and the court—was favorable. It could take a while, but unlike Gorsuch, Roberts was patient. By the time the ultimate goal was in view, he would have managed to move the law so far down the road that the slightest touch could push it over the finish line. The end result would appear to the public as all but inevitable.

So in his Montana opinion, Roberts could respond to the objection in Breyer's dissent that the majority's "several doctrinal innovations" were "misguided and threaten adverse consequences." Not so, Roberts said. "This rule against express religious discrimination is no 'doctrinal innovation.' Far from it. As *Trinity Lutheran* explained, the rule is 'unremarkable in light of our prior decisions.' For innovation, one must look to the dissents."

IN THE AFTERMATH of *Trinity Lutheran*, the Institute for Justice, in partnership with the Christian right First Liberty Institute, filed the new school case in 2018. In its press release announcing the filing in federal district court in Maine, the Institute for Justice quoted Roberts's recent "odious to our Constitution" language. By the time the two organizations filed their Supreme Court petition in February 2021, they of course had *Espinoza* to rely on as well.

While Maine's constitution requires a free public education through twelfth grade, fewer than half the school districts in the state have a high school. For those districts, the state subsidizes the tuition that parents pay to send their children elsewhere, to "the public school or the approved private school of the parent's choice," whether in Maine or in another state. In 1981, acting on the advice of the state's attorney general that the Establishment Clause prohibited the state from subsidizing religious school tuition, the legislature limited the program to "a nonsectarian school in accordance with the First Amendment of the United States Constitution."

The case, *Carson v. Makin*, was filed in federal court on behalf of three couples who wanted to use the tuition assistance at religious schools. Similar lawsuits raising a Free Exercise Clause challenge to the religious school exclusion had been filed years before in the Maine state courts. The lawsuits had failed, and the Supreme Court had twice refused to hear appeals, once in 1999 and once early in Roberts's tenure in 2006. The court's willingness to take up the issue now spoke to how much had changed, both on the court and in the law.

The Maine parents had lost in both the federal district court and the First Circuit, where the unanimous three-judge panel included

David Souter, the retired Supreme Court justice. Souter, who after his retirement in 2009 sat regularly with the First Circuit, had during his tenure on the court often expressed concern about the erosion of the Establishment Clause. An appointee of the first President Bush, Souter had previously served as New Hampshire's attorney general and on the state's supreme court. He was a Republican of the old-fashioned kind, the last nominee of a Republican president not to have any connection with the modern conservative movement.

While the First Circuit was considering the Maine case, the Supreme Court issued the *Espinoza* decision. In his opinion for the panel, Judge David Barron, a former Harvard Law School professor, acknowledged *Espinoza* and then described how Maine's program differed from Montana's. The purpose of Maine's tuition assistance, he explained, was not to enable parent choice in the abstract, but rather to allow parents to provide their children with the education that would have been available had they lived in a district with a public high school. Since Maine provided only a secular education, not a religious one, in its public schools, a secular education was the baseline, Judge Barron concluded; it did not amount to religious discrimination for the state to decline to subsidize anything else. Crucially, the court held that the state's decision not to channel taxpayers' money to religious schools was based not on the schools' religious status but rather was "based on the religious use that they would make of it in instructing children in the tuition assistance program."

Not status, but use. Now, in this third case in the trilogy, the choice for the Supreme Court was unavoidable: Did the Free Exercise Clause require the government to subsidize the religious use of public money, or was the "play in the joints" of the two religion clauses that the Rehnquist court had sought to preserve in *Locke v. Davey* still the law? An answer that would have sounded extreme, even outlandish, not many years before now appeared all but inevitable.

AMONG THE PROJECTS that Antonin Scalia left unfinished when he died in 2016 was to reorient the court's approach to property rights to provide greater constitutional protection for property owners and less room for government regulation. He managed to move the law in his desired direction in the early 1990s, but by the last years of the Rehnquist court in the early 2000s, a majority of his colleagues had become wary of following him as far as he wanted to go.

The major sticking point was over the essential question of how to define a "taking" within the meaning of the Fifth Amendment, which provides "nor shall private property be taken for public use, without just compensation." Clearly, an actual physical appropriation of private property by the government, as with eminent domain, was a "categorical" taking requiring compensation. But what about a land use regulation that deprived the owner of some portion, but not all, of the property's use or value? The classic definition of a "regulatory taking" came in an opinion by Justice Oliver Wendell Holmes in 1922: "While property may be regulated to a certain extent, if regulation goes too far it will be regarded as a taking." How far was "too far"? Later cases applied a balancing test that took into account factors including the economics of the situation, the property owner's reasonable expectations, and the government's reasons for regulating. Only after weighing these factors would a court decide whether a taking had occurred for which compensation was required.

Scalia argued for a more expansive definition of a categorical taking, one that would require compensation even if the regulation did not "take" property in any conventional sense but left it in the owner's hands, albeit with diminished economic value. Scalia's effort ran aground in a case in 2002 involving a government-imposed moratorium on property development along the shores of Lake Tahoe. The majority refused to treat the moratorium as a categorical taking. After that, the court seemed to lose interest in property rights—until the 2020–21 term.

At their conference on November 13—Amy Coney Barrett's third—the justices voted to grant *Cedar Point Nursery v. Hassid*, a property rights case from California. Cedar Point and another sizable fruit grower, Fowler Packing Company, were represented by the Pacific Legal Foundation, long an active player in the property rights movement. The case challenged as a categorical taking a California labor regulation that gave union organizers the right to enter commercial farms for the purpose of talking to the workers before and after the workers' shifts for up to three hours a day on as many as 120 days a year. The growers argued that the regulation amounted to a permanent physical invasion of their property for which compensation was required. The lower federal courts had dismissed the case on the ground that there was no physical taking as defined by the Supreme Court's precedents.

When *Cedar Point* was argued in March, it was clear that the Pacific Legal Foundation sensed that an important victory was at hand and would settle for nothing less. Asked by Justice Kavanaugh whether his clients couldn't prevail more readily under a regulatory taking theory, one that a labor precedent from the 1950s appeared to offer, the growers' lawyer agreed. But he quickly informed Kavanaugh that "I don't think that question is fairly presented by this case." Any state-authorized entry by the union onto the growers' farms was a categorical taking, the lawyer said. Asked by Justice Barrett whether his answer would be the same if the regulation gave the union access for only one hour a day on one day a year, he said yes. The Pacific Legal Foundation was not interested in a balancing test. It wanted a declaration that a regulation of this type was always and automatically an unconstitutional taking.

By a vote of 6 to 3, the court gave the growers what they wanted. Roberts wrote for the majority: "The access regulation appropriates a right to invade the growers' property and therefore constitutes a *per se* physical taking." Compensation was required. Since the lower courts had dismissed the growers' complaint, the decision's effect was to reinstate it; it would now be up to the lower courts to devise a remedy for the constitutional violation.

Breyer, Kagan, and Sotomayor dissented. As the senior justice of the three, Breyer had the prerogative of assigning the dissenting opinion, and he gave the assignment to himself. "The regulation does not *appropriate* anything," he objected. The court's precedents, he continued, "make clear that the regulation before us allows only a *temporary* invasion of a landowner's property and that this kind of temporary invasion amounts to a taking only if it goes 'too far.' In my view, the majority's conclusion threatens to make many ordinary forms of regulation unusually complex or impractical."

Cedar Point received relatively little public attention, for reasons that were understandable: California's regulation, adopted in response to the farmworkers' campaign led by the charismatic Cesar Chavez, was unique among the fifty states, and the decision seemed to have little relevance to most people's lives. But even if the dissenters' warning turned out to be overstated, the decision was a potentially transformational development in the law of property rights. By expanding the definition of a categorical taking, it was likely to hobble government land use regulation and empower property owners far from the fields of California. CEDAR POINT NURSERY V. HASSID QUIETLY REWROTE FOUR DECADES OF TAKINGS CLAUSE DOCTRINE was the headline on a post by Josh Blackman, a conservative blogger who said he would have to revise the book on property law that he was in the midst of writing.

The decision came too late for Antonin Scalia, but it had the full support of his former law clerk who was now the junior justice.

THE COURT HAD one last piece of unfinished business: voting rights. Alito's opinion for a 6-to-3 majority in *Brnovich v. Democratic National Committee*, issued on the term's final day, tracked the flow of the March 2 oral argument with unusual precision. It was no surprise that the justices upheld the two Arizona election laws that were challenged under Section 2 of the Voting Rights Act as discriminatory toward minority voters. Michael Carvin, Arizona's lawyer, had argued that neither the state's ban on the collection of mail-in ballots by third parties nor its disqualification of all votes cast in person by voters who mistakenly found their way to the wrong precinct kept anybody from voting. All the statute required, the lawyer argued, was that voting be "equally open" and that it afford equal "opportunity" to all.

With this Alito heartily agreed. "Mere inconvenience cannot be enough to demonstrate a violation of Section 2," he wrote. In case there was any question about what Alito meant by "mere inconvenience," he offered an analogy. Suppose, he said, "that an exhibit at a museum in a particular city is open to everyone free of charge every day of the week for several months. Some residents of the city who have the opportunity to view the exhibit may find it inconvenient to do so for many reasons—the problem of finding parking, dislike of public transportation, anticipation that the exhibit will be crowded, a plethora of weekend chores and obligations, etc." His implication was that those who missed the exhibit had no one to blame but themselves.

Alito's opinion offered no acknowledgment that the real-world conditions in which voting took place in Arizona meant that rules that appeared neutral and even benign might present racially differential obstacles. Justice Kagan's dissenting opinion, which Breyer and Sotomayor joined, explained why: Precinct locations changed often and seemingly randomly in minority neighborhoods, and the state's far-flung Native American communities were ill served by post offices and public transportation. "Equal voting opportunity is a function of both law and background conditions," she said. In other words, "a voting rule's validity depends on how the rule operates in conjunction with facts on the ground." Kagan then linked this observation to what Congress intended the Voting Rights Act to accomplish. The word "opportunity" in the statute was not an abstraction:

> In using that word, Congress made clear that the Voting Rights Act does not demand equal outcomes. If members of different races have the same opportunity to vote, but go to the ballot box at different rates, then so be it—that is their preference, and Section 2 has nothing to say. But if a law produces different voting opportunities across races—if it establishes rules and conditions of political participation that are less favorable (or advantageous) for one racial group than for others—then Section 2 kicks in. It applies, in short, whenever the law makes it harder for citizens of one race than of others to cast a vote.

The difference between the majority's and dissent's understanding of "opportunity" in the context of voting rights was deeply revealing. It was not just that the two sides disagreed about the meaning of particular statutory language; that happened every day in the course of statutory interpretation. It was that even after a profound threat to the very mechanics of democracy had played out at its doorstep, the court so obviously lacked a shared vision of its role in protecting those mechanics.

Alito's opinion was grudging and ahistorical. It offered a reader no way to understand why Congress in 1965 would have enacted the Voting Rights Act, nor why in 1982 it amended Section 2 to clarify that the section was violated by voting rules that were discriminatory in effect, regardless of intent. Yet the year 1982 played an outsized role in Alito's analysis. He identified 1982 as the "benchmark" for measuring how great a burden a voting procedure imposed. Alito explained that "because voting necessarily requires some effort and compliance with some rules, the concept of a voting system that is 'equally open' and that furnishes an equal 'opportunity' to cast a ballot must tolerate the 'usual burdens of voting.'" (The quotation about burdens was from a 2008 opinion that upheld an Indiana voter identification law.) He continued:

> Because every voting rule imposes a burden of some sort, it is useful to have benchmarks with which the burdens imposed by a challenged rule can be compared. The burdens associated with the rules in widespread use when Section 2 was adopted are therefore useful in gauging whether the burdens imposed by a challenged rule are sufficient to prevent voting from being equally "open" or furnishing an equal "opportunity" to vote in the sense meant by Section 2.

This was a surprising account of how to evaluate a voting restriction. It was, as Kagan objected in dissent, counter to the basic thrust of the law: "The 1982 state of the world is no part of the Section 2 test. An election rule prevalent at that time may make voting harder for minority than for white citizens; Section 2 then covers such a rule, as it covers any other. And contrary to the majority's unsupported speculation, Congress intended exactly that." She added: "Section 2 was meant to disrupt the status quo, not to preserve it—to eradicate then current discriminatory practices, not to set them in amber."

In contrast to Alito, Kagan gave readers a history lesson. Her opinion talked about Selma's "Bloody Sunday" in 1965. She quoted John Lewis and Lyndon Baines Johnson and Ruth Bader Ginsburg. "If a single statute represents the best of America, it is the Voting Rights Act," she wrote. Section 2 was "extraordinary," "ambitious," "as broad as broad can be." "But the majority today lessens the law—cuts Section 2 down to its own preferred size," she wrote. The majority opinion "mostly inhabits a law-free zone."

For Alito, history wasn't the point. He was drawing a road map for like-minded lower court judges to follow when Section 2 cases came their way. The dissenters' project was different. They were serving as witnesses, writing to make the public understand what had just taken place. Had the court been meeting in person, Kagan no doubt would have announced her dissent from the bench. Even residing only on the page, her opinion exemplified what the Harvard law professor Lani Guinier, in a famous article, labeled "demosprudence through dissent," using an unfamiliar word to suggest a jurisprudence emanating not from judges but from the wisdom of ordinary people. Guinier's 2008 article, published in the *Harvard Law Review*, opened with the scene in the Supreme Court courtroom on the final day of the previous term, when Stephen Breyer had delivered an impassioned twenty-one-minute oral dissent from the opinion by John Roberts in the *Parents Involved* case that invalidated racially conscious student placement plans designed to maintain integration in two formerly segregated public school systems. "Although few legal actors actually heard Justice Breyer's *cri de coeur*," Guinier wrote, "it represented a gestational move in the direction of greater democratic accountability."

While Breyer's oral dissent was never published, Kagan's written dissent in *Brnovich* was instantly available on the court's website. An indication of its power, and of how it unsettled some on the right, came several days later in a commentary on the *National Review*'s website. JUSTICE KAGAN'S RHETORIC DIMINISHES THE COURT was the headline, the author evidently having missed or forgotten pronouncements from a dissenting Justice Scalia such as his assertion in the court's same-sex marriage case that "I would hide my head in a bag" before joining Justice Kennedy's majority opinion.

Elena Kagan was the second of President Obama's two Supreme Court nominees, following Sonia Sotomayor by a year. She had been Obama's solicitor general, the first woman to hold that position, and before that had been dean of Harvard Law School, the first woman in that job as well, where she became known for bringing a measure of peace and comity to a faculty riven for years by bitter ideological disputes. When she became dean, the law school's faculty was so divided that new appointments had nearly come to a halt. Some people had taken to calling Harvard Law School "Beirut on the Charles." Kagan calmed the waters with good humor and a robust budget that enabled her to hire prominent conservative and liberal professors away from other law schools.

Like five of her fellow justices, she had clerked on the Supreme Court (for Justice Thurgood Marshall). Unlike all the others, she had never before been a judge. While prior judicial service had not been seen historically as a prerequisite for the Supreme Court, it had come to be one almost by default, given the desire of presidents and senators for a demonstrable credential as well as some hint of how a nominee might behave on the bench; of course, as presidents and senators knew, the nearly limitless discretion enjoyed by Supreme Court justices made their prior service of dubious predictive value.

Impassioned dissents from Kagan were rare. She typically held her fire, deploying a disarming wit and a refreshingly conversational writing style. Earlier in the term, for example, she dissented from a Kavanaugh opinion that declined to make retroactive a decision from the previous year that required unanimous juries for felony convictions in state courts. "The majority argues," Kagan wrote, "that the jury unanimity rule is not so fundamental because. . . . Well, no, scratch that. Actually, the majority doesn't contest anything I've said about the foundations and functions of the unanimity requirement. Nor could the majority reasonably do so." In part because they were so infrequent, her strong dissenting opinions were noticed. They usually meant that she had worked to find common ground with colleagues to her right and had failed. If she had tried in the voting rights case, she had nothing to show for it. The members of the majority knew what they wanted. The chief justice, for one, had wanted it for a very long time.

By mid-June, with vaccinations increasing, COVID infections plunging (down by nearly 75 percent since the January peak), and many restrictions expiring, it seemed the justices would not be receiving additional shadow docket COVID cases. But the pandemic's aftermath was still playing out in court. A group of Alabama landlords had sued the Department of Health and Human Services, arguing that a nationwide moratorium on evictions imposed by the Centers for Disease Control and Prevention exceeded the agency's authority. A federal district judge in Washington agreed with the plaintiffs but issued a stay of her ruling to permit the government to appeal. The landlords asked the Supreme Court to lift the stay. "The state of the pandemic has improved to the point where vaccinated Americans can safely gather inside without restriction," the landlords' emergency application asserted. "Forcing landlords to provide free housing for vaccinated Americans may be good politics, but it cannot be called health policy."

The action the landlords sought required five votes, and they got four: Thomas, Alito, Gorsuch, and Barrett. Roberts and Kavanaugh joined the liberal justices to deny the application. Of the nine justices, only Kavanaugh explained his vote when the court issued its order on June 29. He said that while he agreed with the district court, he was voting to allow the moratorium to expire on its own, as scheduled, on

July 31. "Those few weeks will allow for additional and more orderly distribution of the congressionally appropriated rental assistance funds," he wrote.

The administration had informed the court that the CDC would not seek to extend the moratorium beyond its scheduled July 31 expiration. But as that day approached, COVID cases were rising sharply once again and President Biden faced enormous political pressure from the Democratic base to give renters continued relief. Swift congressional action would have alleviated Kavanaugh's concern that the CDC was acting without legal authority, but congressional leaders were resistant. On August 3, with some renters already having received eviction notices, the president announced a new, limited eviction moratorium for areas of the country hardest hit by the new surge of illness. The landlords, reprising their earlier argument, immediately filed suit. Conservative scholars predicted that the Supreme Court's recent *Cedar Point* decision, in expanding the definition of a governmental "taking" of private property to include even temporary limitations on owners' use of their property, would prove useful in the landlords' case.

ON JUNE 30, Attorney General Merrick Garland announced that the Justice Department was suspending the federal death penalty to give itself time to review the changes the previous administration had made in protocols for federal executions. This was followed later in July with the announcement that seven men charged by the Trump administration with capital murder would no longer face the death penalty. In the heat of midsummer, it was not easy to recall Trump's bizarre rush to execute federal inmates, thirteen in all, in the closing months and days of his administration. Of the seventeen executions nationwide in 2020, the federal government carried out ten, more than the fifty states combined.

Now a new attorney general was closing the book on the execution "spree" that a divided court had enabled over Sonia Sotomayor's passionate dissents. In many quarters, the Trump legacy might already be fading. But not within the judiciary in general, nor in particular on the Supreme Court. In interviews at Mar-a-Lago, the former president regularly gave vent to his anger that his handpicked justices had let him down. "I was disappointed, and that's the way it goes," he told one interviewer in late June. "Very disappointed. I fought very hard for them." At a campaign-style rally in Ohio at which he vowed to "never stop fighting" the 2020 election result, Trump complained: "Many of our judges are gutless, and our Supreme Court, I am ashamed."

His handpicked justices had not saved him. They had, perhaps, helped save the court.

THE BROKEN FOURTH WALL

TRUTH TELLER THAT SHE WAS, Justice Ruth Bader Ginsburg once violated a basic norm of judicial opinion writing. The year was 2007. Seven years earlier, the Supreme Court had declared unconstitutional a Nebraska law that prohibited a particular medical procedure for terminating a pregnancy, a method to which abortion opponents had attached the cringeworthy name "partial-birth abortion." The vote to strike down the state law was 5 to 4. In the 2007 decision, *Gonzales v. Carhart*, the court confronted the same issue, this time in a federal statute enacted after the Nebraska ruling. Notwithstanding the earlier decision, the vote was 5 to 4 the other way. The federal Partial-Birth Abortion Ban Act of 2003 was upheld. The purported distinction between the state and federal laws was "flimsy and transparent," Ginsburg wrote in her dissenting opinion. What had happened during the intervening seven years to account for the reversal? Only this: Justice Sandra Day O'Connor, who voted with the majority in the first case, had retired, and Justice Samuel Alito had taken her place. "Though today's opinion does not go so far as to discard *Roe* or *Casey*," Ginsburg wrote, "the Court, differently composed than it was when we last considered a restrictive abortion regulation, is hardly faithful to our earlier invocations of 'the rule of law' and the 'principles of *stare decisis.*'"

"Differently composed than it was." For a justice to include this phrase in a dissenting opinion is the judicial equivalent of an actor's breaking the "fourth wall" by acknowledging the audience and thus dispensing with the fiction that the action on stage is anything other than a play.

In a legal system governed by precedent—the Latin *stare decisis* means "to stand by what has been decided"—the basic premise is that one decision leads logically, even inexorably, to the next. This construct enabled Chief Justice John Roberts to claim that there was no new law, just a routine application of precedent, in the move he made from *Trinity Lutheran*, the case about state funding of church playgrounds, to *Espinoza*, the case about state funding of church schools.

Members of a majority and a dissent will of course debate the relevance or interpretation of a particular precedent. But that debate takes place within a shared frame of assumption—or pretense—that law is all that matters, that the correct answer will reveal itself from the right line of precedent or the accurate reading of a statute's text. The system's actors stay on script, behaving as if external events—the departure of one justice, the arrival of another—are just that, extraneous to the action on the stage.

2020–21 was the term the fourth wall disappeared. It could hardly have been otherwise, beginning as the term did in the shadow of Justice Ginsburg's death and ending with the country holding its breath over whether Justice Stephen Breyer would retire. How could the fourth wall have survived a president's declaration that he urgently needed to fill a vacancy so his court would be at full strength to protect his forthcoming fraudulent claim to having been reelected? To his evident bafflement and lasting anger, the court did not oblige Donald Trump. It was not his court after all. But when Amy Coney Barrett's Thanksgiving eve vote, only weeks after her confirmation, abruptly shifted the balance the court had previously struck between religion and public health in the context of the COVID pandemic, the country saw what it meant to have a court "differently composed than it was."

And if it wasn't Trump's court, whose was it?

In one sense, it was a court in regression to an earlier mean of judicial behavior, to a time before there was a single "swing justice" occupying the ideological center to whom any argument had to be addressed if it was to succeed. That configuration lasted decades, beginning with Justice Lewis Powell in the central role in the late 1970s to mid-'80s; moving to Sandra Day O'Connor until her retirement in early 2006; and then for the next twelve years shifting to Anthony Kennedy, followed briefly by John Roberts.

Each of these median justices was appointed by a Republican president, and each one who filled the role was more conservative than the one before, a measure of the court's steady move to the right. In the 2020–21 term, however, a swing justice was missing. Rather, there were pairs or trios of justices who came together in case-specific coalitions. When the six conservatives were divided, as they were most notably in the Affordable Care Act case and in the religion case from Philadelphia, what separated them was not primarily ideology or methodology. It was rather their level of concern, or perhaps even awareness, that the fourth wall's disappearance had left the court exposed, vulnerable to being written off as just another political branch of government.

From the left, Justice Breyer did his best to warn about what he saw as the threat to the court's legitimacy. In an April 2021 Harvard Law School lecture titled "The Authority of the Court and the Peril of Politics," Breyer avoided direct criticism of his colleagues. But he observed pointedly that "if the public sees judges as 'politicians in robes,' its confidence in the courts, and in the rule of law itself, can only diminish, diminishing the court's power, including its power to act as a 'check' on the other branches."

It was a concern that John Roberts had long shared, although he evidently put such worries aside when it came to the Voting Rights Act, whether in his own highly disruptive *Shelby County* decision in 2013, which eviscerated the law's protection against discriminatory voting changes under the Section 5 "preclearance" requirement, or his full support of Alito's context-free approach to the statute's Section 2 in the 2021 case from Arizona. Roberts's concern about public perception may have accounted for the court's unanticipated action in June in a high-profile challenge to affirmative action in university admissions. The case, *Students for Fair Admissions v. President and Fellows of Harvard College,* had been designed for the specific purpose of presenting the Supreme Court with an irresistible vehicle for reconsidering precedents that for more than forty years had enabled colleges to take race into account in the admissions process. The claim, which two lower courts had rejected, was that Harvard discriminated against Asian Americans in favor of Black and Latino applicants. The Trump administration supported the plaintiffs both in the federal district court in Boston, which held a fifteen-day trial, and on appeal to the First Circuit.

The Supreme Court petition that Students for Fair Admissions filed in March had an opening that could best be described as cheeky: "It is a sordid business, this divvying us up by race." Directly aimed at Chief Justice Roberts, this was a line from one of his earliest opinions, a dissent from a 2006 decision that a congressional redistricting plan in Texas violated Section 2 of the Voting Rights Act by splitting a growing Latino community and diluting its voting strength. The line, deep in a lengthy opinion in which Roberts took issue with the majority's approach to Section 2, quickly became one of the new chief justice's best known. And now here it was, in a case that had nothing to do with voting rights, deployed as a dare to the chief justice: If you still mean now what you said then, you will grant this case.

Instead, the June 14 order list contained this entry under the case's name: "The Acting Solicitor General is invited to file a brief in this case expressing the views of the United States." Such an "invitation" is not one that any solicitor general would think of disregarding. In all likelihood, the Justice Department immediately began the process of disentangling the government from the case against Harvard. That surely is what the justices anticipated. Could there be any question about the position the Biden administration would take? And if not, why issue the "invitation"? If the case were granted, the administration would be free to file a brief on the merits expressing its views.

Perhaps the justices were using the invitation as a deferral device. They had already accepted both the New York gun case and Mississippi's abortion appeal for the next term. Might not affirmative action be one culture war issue too many? For an invitation issued in June, the solicitor general would ordinarily respond by December, in order for the justices to grant review, if they were so inclined, in time to hear the case during the spring and decide it by the end of the term. So the deferral would not necessarily be a long one. But at the very least, it gave the justices what they—and the country—needed in the closing weeks of this tumultuous term: some breathing room.

WITH THE COVID pandemic roaring back due to the vulnerability of the millions of unvaccinated Americans to the highly transmissible Delta variant, schools, universities, employers, and public agencies began to require vaccination. Not surprisingly, the requirements led to lawsuits. Eight students sued Indiana University, claiming that its vaccination mandate "violates the liberty protected by the Fourteenth Amendment to the United States Constitution, which includes the rights of personal autonomy and bodily integrity and the right to reject medical treatment." The lawyer who filed the fifty-five-page complaint was James Bopp, Jr. His invocation of "liberty" and "autonomy" was striking, given that Bopp had earned a national reputation representing antiabortion interests in the decades following *Roe v. Wade*. His Bopp Law Firm in Terre Haute remained a strategic center for generating antiabortion litigation; after the Supreme Court granted the Mississippi abortion case, Bopp had filed a brief for the state on behalf of the National Right to Life Committee. While "liberty" and "autonomy" were familiar words in the abortion context, they were invariably deployed in defense of abortion rights.

The students' lawsuit against Indiana University produced the first federal court decision on the subject of mandatory COVID vaccination. A federal district judge in South Bend—until recently, Amy Barrett's home—refused to issue the temporary injunction that Bopp sought. "The states don't have arbitrary power, but they have discretion to act reasonably in protecting the public's health," Judge Damon R. Leichty wrote on July 18.

Although the university offered students the option to request a religious exemption, and six of the eight plaintiffs had applied for and obtained one, Bopp added a Free Exercise claim to the complaint. Judge Leichty, a Trump appointee to the district court, rejected the claim. The legal authority he invoked was *Employment Division v. Smith*, the much disputed but still controlling decision under which the Free Exercise Clause requires no exemption from a law that applies to all. "The vaccine mandate is a neutral rule of general applicability," Judge Leichty wrote. "It applies to all students, religious or not. It doesn't discriminate among religions. Indeed the university has chosen to *enable* the practice of religion by providing a religious exemption to this vaccination requirement—one that the university, on this record, has freely granted to students if they request it, no questions asked. This is consistent with the Constitution."

A panel of the Seventh Circuit refused the students' request for a stay pending appeal. Judge Frank Easterbrook, one of the federal judiciary's best-known conservatives, was decidedly unsympathetic in his brief opinion for the appeals court. "People who do not want to be vaccinated may go elsewhere," he wrote on August 2. "Plaintiffs have ample educational opportunities." Bopp turned immediately to the Supreme Court with an "emergency application for writ of injunction." In this filing, the lawyer who had spent his career attacking legalized abortion made an astonishing argument. Seeking to bolster the case for protecting the students' "bodily integrity and autonomy," he cited to the justices two precedents that had accorded just such protection for women seeking to terminate a pregnancy: *Roe* and *Casey*. This truly was a world turned upside down.

Bopp requested a response from the court by August 13. On the night of August 12, he got his answer from Justice Barrett, acting in her capacity as "circuit justice" for the Seventh Circuit. The order consisted of one word: Denied.

RELIGION HAD BEEN the justices' companion throughout the term, and now it was following them into the summer recess and beyond. It had long been a staple of the court's docket, of course. The difference was that the cases had looked in both directions and the outcome had not been predictable; Rehnquist's "play in the joints" of the two religion clauses was an apt metaphor. As the term ended, it had been just short of forty years since President Ronald Reagan had named Sandra Day O'Connor to the court. Religion was a polarizing issue then as now, and O'Connor had taken it upon herself during her twenty-four-year tenure to try to help the court find a workable middle ground. Her instincts were strongly against absolutes, a reflection—and perhaps a cause as well—of her successful career in Arizona electoral politics before she became a judge. That background in elective office, once common for Supreme Court justices, was shared by no other member of the court of her day, or since.

One of O'Connor's last opinions, in June 2005, was a short concurrence in a case concerning a display of the Ten Commandments on the wall of a Kentucky courthouse. The long-running dispute over successive iterations of this religious exhibit had captured public attention, and the case was closely watched. Justice David Souter's opinion for the majority invalidated the display as a violation of the Establishment Clause. The vote was 5 to 4, with O'Connor joining the majority with four justices who were typically to her left. It was a week before she surprised the country by announcing her retirement, and she had something to say. "At a time when we see around the world the violent consequences of the assumption of religious authority by government," she wrote, "Americans may count themselves fortunate: Our regard for constitutional boundaries has protected us from similar travails while allowing private religious exercise to flourish."

She continued: "Those who would renegotiate the boundaries between church and state must therefore answer a difficult question: Why would we trade a system that has served us so well for one that has served others so poorly?"

Would any Republican nominee since O'Connor have even posed such a question? Indeed, would any who answered the question as she did, perhaps on a lower court, have even been nominated? Renegotiating the boundary between church and state was part of the unstated charge to the most recent nominees, so the degree to which religion dominated the 2020–21 term came as no surprise. Gorsuch took up his mission with enthusiasm, Kavanaugh more hesitantly. Amy Barrett mainly watched and waited. If the chief justice had the court's legitimacy to worry about, the newest justice had her own. But she had plenty of time.

It's tempting to think of a single term as a snapshot of a fixed period in the Supreme Court's life. A more accurate image is that of a series of frames in a moving picture in which members of the court continually navigate among past, present, and future, deciding cases they accepted during the previous term and adding new cases for decision in the next. The end of a term is in no real sense an ending, just a pause in a steady flow.

The death of the court's leading liberal and her nearly instantaneous replacement by Amy Coney Barrett, a conservative forty years her junior, jolted the flow off course, upending expectations for the term that was just getting under way in the shadow of a dangerous pandemic and a contested national election. Cases already accepted for decision—healthcare, religion—under one set of assumptions suddenly looked different, either more hopeful or more dangerous, depending on one's perspective. New petitions the court might have passed over—guns, abortion—now tempted. The term flowed on in its new course.

In the end, it was not quite the term conservatives had hoped for, nor the term that liberals had most feared. A Gallup poll released in late July revealed an unexpected turn in public opinion. What was surprising was not that overall approval of the court's performance had dipped to just under 50 percent, down from 58 percent a year earlier; all institutions of government took a hit during a tumultuous year. What was startling was that after all that had happened, Democrats and Republicans shared an identical view of the court. This was a sharp contrast to just a few years earlier, when in 2018, midway through Donald Trump's term, Republican approval of the court soared to 72 percent while Democratic approval fell to 38 percent. The change was "notable," the Gallup analyst wrote, perhaps reflecting the particular mix of rulings that "may have helped keep Republicans from viewing the court as a conservative ally, or Democrats from perceiving it as too ideologically extreme." But he added: "Today's symmetry in Republicans' and Democrats' ratings of the court may be put to the test in the court's next term."

Everyone had something to hope and something to fear from a court on the brink.

THE STEADY STREAM of op-eds urging Stephen Breyer to retire while the Democrats controlled the Senate and holding up Ruth Ginsburg as an example of an aging justice who waited too long did not persuade him. Neither did the truck with the words BREYER, RETIRE painted on the side, hired by the liberal advocacy group Demand Justice to drive around the closed Supreme Court's block. Breyer's Harvard Law School lecture, with its warning against politicizing the court, led to frantic speculation over whether he intended it as a valedictory or as an oblique explanation for why he would not time his retirement to optimize President Biden's chance to replace him.

Justice Kennedy had announced his retirement on the afternoon of the term's final day in 2018, hours after the justices had left the bench. The Breyer frenzy grew as late June turned into early July. From the justice, there was silence. On July 15, the journalist Joan Biskupic scored an interview with Breyer near his summer retreat in New Hampshire. He talked about the pleasure he took in his new role as the senior justice among the liberals, a position Ginsburg had held for ten years; under the court's rigid culture of seniority, it meant that he spoke in conference before either Sotomayor or Kagan and so got to shape the liberal response to whatever the majority was proposing.

He hadn't decided when to retire, Breyer said, but one thing was clear: It was not about to happen. He would be there at the start of the new term, his twenty-eighth. Everything would be the same.

Wouldn't it?

August 13, 2021

AUTHOR'S NOTE AND ACKNOWLEDGMENTS

THE SUPREME COURT'S 2020–21 TERM was barely under way, and my head was still spinning from the events of the previous weeks, from Justice Ruth Bader Ginsburg's death to the breathtakingly fast nomination and confirmation of her successor, Amy Coney Barrett. Taking on a book project was the furthest thing from my mind when my agent, Wendy Strothman, and David Ebershoff, vice president and executive editor at Random House, proposed a chronicle of what promised to be a fascinating and consequential Supreme Court term. My first thought was: *But I'm waiting out the pandemic in the Berkshires of western Massachusetts—I can't watch the court in action.* It quickly dawned on me that neither could anyone else. The court was closed to the public and the justices were hearing arguments over an open telephone line that the world could listen in on. I said yes.

I'm immensely grateful to both Wendy and David for bringing me the perfect pandemic project, especially to David for his deft editor's touch. I had nine months to write the book. It took every one of those months, plus the previous four decades of immersion in the life of the Supreme Court as a journalist, writer, and teacher.

I also thank two colleagues who read parts of the work in progress: Professor Reva Siegel of Yale Law School, who has taught me a great deal over the twelve years we have been writing and teaching together, and Andrew Pincus, my teaching partner in Yale's Supreme Court Clinic, whose practitioner's knowledge of the court has enriched my own understanding over the decades. And of course I thank my in-house editor, my husband, Eugene Fidell, who read every chapter at whatever hour I presented him with one and who despite many years of law practice thankfully does not write like a lawyer. I also thank Emily DeHuff for her lightning-fast and sure-handed copyediting, so important given the unusually fast production schedule.

This book is an account of the term as I processed it from day to day and month to month. I wrote in real time. Once I finished a chapter, that chapter was closed. There was no cheating, no going back to make my account of an argument in March look smart by tweaking it in light of how the case turned out in June. That was the challenge. It was a little scary and a lot of fun.

NOTES AND SOURCES

PROLOGUE: THE CHOSEN ONE

xx **The Truman Balcony tableau** Nick Whigam, "US Election 2020: Democrats Fume at Trump's Unusual Photo-Op," *Yahoo! News*, Oct. 27, 2020, au .news.yahoo.com/us-election-2020-democrats-fume-trumps-balcony-moment -072028574.html.

xxi **"I'm saving her for Ginsburg"** Jonathan Swan and Sam Baker, "Scoop: Trump 'Saving' Judge Amy Barrett for Ruth Bader Ginsburg Seat," *Axios*, March 31, 2019, axios.com/supreme-court-trump-judge-amy-barrett-ruth -bader-ginsburg-11d25276-a92e-4094-8958-eb2d197707c8.html.

xxi **Barely an hour after word came** Mark Landler and Peter Baker, "Battle Begins over Naming Next Justice," *New York Times*, Feb. 14, 2016.

xxii **But whenever the basically conservative court had tilted** The cases mentioned were: same-sex marriage, Obergefell v. Hodges, 576 U.S. 644 (2015); abortion, Planned Parenthood of Southeastern Pennsylvania v. Casey, 505 U.S. 833 (1992); enemy combatants, Boumediene v. Bush, 553 U.S. 723 (2008); affirmative action, Fisher v. University of Texas, 570 U.S. 297 (2013).

xxii **Justice Scalia was a dissenter** John O. McGinnis, "2020: A Mixed Bag for Classical Liberalism," *Law & Liberty*, Dec. 31, 2020, lawliberty.org/2020-a -mixed-bag-for-classical-liberalism/.

xxii **The week after the term ended** "Statement from Justice Ruth Bader Ginsburg," July 17, 2020, supremecourt.gov/publicinfo/press/pressreleases/pr_07 -17-20.

The full statement read as follows:

For Immediate Release   For Further Information Contact:

July 17, 2020   Kathleen Arberg (202) 479-3211

Statement from Justice Ruth Bader Ginsburg:

On May 19, I began a course of chemotherapy (gemcitabine) to treat a recurrence of cancer. A periodic scan in February followed by a biopsy revealed lesions on my liver. My recent hospitalizations to remove gall stones and treat an infection were unrelated to this recurrence.

Immunotherapy first essayed proved unsuccessful. The chemotherapy course, however, is yielding positive results. Satisfied that my treatment course is now clear, I am providing this information.

My most recent scan on July 7 indicated significant reduction of the liver lesions and no new disease. I am tolerating chemotherapy well and am encouraged by the success of my current treatment. I will continue bi-weekly chemotherapy to keep my cancer at bay, and am able to maintain an active daily routine. Throughout, I have kept up with opinion writing and all other Court work.

I have often said I would remain a member of the Court as long as I can do the job full steam. I remain fully able to do that.

xxiii **Nina Totenberg of NPR** Phillip Ewing, "Granddaughter Presages Battle Royale: When Will New Justice Be Confirmed?" NPR, Sept. 18, 2020, npr .org/sections/death-of-ruth-bader-ginsburg/2020/09/18/914643289/ .granddaughter-presages-battle-royale-when-will-new-justice-be-confirmed.

xxiii **For Senator McConnell, this was a time** Patrice Taddonio, "On Night of Ginsburg's Death, McConnell Pushed Trump to Nominate Amy Coney Barrett," *Frontline*, Nov. 24, 2020, pbs.org/wgbh/frontline/article/on-night-of -ginsburgs-death-mcconnell-pushed-trump-to-nominate-amy-coney-barrett/.

xxiii **Why Amy Barrett?** Extensive reporting in *The New York Times* is the source for most of the biographical information. See Elizabeth Dias, Rebecca R. Ruiz, and Sharon LaFraniere, "Rooted in Faith, Amy Coney Barrett Represents a New Conservatism," *New York Times*, Oct. 11, updated Oct. 14, 2020.

xxv **"I'm a Catholic, and I always grew up loving Notre Dame"** Ibid.

xxv **A commencement speech** Elizabeth Dias and Adam Liptak, "To Conservatives, Barrett Has 'Perfect Combination' of Attributes for Supreme Court," *New York Times*, Sept. 20, updated Oct. 26, 2020.

xxv **It was in South Bend, Indiana** Michael J. O'Loughlin, "Explainer: Amy Coney Barrett's Relationship with People of Praise," *America*, Sept. 24, 2020.

xxvi **In 2013, on the fortieth anniversary** University Faculty for Life and Notre Dame Fund to Protect Human Life, "Paid Advertisement," *Notre Dame Observer*, Jan. 22, 2013.

xxvii **The previous year, she had signed a statement** becketlaw.org/media/ unacceptable/.

xxvii **The decision, *Little Sisters of the Poor*** 140 S. Ct. 2367 (2020).

xxvii **Among other public statements** "Letter to Synod Fathers from Catholic Women," Ethics and Public Policy Center, Oct. 1, 2015, eppc.org/synodletter/.

xxviii **In 2016, the University Faculty for Life** This statement has recently been removed from the University Faculty for Life website. The paragraph quoted in the text read in full:

Saying that Mr. Biden rejects Church teaching could make it sound like he is merely disobeying the rules of his religious group. But the Church teaching about the sanctity of life is *true*. And so the Vice-President rejects the truth that human life begins at conception. He rejects the *truth* that every human life deserves protection, from conception until natural death. He rejects the *truth* that public officials like him have an especially grave duty to preserve the least of our brothers and sisters from harm. [Emphasis in original.]

xxix **Senator Feinstein asked her** Aaron Blake, "Did Dianne Feinstein Accuse a Judicial Nominee of Being Too Christian?" *Washington Post*, Sept. 7, 2017.

xxx **"The notion that Catholics"** Sohrab Ahmari, "The Dogma of Dianne Feinstein," *New York Times*, Sept. 11, 2017.

xxx **When Don McGahn spoke** Elizabeth Dias, Rebecca R. Ruiz, and Sharon LaFraniere, "Rooted in Faith, Amy Coney Barrett Represents a New Conservatism," *New York Times*, Oct. 11, updated Oct. 14, 2020.

xxx **Cathleen Kaveny** Cathleen Kaveny, "No, Dianne Feinstein Is Not an Anti-Catholic Bigot," *Washington Post*, Sept. 21, 2017.

xxxii **"Thank you from the bottom of my heart"** Josh Gerstein, "Gorsuch Takes Victory Lap at Federalist Dinner," *Politico*, Nov. 16, 2017, politico.com/story/2017/11/16/neil-gorsuch-federalist-society-speech-scotus-246538.

xxxii **The organization was started** Michael Kruse, "The Weekend at Yale That Changed American Politics," *Politico Magazine*, Sept.–Oct. 2018, politico.com/magazine/story/2018/08/27/federalist-society-yale-history-conservative-law-court-219608.

xxxiii **Blackwell's speech** Steven M. Teles, *The Rise of the Conservative Legal Movement: The Battle for Control of the Law* (Princeton, N.J.: Princeton University Press, 2008), p. 3.

xxxiii **In their 2013 book** Michael Avery and Danielle McLaughlin, *The Federalist Society: How Conservatives Took the Law Back from Liberals* (Nashville, Tenn.: Vanderbilt University Press, 2013), p. 2.

xxxiv **In a 2019 talk** Elizabeth Dias, Rebecca R. Ruiz, and Sharon LaFraniere, "Rooted in Faith, Amy Coney Barrett Represents a New Conservatism," *New York Times*, Oct. 11, updated Oct. 14, 2020.

xxxiv **One of her other law school mentors** John H. Garvey and Amy V. Coney, "Catholic Judges in Capital Cases," *Marquette Law Review* 81, no. 2 (Winter 1998), pp. 303–50.

xxxv **In 1997, the conservative Olin Foundation** Teles, *Rise of the Conservative Legal Movement*, pp. 173–78. Because the book was published in 2008, the fellowship data includes only the program's first nine years, 1997–2006. It is highly likely that the fellows' success rate in finding academic positions grew over time.

xxxvi **Her connection to the Federalist Society** Barrett's speeches are listed in her Senate Judiciary Committee questionnaire, apps.npr.org/documents/document.html?id=7220197-Amy-Coney-Barrett-Senate-Questionnaire.

xxxvii **When she provided a fifth vote** Roman Catholic Diocese of Brooklyn v. Cuomo, on application for injunctive relief 20A87, Nov. 25, 2020, 141 S. Ct. 63 (2020), supremecourt.gov/opinions/20pdf/20a87_4g15.pdf.

xxxvii **"We do not have Obama judges"** Adam Liptak, "Chief Justice Defends Judicial Independence After Trump Attacks 'Obama Judge,'" *New York Times*, Nov. 21, 2018, nytimes.com/2018/11/21/us/politics/trump-chief-justice-roberts -rebuke.html.

CHAPTER ONE: JULY · THE TRIUMPH OF JOHN ROBERTS

3 **Of the term's fifty-three cases** The two cases were Ramos v. Louisiana, 140 S. Ct. 1390 (2020), supremecourt.gov/opinions/19pdf/18-5924_n6io.pdf, holding that the Sixth Amendment requires a unanimous jury for conviction of a felony in state court (as has long been the case in federal court), and McGirt v. Oklahoma, 140 S. Ct. 2452 (2020), supremecourt.gov/opinions/ 19pdf/18-9526_9okb.pdf, holding that much of eastern Oklahoma, including Tulsa, remains Indian country, in which the state lacks jurisdiction to prose-cute Native Americans. The chief justice filed his only written dissenting opinion in that case.

3 **The easiest way to keep track** The decisions referred to are: presidential immunity, Trump v. Vance, 140 S. Ct. 2412 (2020), supremecourt.gov/ opinions/19pdf/19-635_07jq.pdf (majority opinion by Roberts); immigration policy, Department of Homeland Security v. Regents of the University of California, 140 S. Ct. 1891 (2020), supremecourt.gov/opinions/19pdf/18 -587_5ifl.pdf (majority opinion by Roberts); religion, Espinoza v. Montana Department of Revenue, 140 S. Ct. 2246 (2020), supremecourt.gov/opinions/ 19pdf/18-1195_g314.pdf (majority opinion by Roberts); religion, Our Lady of Guadalupe School v. Morrissey-Berru, 140 S. Ct. 2049 (2020), supreme court.gov/opinions/19pdf/19-267_1an2.pdf; religion, Little Sisters of the Poor v. Pennsylvania, 140 S. Ct. 2367 (2020), supremecourt.gov/opinions/ 19pdf/19-431_5i36.pdf; abortion, June Medical Services v. Russo, 140 S. Ct. 2103 (2020), supremecourt.gov/opinions/19pdf/18-1323_c07d.pdf (concur-ring opinion by Roberts); LGBT protections, Bostock v. Clayton County, 140 S. Ct. 1731 (2020), supremecourt.gov/opinions/19pdf/17-1618_hfci.pdf.

4 **Race would certainly be back** The new cases were Brnovich v. Democratic National Committee, No. 19-1257, and Arizona Republican Party v. Demo-cratic National Committee, No. 19-1258. The court consolidated the two cases and on July 1, 2021, decided them in one opinion, Brnovich v. Demo-cratic National Committee, supremecourt.gov/opinions/20pdf/19-1257_new _4g15.pdf.

5 **These internal memos** Ari Berman, "Inside John Roberts' Decades-Long Crusade Against the Voting Rights Act," *Politico Magazine*, Aug. 10, 2015, politico.com/magazine/story/2015/08/john-roberts-voting-rights-act-121222.

See also the summary of his activities on race issues during his service in the Reagan administration in Joan Biskupic's biography *The Chief: The Life and Turbulent Times of Chief Justice John Roberts* (New York: Basic Books, 2019), pp. 67–81.

5 **A case known by the shorthand** Parents Involved in Community Schools v. Seattle School District No. 1, 551 U.S. 701 (2007).

7 *Regents of the University* Regents of the University of California v. Bakke, 438 U.S. 265 (1978).

8 *United Steelworkers of America v. Weber* United Steelworkers of America v. Weber, 443 U.S. 193 (1979).

9 **Ruth Ginsburg, who referred to him fondly** "Statements from the Supreme Court Regarding the Death of Chief Justice William H. Rehnquist," supremecourt.gov/publicinfo/press/pressreleases/pr_09-04-05b.

11 **A small Texas utility district** The case, usually referred to as NAMUDNO, was Northwest Austin Municipal Utility District No. One v. Holder, 557 U.S. 193 (2009).

12 **Not surprisingly, the court's invitation** The case was Shelby County v. Holder, 570 U.S. 509 (2013).

13 **Southern governors and legislatures responded** Brennan Center for Justice, "The Effects of Shelby County v. Holder," Aug. 6, 2018, brennancenter .org/our-work/policy-solutions/effects-shelby-county-v-holder.

14 **In one of Rehnquist's last major opinions** Locke v. Davey, 540 U.S. 712 (2004).

14 **The first step came in late 2015** Trinity Lutheran Church of Columbia, Inc. v. Comer, 137 S. Ct. 2012 (2017), supremecourt.gov/opinions/16pdf/15 -577_khlp.pdf.

16 **The new case was from Montana** Espinoza v. Montana Department of Revenue, 140 S. Ct. 2246 (2020), supremecourt.gov/opinions/19pdf/18 -1195_g314.pdf.

17 **The Institute for Justice had won a major Supreme Court victory** Zelman v. Simmons-Harris, 536 U.S. 639 (2002).

18 **Roberts himself was a graduate** For biographical details here and later in this chapter, I relied on Joan Biskupic's biography *The Chief: The Life and Turbulent Times of Chief Justice John Roberts* (New York: Basic Books, 2019).

18 **The first Catholic justice** The Catholic judges and their dates of service: Roger B. Taney, 1836–64; Edward Douglass White, 1894–1921; Joseph McKenna, 1898–1925; Pierce Butler, 1923–39; Frank Murphy, 1940–49; Sherman Minton, 1949–56; William J. Brennan, Jr., 1956–90; Antonin Scalia, 1986–2016; Anthony Kennedy, 1988–2018; Clarence Thomas, 1991–; John Roberts, 2005–; Samuel Alito, 2006–; Sonia Sotomayor, 2009–; Brett Kavanaugh, 2018–; and Amy Coney Barrett, 2020–. This list does not include Neil Gorsuch, 2017–, who was raised in the Catholic church but is now an Episcopalian.

19 **But since the advent of the Roberts court** Lee Epstein and Eric Posner, "How the Religious Right Has Transformed the Supreme Court," *New York Times*, Sept. 22, 2020.

20 **The court had already ruled that churches** Hosanna-Tabor Evangelical Lutheran Church and School v. Equal Employment Opportunity Commission, 565 U.S. 171 (2012).

21 **Winnifred Fallers Sullivan** Winnifred Fallers Sullivan, *Church State Corporation: Construing Religion in U.S. Law* (Chicago: University of Chicago Press, 2020), p. 21.

21 **There were two cases** Our Lady of Guadalupe School v. Morrissey-Berru, 140 S. Ct. 2049 (2020), supremecourt.gov/opinions/19pdf/19-267_1an2.pdf.

22 *Little Sisters of the Poor* Little Sisters of the Poor v. Pennsylvania, 140 S. Ct. 2367 (2020), supremecourt.gov/opinions/19pdf/19-431_5i36.pdf.

23 **In the** *Hobby Lobby* **case** Burwell v. Hobby Lobby Stores, 573 U.S. 682 (2014).

23 **Instead, in an unusual and unanimous ruling** Zubik v. Burwell, 136 S. Ct. 1557 (2016), supremecourt.gov/opinions/15pdf/14-1418_8758.pdf.

24 **In short order, his administration issued new rules** 83 Fed. Reg. 57536 and 57592, codified at 45 C.F.R. pt. 147 (2018).

24 **It was one of Ruth Ginsburg's specialties** McNabb v. United States, 318 U.S. 332 (1943).

24 **One, in the previous term** Department of Commerce v. New York, 139 S. Ct. 2551 (2019), supremecourt.gov/opinions/18pdf/18-966_bq7c.pdf.

25 **Would the court ignore the promise** For law's treatment of religious complicity claims, see Douglas NeJaime and Reva B. Siegel, "Conscience Wars: Complicity-Based Conscience Claims in Religion and Politics," *Yale Law Journal* 124, no. 7 (2015), pp. 2516–91.

25 **The Becket Fund understandably kept** Becket Fund for Religious Liberty, "Little Sisters Ask Supreme Court to Protect Their Ministry to the Elderly Poor Once and for All," press release, May 6, 2020, becketlaw.org/media/little-sisters-ask-supreme-court-protect-ministry-elderly-poor/.

26 **In February, the court had agreed to hear** Fulton v. City of Philadelphia, 19-123, cert. granted Feb. 24, 2020.

26 **The fund brought the case** Becket Fund for Religious Liberty, "Heroic Foster Moms Fight for the Oldest Foster Care Agency in Philadelphia," press release, Sept. 16, 2020, becketlaw.org/media/heroic-foster-moms-fight-for-oldest-foster-care-agency-philadelphia/.

27 **He dissented in 2016** Whole Woman's Health v. Hellerstedt, 136 S. Ct. 2292 (2016), supremecourt.gov/opinions/15pdf/15-274_new_e18f.pdf.

27 **This balancing exercise showed** Planned Parenthood of Southeastern Pennsylvania v. Casey, 505 U.S. 833 (1992).

28 **The Fifth Circuit panel overturned** June Medical Services v. Gee, 905 F. 3d 787 (2018).

28 **Roberts joined them** June Medical Services v. Gee, on application for stay, 18A774, Feb. 7, 2019, 139 S. Ct. 663 (2019), supremecourt.gov/opinions/18pdf/18a774_3ebh.pdf.

28 **By the time** *June Medical Services v. Russo* **was argued** June Medical Ser-

vices v. Russo, 140 S. Ct. 2103 (2020), supremecourt.gov/opinions/19pdf/18
-1323_c07d.pdf.

30 **There was considerable ambiguity** Two federal circuits resolved pending
cases by declaring that Roberts's separate opinion in *June Medical* now stated the
law of abortion: the Eighth Circuit in Hopkins v. Jegley, 968 F. 3d 912, and the
Sixth Circuit in EMW Women's Surgical Center, P.S.C. v. Friedlander, 978 F.
3d 418. The Fifth Circuit, by contrast, ruled that *Whole Woman's Health* remained binding: Whole Woman's Health v. Paxton, 972 F. 3d 649.

31 A BLOCKBUSTER TURN Adam Liptak, "A Blockbuster Turn to the Center
Led by a Chief Justice at Center Stage," *New York Times*, July 10, 2020.

31 **The court had not permitted the president** The cases mentioned in this
paragraph are: president's financial records, Trump v. Vance, 140 S. Ct. 2412
(2020), supremecourt.gov/opinions/19pdf/19-635_07jq.pdf; protections for
the Dreamers, Department of Homeland Security v. Regents of the University of California, 140 S. Ct. 1891 (2020), supremecourt.gov/opinions/
19pdf/18-587_5ifl.pdf; LGBT employment protections, Bostock v. Clayton
County, 140 S. Ct. 1731 (2020), supremecourt.gov/opinions/19pdf/17-1618
_hfci.pdf.

32 **"An alien appears to have occupied the body"** Editorial Board, "Gorsuch
vs. Gorsuch: An Alien Legal Being Seems to Have Captured the Justice," *Wall
Street Journal*, June 16, 2020.

32 **A senator from Missouri** Josh Hawley, "Was It All for This? The Failure of
the Conservative Legal Movement," *Public Discourse*, June 16, 2020.

33 **During the 2016 presidential campaign** Mark Sherman, Associated Press,
"'Absolute Disaster' Chief Justice Roberts, Trump to Share Center Stage,"
Jan. 20, 2017, reviewjournal.com/news/politics-and-government/absolute
-disaster-chief-justice-roberts-trump-to-share-center-stage/.

33 **Vice President Pence called him merely** William Cummings, "Vice President Mike Pence Calls Supreme Court Chief Justice John Roberts 'A Disappointment to Conservatives,'" *USA Today*, Aug. 6, 2020.

33 **The theme from the right** Varad Mehta and Adrian Vermeule, "John
Roberts's Self-Defeating Attempt to Make the Court Appear Nonpolitical,"
Washington Post, Dec. 17, 2020, washingtonpost.com/outlook/john-roberts
-self-defeating-attempt-to-make-the-court-appear-nonpolitical/2020/12/17/
d3d1df5a-3fd5-11eb-9453-fc36ba051781_story.html.

33 **Since the *Heller* decision** District of Columbia v. Heller, 554 U.S. 570
(2008).

33 **The court regularly refused** Linda Greenhouse, "A Call to Arms at the
Supreme Court," *New York Times*, Jan. 3, 2019, nytimes.com/2019/01/03/
opinion/guns-second-amendment-supreme-court.html.

33 **Finally, the court had agreed to hear** New York State Rifle & Pistol
Association, Inc. v. City of New York, 140 S. Ct. 1525 (2020), https://www
.supremecourt.gov/opinions/19pdf/18-280_ba7d.pdf. The filings in the case are
posted on the court's website, supremecourt.gov, under docket number 18-280.

34 **"Rather than prolonging"** Rogers v. Grewal, 18-824, Thomas and Kavanaugh dissenting from the denial of certiorari, June 15, 2020, supremecourt .gov/opinions/19pdf/18-824_2cp3.pdf.

35 **The first case arrived in May** South Bay United Pentecostal Church v. Newsom, 19A1044, on application for injunctive relief,140 S. Ct. 1613 (2020), supremecourt.gov/opinions/19pdf/19a1044_poko.pdf.

36 **Another case arrived** Calvary Chapel Dayton Valley v. Sisolak, 19A1070, on application for injunctive relief, 140 S. Ct. 2603 (2020), supremecourt.gov/ opinions/19pdf/19a1070_o8l1.pdf#page=13.

CHAPTER TWO: AUGUST–SEPTEMBER · AN ENDING AND A BEGINNING

37 **In midsummer** Rosa Cartagena, "These New 'Wear a Mask' Signs Invoke RBG, and They're Awesome," *Washingtonian*, July 16, 2020, washingtonian .com/2020/07/16/rbg-wear-a-mask-signs-adams-morgan/.

37 **Because immunotherapy had proved unsuccessful** Supreme Court press release, "Statement from Justice Ginsburg," July 17, 2020, supremecourt.gov/ publicinfo/press/pressreleases/pr_07-17-20.

38 **A video of Ginsburg** Yohana Desta, "See Ruth Bader Ginsburg Barely Tolerate a Workout with Stephen Colbert," *Vanity Fair*, March 22, 2018, vanity fair.com/hollywood/2018/03/ruth-bader-ginsburg-workout-stephen-colbert.

38 **Even in her final weeks** Marcia Coyle, "Supreme Court Brief," *National Law Journal*, March 17, 2021.

38 **Randall Kennedy** Randall Kennedy, "The Case for Early Retirement," *New Republic*, April 28, 2011.

39 **"So tell me who the president could have nominated"** Joan Biskupic, "U.S. Justice Ginsburg Hits Back at Liberals Who Want Her to Retire," *Reuters*, July 31, 2014, reuters.com/article/us-usa-court-ginsburg/u-s-justice -ginsburg-hits-back-at-liberals-who-want-her-to-retire-idUSKBN0G12V02 0140801.

39 **Two years later** Mark Sherman, "AP Interview: Ginsburg Reflects on Big Cases, Scalia's Death," *AP News*, July 8, 2016, apnews.com/article/0da3a6411 90742669ccod01b90cd57fa.

40 **It was during those crucial years** Irin Carmon and Shana Knizhnik, *Notorious RBG: The Life and Times of Ruth Bader Ginsburg* (New York: HarperCollins, 2015).

40 **But it was Ginsburg** Debbie Levy, *I Dissent: Ruth Bader Ginsburg Makes Her Mark* (New York: Simon & Schuster, 2016).

41 **She spoke out in dissent** On abortion: Gonzales v. Carhart, 550 U.S. 124 (2007). On discrimination: Ledbetter v. Goodyear Tire & Rubber Co., 550 U.S. 618 (2007).

41 **A Harvard law professor** Lani Guinier, "Foreword: Demosprudence Through Dissent," *Harvard Law Review* 122, no. 1 (2008), pp. 4–138.

41 **It's clear in retrospect** Shelby County v. Holder, 570 U.S. 529 (2013).

41 **Her route to that exalted final chapter** Among recent biographical treatments are Jane Sherron De Hart's *Ruth Bader Ginsburg: A Life* (New York: Alfred A. Knopf, 2018) and Linda Hirshman's *Sisters in Law: How Sandra Day O'Connor and Ruth Bader Ginsburg Went to the Supreme Court and Changed the World* (New York: HarperCollins, 2015).

42 **To open the eyes of the nine men** Weinberger v. Wiesenfeld, 420 U.S. 636 (1975).

42 **In another case, a female Air Force officer** Frontiero v. Richardson, 411 U.S. 677 (1973).

43 **Before Jimmy Carter became president** Gwyneth Kelly, "Jimmy Carter's Most Important Legacy: Female Judges," *New Republic*, Aug. 13, 2015.

43 **But the opportunity came to Ginsburg** United States v. Virginia, 518 U.S. 515 (1996).

44 **Before Ginsburg spoke** Ariane de Vogue, "At VMI, Ruth Bader Ginsburg Reflects on a Monumental Ruling," CNN, Feb. 2, 2017. (Lara Tyler Chambers's name is misspelled in this account.)

46 **Trump had been lagging in the polls** Jennifer Rubin, "What Do the Polls Tell Us?" *Washington Post*, Sept. 7, 2020.

47 **Drawing particular attention** Amy Coney Barrett, "Countering the Majoritarian Difficulty," *Constitutional Commentary* 32, no. 1 (Winter 2017), pp. 61–84.

47 **The actual phrase** Alexander Bickel, *The Least Dangerous Branch: The Supreme Court at the Bar of Politics* (New York: Bobbs-Merrill, 1962).

47 **Barrett's essay approached this topic** Randy E. Barnett, *Our Republican Constitution: Securing the Liberty and Sovereignty of We the People* (New York: HarperCollins, 2016).

47 **His claim to fame** National Federation of Independent Business v. Sebelius, 567 U.S. 519 (2012).

48 **The case, *State of California*** California v. Texas, 141 S. Ct. 2104 (2021), supremecourt.gov/opinions/20pdf/19-840_new_5hdk.pdf.

50 **A federal district judge in Fort Worth** Texas v. United States, 340 F. Supp. 3d 579 (N.D. Tex. 2018).

50 **On appeal** Texas v. United States, 945 F. 3d 355 (5th Cir. 2019).

51 **For others, including the president** Dartunorro Clark, "Fauci Calls Amy Coney Barrett Ceremony in Rose Garden 'Superspreader Event,'" *Yahoo! News*, Oct. 9, 2020, yahoo.com/now/fauci-calls-amy-coney-barrett-212733107.html.

51 **Trump introduced his nominee as** Daily Comp. Pres. Docs., 2020DCPD No. 00728, "Remarks on the Nomination of Amy Coney Barrett to be a United States Supreme Court Associate Justice," Sept. 26, 2020.

52 **In her own brief remarks** "Full Transcript: Read Judge Amy Coney Barrett's Remarks," *New York Times*, Sept. 26, 2020.

CHAPTER THREE: OCTOBER · WAITING FOR JUSTICE BARRETT

53 **ORDER IN PENDING CASE** supremecourt.gov/orders/courtorders/101920zr _3fb4.pdf.

55 *Davis v. Ermold* **was one of hundreds** The petition and other filings are posted on the Supreme Court's website, supremecourt.gov, under docket number 19-926.

56 **The court's same-sex marriage decision** Obergefell v. Hodges, 576 U.S. 644 (2015).

56 **the Vatican put out a highly unusual statement** "Vatican: Pope Did Not Show Support for Kim Davis," *The Guardian*, Oct. 2, 2015, theguardian.com/ world/2015/oct/02/vatican-pope-kim-davis-same-sex-marriage.

57 **"This petition implicates important questions"** Davis v. Ermold, State-ment of Justice Thomas, with whom Justice Alito joins, respecting the denial of certiorari, 141 S. Ct. 3 (2020), supremecourt.gov/opinions/20pdf/19-926 _5hdk.pdf.

58 **The idea seemed outlandish** U.S. Census Bureau release no. CB-19-TPS.51, Nov. 19, 2019, "U.S. Census Bureau Releases CPS Estimates of Same-Sex Households," census.gov/newsroom/press-releases/2019/same-sex -households.html.

58 *Fulton v. City of Philadelphia* 141 S. Ct. 1868 (2021), supremecourt.gov/ opinions/20pdf/19-123_g3bi.pdf.

60 **It was equally unsurprising** The Fifth Circuit issued two opinions, both captioned In re Abbott: 954 F. 3d 772 (5th Cir. 2020) and 956 F. 3d 696 (5th Cir. 2020).

60 **The court granted the request** Planned Parenthood Center for Choice v. Abbott, No. 20-305, vacated Jan. 25, 2021.

60 **In July, U.S. District Judge Theodore D. Chuang** American College of Obstetricians and Gynecologists v. U.S. Food and Drug Administration, 472 F. Supp. 183 (D. Md. 2020).

61 **The administration's brief cited** Harris v. McRae, 448 U.S. 297 (1980).

61 **On October 8, an unusual order** Food and Drug Administration v. Ameri-can College of Obstetricians and Gynecologists, No. 20A34, on application for stay, Oct. 8, 2020, supremecourt.gov/opinions/20pdf/20a34_nmjp.pdf.

62 **The term's first order in an election case** Andino v. Middleton, No. 20A55, on application for stay, Oct. 5, 2020, 141 S. Ct. 9 (2020), supremecourt.gov/ opinions/20pdf/20a55_dc8e.pdf.

63 **A case from Alabama involved curbside voting** Merrill v. People First of Alabama, No. 20A67, on application for stay, Oct. 21, 2020, 141 S. Ct. 25 (2020), supremecourt.gov/opinions/20pdf/20a67_3e04.pdf.

64 **A case from Wisconsin presented** Democratic National Committee v. Wis-consin State Legislature, No. 20A66, on application to vacate stay, Oct. 26, 2020, 141 S. Ct. 493 (2020), supremecourt.gov/opinions/20pdf/20a66_new _m6io.pdf.

65 **One of those cases was from North Carolina** Moore v. Circosta, No.

20A72, on application for injunctive relief, Oct. 28, 2020, 141 S. Ct. 46 (2020), supremecourt.gov/opinions/20pdf/20a72_5hek.pdf.

65 **The other case was from Pennsylvania** Republican Party of Pennsylvania v. Boockvar, No. 20-542, on motion to expedite consideration of the petition for writ of certiorari, Oct. 28, 2020, 141 S. Ct. 643 (2020), supremecourt.gov/opinions/20pdf/20-542(1)_3e04.pdf.

67 **In 1995, when she was just an assistant professor** Elena Kagan, "Confirmation Messes, Old and New," *University of Chicago Law Review* 62, no. 2 (Spring 1995), pp. 919–42.

67 **There were no similar light moments** The transcript of the confirmation hearing is available on the C-SPAN website (c-span.org) and from a digital archive maintained by the library at the University of California at San Diego.

73 **"A New Feminist Icon"** Erika Bachiochi, "Amy Coney Barrett: A New Feminist Icon," *Politico Magazine*, Sept. 27, 2020.

73 **"This is the first time"** Jane Sloan Peters, "I See My Own Pro-Life Feminism in Amy Coney Barrett," *America*, Oct. 14, 2020.

73 **During the spring of 2020** The definitive biography of Phyllis Schlafly is Donald T. Critchlow's *Phyllis Schlafly and Grassroots Conservatism: A Woman's Crusade* (Princeton, N.J.: University of Princeton Press, 2005). A more recent treatment places Schlafly in the specific context of the 1970s battle over women's rights: Marjorie J. Spruill, *Divided We Stand: The Battle over Women's Rights and Family Values That Polarized American Politics* (New York: Bloomsbury, 2017).

CHAPTER FOUR: NOVEMBER · TURNING POINT

75 **Yet of course** *Fulton* Fulton v. City of Philadelphia, 141 S. Ct. 1868 (2021), supremecourt.gov/opinions/20pdf/19-123_new_6kg7.pdf.

75 **Expressed most recently** Employment Division v. Smith, 494 U.S. 872 (1990).

76 **He reached back** Reynolds v. United States, 98 U.S. 145 (1879).

76 **In a handful of cases** The two leading cases requiring accommodation of this sort are Sherbert v. Verner, 374 U.S. 398 (1963), and Wisconsin v. Yoder, 406 U.S. 205 (1972).

77 **While Congress of course cannot** The act provides that "Governments shall not substantially burden religious exercise without compelling justification."

77 **But the court ruled in 1997** City of Boerne v. Flores, 521 U.S. 507 (1997).

78 **Citing** *Employment Division v. Smith* District court: Fulton v. City of Philadelphia, 320 F. Supp. 3d 661 (E.D. Pa. 2018). Appeals court: Fulton v. City of Philadelphia, 922 F. 3d 140 (3d Cir. 2019).

78 **Surprisingly, the November 4 argument** supremecourt.gov/oral_arguments/argument_transcripts/2020/19-123_0758.pdf.

81 **If the court could find that the city** Church of Lukumi Babalu Aye, Inc. v. City of Hialeah, 508 U.S. 520 (1993).

82 **Coming so soon after** Masterpiece Cakeshop, Ltd. v. Colorado Civil Rights Commission, 138 S. Ct. 1719 (2018).

82 **Neither in the first of the COVID cases** South Bay United Pentecostal Church v. Newsom, 140 S. Ct. 1613 (2020); Calvary Chapel Dayton Valley v. Sisolak, 140 S. Ct. 2603 (2020).

84 **The Democrats hadn't managed to defeat** California v. Texas, argument: supremecourt.gov/oral_arguments/argument_transcripts/2020/19-840 _1a72.pdf, decision: 141 S. Ct. 2104 (2021), supremecourt.gov/opinions/ 20pdf/19-840_new_5hdk.pdf.

85 **Roberts himself had paid a price** National Federation of Independent Business v. Sebelius, 567 U.S. 519 (2012). Three years later, Roberts wrote the majority opinion that turned back another attack on the ACA: King v. Burwell, 576 U.S. 473 (2015).

87 **Alito addressed the convention** There is no official transcript of Alito's speech to the Federalist Society's 2020 National Lawyers Convention. There is a video link at youtube.com/watch?v=tYLZL4GZVbA.

88 **The Little Sisters of the Poor** Little Sisters of the Poor v. Pennsylvania, 140 S. Ct. 2367 (2020).

89 **An article in *The American Spectator*** Matthew Walther, "Sam Alito: A Civil Man," *American Spectator*, April 21, 2014.

89 **Michael Stokes Paulsen** Michael Stokes Paulsen, "2014 Supreme Court Roundup," *First Things*, Nov. 2014.

90 **Applying for a job** Alito's childhood affinities came to light in one of the documents produced during his Supreme Court confirmation process. In 1985, when Alito was a lawyer in the solicitor general's office, he applied for a higher-level position in the Justice Department and on his application discussed his lifelong conservatism. The application is part of the file posted at archives.gov/files/news/samuel-alito/accession-060-97-761/Acc060-97-761 -box1-Alito.pdf.

91 **In 1998, when Amy Coney Barrett** John H. Garvey and Amy V. Coney, "Catholic Judges in Capital Cases," *Marquette Law Review* 81, no. 2 (Winter 1998), pp. 303–50.

92 **The federal government had not executed** The decision was announced in a Department of Justice press release on July 25, 2019, "Federal Government to Resume Capital Punishment After Nearly Two Decade Lapse," Department of Justice Public Affairs, press release no. 19-807, justice.gov/opa/ pr/federal-government-resume-capital-punishment-after-nearly-two -decade-lapse. The release included the names of five men to be executed. Others were added to the list in subsequent months.

92 **Barrett was a member** Peterson v. Barr, 965 F. 3d 549 (7th Cir. 2020).

92 **Simultaneously, in a separate proceeding** In re Federal Bureau of Prisons' Execution Protocol Cases, No. 19-mc-145 (D.D.C., July 13, 2020).

92 **By a vote of 5 to 4** Barr v. Lee, 20A8 (per curiam), July 14, 2020, supreme
court.gov/opinions/19pdf/20a8_970e.pdf.

93 **A district judge in Washington, D.C.** In re Federal Bureau of Prisons' Execution Protocol Cases, No. 19-mc-145 (D.D.C., Nov. 19, 2020).

93 **The court lifted the stay** Barr v. Hall, 20A102, Nov. 19, 2020, 141 S. Ct.
869 (2020), supremecourt.gov/orders/courtorders/111920zr_4hd5.pdf.

93 **There was something deeply discordant** United States v. Higgs, No. 20-
927 (20A134), Sotomayor dissenting ("an expedited spree of executions"), 141
S. Ct. 645, supremecourt.gov/opinions/20pdf/20-927_i42k.pdf.

93 **Only seven nonfederal death sentences** "The Death Penalty in 2020: Year
End Report: Death Penalty Hits Historic Lows Despite Federal Execution
Spree," Death Penalty Information Center, Dec. 16, 2020, deathpenaltyinfo
.org/facts-and-research/dpic-reports/dpic-year-end-reports/the-death
-penalty-in-2020-year-end-report.

94 **Justices' papers from that time** See, e.g., the account of this period in Linda
Greenhouse, *Becoming Justice Blackmun: Harry Blackmun's Supreme Court Journey* (New York: Times Books/Henry Holt, 2005), pp. 160–75.

94 **Rehnquist dissented** Coleman v. Balkcom, 451 U.S. 949 (1981).

95 **After becoming chief justice** The 1996 law codified much of the limitation
on federal court jurisdiction imposed by the 1989 Supreme Court decision
Teague v. Lane, 489 U.S. 288 (1989).

96 **The case was from New York City** Roman Catholic Diocese of Brooklyn v.
Cuomo, 141 S. Ct. 63 (2021), supremecourt.gov/opinions/20pdf/20a87_4g15
.pdf.

96 **They lost in federal district court** Roman Catholic Diocese of Brooklyn v.
Cuomo, 495 F. Supp. 3d 118 (E.D.N.Y. 2020).

96 **On November 9** The Second Circuit decided the appeals of both the diocese and Agudath Israel in a single opinion, Agudath Israel of America v.
Cuomo, 979 F. 3d 177 (2d Cir. 2020).

100 **The Third Circuit's treatment** Donald J. Trump for President, Inc. v. Secretary Commonwealth of Pennsylvania, 830 F. App'x 377 (3d Cir. 2020).
www2.ca3.uscourts.gov/opinarch/203371np.pdf.

CHAPTER FIVE: DECEMBER · TESTING TIME

101 **In 1998, in a decision** New Jersey v. New York, 523 U.S. 767 (1998).

102 **But that was the essence** All the filings in the Texas case can be found on
the Supreme Court's website under docket number 22O155, supremecourt
.gov/search.aspx?filename=/docket/docketfiles/html/public/22o155.html.
The Paxton motion with accompanying brief is at supremecourt.gov/Docket
PDF/22/22O155/162953/20201207234611533_TX-v-State-Motion-2020
-12-07%20FINAL.pdf. The quoted language is from the second (unnum-
bered) page of the Motion for Leave to File.

102 **total of 62 electoral votes** The four states' electoral votes were Georgia 16, Michigan 16, Pennsylvania 20, and Wisconsin 10.

103 **Two days later** The Trump motion to intervene is at supremecourt.gov/ DocketPDF/22/22O155/163234/20201209155327055_No.%2022O155% 20Original%20Motion%20to%20Intervene.pdf. The quoted language is on page 9.

103 **He had come to public attention** John C. Eastman, "Some Questions for Kamala Harris About Eligibility," *Newsweek*, Aug. 12, 2020.

103 **Three days after publishing the op-ed** Mark Kennedy, "Newsweek Apologizes for Op-ed Questioning Harris Eligibility," *Washington Post*, Aug. 15, 2020.

103 **In January 2021** Andrea Salcedo, "Law Professor John Eastman Spoke at Rally Before Capitol Riots. Facing Outrage, He Won't Return to His University," *Washington Post*, Jan. 14, 2021.

103 **Others jumped on the Texas bandwagon** See the motions collected on the Supreme Court's website at supremecourt.gov/search.aspx?filename=/docket/docketfiles/html/public/220155.html.

104 **Josh Shapiro, attorney general of Pennsylvania** Pennsylvania's opposition to motion for leave to file bill of complaint. The quoted language is from page 1.

104 **WHY THE TEXAS LAWSUIT** Amber Phillips, "Why the Texas Lawsuit to Overturn the 2020 Election May Be the Most Outlandish Effort Yet," *Washington Post*, Dec. 10, 2020.

104 **William Barr** Katie Benner and Michael S. Schmidt, "Barr Acknowledges Justice Department Has Found No Widespread Voter Fraud," *New York Times*, Dec. 1, 2020.

105 **Early on the evening of December 11** Texas v. Pennsylvania, No. 155, Orig., 141 S. Ct. 1230 (2020), supremecourt.gov/orders/courtorders/121120zr_p860.pdf.

105 **"The Court has provided scant"** Arizona v. California, No. 150, Orig., 140 S. Ct. 684 (2020), supremecourt.gov/opinions/19pdf/150orig_3e04.pdf.

106 **That night, Trump naturally turned** Mary Papenfuss, "Trump Rants About Getting 'Screwed' by Supreme Court in Twitter Meltdown," *HuffPost*, Dec. 12, 2020, huffingtonpost.co.uk/entry/trump-rants-about-getting-screwed -supreme-court-twitter-meltdown_uk_5fd4ba2cc5b690d5d3045160.

106 **It emerged later** Jess Bravin and Gurman Sadie, "Trump Pressed Justice Department to Go Directly to Supreme Court to Overturn Election Results," *Wall Street Journal*, Jan. 23, 2021.

106 **"The U.S. Supreme Court has been"** Evan Semones, "Trump Rails at Justice Dept., Supreme Court as Stimulus Bill Deadline Nears," *Politico*, Dec. 26, 2020, politico.com/news/2020/12/26/trump-stimulus-bill-doj-supreme -court-450497.

106 **In mid-November** "Gov. Beshear Implements New Restrictions to Save Lives," official press release, kentucky.gov/Pages/Activity-stream.aspx?n=Gover norBeshear&prId=475.

107 **U.S. District Judge Gregory** Danville Christian Academy v. Beshear, 503 F. Supp. 3d 516 (E.D. Ky. 2020). The lower court opinions and all the Supreme Court filings in the case are posted on the Supreme Court's website under docket number 20A-96, supremecourt.gov/search.aspx?filename=/docket/docketfiles/html/public/20a96.html.

108 **Governor Beshear filed an emergency appeal** Commonwealth of Kentucky v. Beshear, 957 F. ed 610 (6th Cir. 2020), www.opn.ca6.uscourts.gov/opinions.pdf/20a0371p-06.pdf.

108 **On December 1** Danville Christian Academy v. Beshear, Emergency Application to Vacate the Sixth Circuit's Stay, 20A96, supremecourt.gov/Docket PDF/20/20A96/162186/20201201110258420_Filed%20Application.pdf. The quoted language is on pp. 29–30.

109 **Among the school's lawyers** First Liberty Institute, firstliberty.org/about-us/.

109 **His case against the school district** Kennedy v. Bremerton School District. The petition and the other filings in the case are available on the Supreme Court's website under docket number 18-12, supremecourt.gov/search.aspx?filename=/docket/docketfiles/html/public/18-12.html.

109 **The denial was accompanied** Kennedy v. Bremerton School District, No. 18-12, Statement of Alito, supremecourt.gov/opinions/18pdf/18-12_d18e.pdf.

109 **First Liberty promptly accepted** The U.S. District Court for the Western District of Washington granted summary judgment to the school district in March 2020. Kennedy v. Bremerton School District, 443 F. Supp. 3d 1223 (W.D. Wash. 2020). On March 18, 2021, the U.S. Court of Appeals for the Ninth Circuit rejected Kennedy's renewed appeal, ruling that his dismissal was justified by the school district's desire to avoid violating the First Amendment's Establishment Clause. Kennedy v. Bremerton School District, 991 F. 3d 1004 (9th Cir. 2021). The court observed: "At the outset, we address Kennedy's repeated contention that the practice he sought to engage in was a brief, personal, and private prayer. While his prayer may have been brief, the facts in the record utterly belie his contention that the prayer was personal and private. As noted, Kennedy engaged in a media blitz . . ."

110 **The justices turned down the *Danville Christian* case** 141 S. Ct. 527 (2020), supremecourt.gov/opinions/20pdf/20a96_e29g.pdf (the order includes the dissenting opinions).

111 **The Trump administration carried out two executions** "Federal Government Carries Out Two More Executions, Capping Deadliest Federal Death Penalty Year Since the 1890s," Death Penalty Information Center, Dec. 11, 2020, deathpenaltyinfo.org/news/federal-government-carries-out-two-more-executions-capping-deadliest-federal-death-penalty-year-since-the-1890s.

111 **In the *Bernard* case** Brandon Bernard v. United States, No. 20A110, 20-6570, Sotomayor dissenting, supremecourt.gov/opinions/20pdf/20a110_1972.pdf.

112 **Kagan joined Sotomayor's dissent** Bourgeois v. Watson, No. 20A104,

20-6500, Sotomayor dissenting, 141 S. Ct. 507 (2020), supremecourt.gov/opinions/20pdf/20a104_l537.pdf.

113 **In June 2016** Henderson v. Adams, 209 F. Supp. 3d 1059 (S.D. Ind. 2016).

113 **While the appeal was pending** Pavan v. Smith, 137 S. Ct. 2075 (2017).

114 **Indiana lost its appeal** Henderson v. Box, 947 F. 3d 482 (7th Cir. 2020).

114 **It filed a Supreme Court appeal** Box v. Henderson, No. 19-1385, supreme court.gov/search.aspx?filename=/docket/docketfiles/html/public/19-1385.html.

115 **On Monday, December 14** Chris Johnson, "Supreme Court Rejects Challenge to Same-Sex Parents on Birth Certificates," *Washington Blade*, Dec. 14, 2020.

115 **December was the worst month** covidtracking.com/data/national/deaths.

CHAPTER SIX: JANUARY · ACROSS THE STREET

116 **Halfway into his hourlong speech** rev.com/blog/transcripts/donald-trump -speech-save-america-rally-transcript-january-6.

117 **From 1860 to 1935** The semicircular room is known as the Old Senate Chamber because the Senate met there from 1819 until 1859. It was home to the Supreme Court for twice as long.

118 **The ten federal executions** The nonprofit Death Penalty Information Center, deathpenaltyinfo.org, continually updates its website with information about federal and state executions. For a historical overview, see death-penaltyinfo.org/news/dpic-analysis-federal-government-to-conduct-first -lame-duck-federal-executions-in-more-than-a-century.

119 **A campaign document titled** See joebiden.com/justice/.

119 **The U.S. District Court for the Southern District** The leading precedent on the death penalty and mental illness is Ford v. Wainwright, 477 U.S. 399 (1986).

120 **After the Seventh Circuit vacated** United States v. Montgomery. The lower court opinions and Supreme Court filings in the Lisa Montgomery case are posted on the Supreme Court's website, supremecourt.gov, under docket number 20A125.

120 **Another of the final three, Corey Johnson** United States v. Johnson and Johnson v. Rosen. The lower court opinions and Supreme Court filings in Corey Johnson's two cases are posted on the Supreme Court's website, supreme court.gov, under dockets number 20A130 and 20A131.

120 **His lawyers sought to show** Among several important precedents on the death penalty and intellectual disability are Atkins v. Virginia, 536 U.S. 304 (2002), and Moore v. Texas, 137 S. Ct. 1039 (2019).

120 **Troubling as those cases were** United States v. Higgs. The lower court opinions and Supreme Court filings are posted on the Supreme Court's website, supremecourt.gov, under dockets number 20A134 and 20-927. The dis-

senting opinions by Justices Breyer and Sotomayor are attached to this order: 141 S. Ct. 645 (2021), supremecourt.gov/opinions/20pdf/20-927_i42k.pdf.

121 **Justice Breyer, who in 2015** Breyer's call for reconsideration of the death penalty came in his dissenting opinion in Glossip v. Gross, 576 U.S. 863, 945–946 (2015).

122 **"Judge Sonia Sotomayor has lived"** The White House press release: obamawhitehouse.archives.gov/the-press-office/background-judge-sonia-sotomayor.

124 **One such opinion came** Kaur v. Maryland, 141 S. Ct. 5 (2021). The lower court opinion and the Supreme Court filings are posted on the Supreme Court's website, supremecourt.gov, under docket number 19-1045. Justice Sotomayor's opinion is here: supremecourt.gov/opinions/20pdf/19-1045_d1pf.pdf.

125 **Clarence Thomas's solitary dissenting and concurring opinions** Brown v. Entertainment Merchants Assoc., 564 U.S. 786 (2011).

126 **One striking example was** Little Sisters of the Poor v. Pennsylvania, 140 S. Ct. 2367 (2020), supremecourt.gov/opinions/19pdf/19-431_5i36.pdf.

126 **She gave no indication** The Hobby Lobby case, requiring accommodation of employers' religious objections to contraception, was Burwell v. Hobby Lobby Stores, 573 U.S. 682 (2014).

127 **She would write a bestselling memoir** Sonia Sotomayor, *My Beloved World/ Mi Mundo Adorado* (New York: Alfred A. Knopf, 2013).

127 **Later came a children's edition** Sonia Sotomayor, *Sonia Sotomayor's Beloved World* (New York: Delacorte Press, 2018). Sonia Sotomayor, *Just Ask! Be Different, Be Brave, Be You* (New York: Penguin Young Readers Group, 2019).

128 **She would be "the people's justice"** David Fontana, "The People's Justice?" *Yale Law Journal Forum*, March 24, 2014, pp. 447–78, yalelawjournal .org/forum/the-peoples-justice.

128 **Within the court** Joan Biskupic, *Breaking In: The Rise of Sonia Sotomayor and the Politics of Justice* (New York: Sarah Crichton/Farrar, Straus & Giroux, 2014), pp. 200–201.

128 **Nine years earlier** Grutter v. Bollinger, 539 U.S. 302 (2003).

128 **The case,** *Fisher* 570 U.S. 297 (2013).

129 **On remand, the U.S. Court of Appeals** Fisher v. University of Texas (Fisher II), 136 S. Ct. 2198 (2016).

129 **The case was** *Schuette v. BAMN* 572 U.S. 291 (2014).

130 **In the** *Parents Involved* **case** Parents Involved in Community Schools v. Seattle School District No. 1, 551 U.S. 701 (2007).

130 **The line was not original** The line originated with Judge Bea's opinion in Parents Involved in Community Schools v. Seattle School District No. 1, 426 F. 3d 1162, 1222 (9th Cir. 2005) (Bea, J., dissenting). See also Linda Greenhouse, "A Tale of Two Justices," *Green Bag*, second series, vol. 11 (Autumn 2007), pp. 37–41.

131 **In July, a federal district judge** American College of Obstetricians and Gynecologists v. U.S. Food and Drug Administration, 472 F. Supp. 3d 183 (D. Md. 2020).

131 **In October, over an angry dissent** The opinions and briefs in the case are posted on the Supreme Court's website, supremecourt.gov, under docket number 20A34. 141 S. Ct. 10 (2020), supremecourt.gov/opinions/20pdf/20a34 _nmjp.pdf.

132 **In an opinion issued on December 9** American College of Obstetricians and Gynecologists v. U.S. Food and Drug Administration, Dist. of Maryland Case 8:20-cv-01320—TDC Document 144.

132 **The court's answer came late** Food and Drug Administration v. American College of Obstetricians and Gynecologists, 141 S. Ct. 578 (2021), supreme court.gov/opinions/20pdf/20a34_3f14.pdf.

134 **Sotomayor ended her opinion** Gonzales v. Carhart, 550 U.S. 124 (2007).

135 **On the agenda were two petitions** Trump v. CREW (No. 20-330) and Trump v. District of Columbia (No. 20-331). The briefs are posted on the Supreme Court's website, supremecourt.gov.

CHAPTER SEVEN: FEBRUARY · CHOOSING SIDES

137 *Salinas v. United States Railroad Retirement Board* 141 S. Ct. 691 (2021), supremecourt.gov/opinions/20pdf/19-199_07jq.pdf. The briefs in the case are posted on the Supreme Court's website, supremecourt.gov, under docket number 19-199. (On July 21, 2021, the Fifth Circuit ruled in a brief unpublished opinion that the appeals court, after considering the Supreme Court's ruling, had decided against reopening Salinas's case, www.ca5.uscourts.gov/opinions/unpub/18/18-60702.1.pdf.)

138 **Resolving such a dispute** See Rule 10, Rules of the Supreme Court (edition of July 2019), supremecourt.gov/ctrules/2019RulesoftheCourt.pdf.

139 **In 2016, as a judge on the D.C. Circuit** Stovic v. Railroad Retirement Board, 826 F. 3d 500 (D.C. Cir. 2016).

140 **It was a Railroad Retirement Board case** Szostak v. Railroad Retirement Board, 370 F. 2d 253 (2d Cir. 1966).

140 **But in December 2005** The Roberts opinion was Martin v. Franklin Capital Corp., 546 U.S. 132 (2005). Judge Friendly's article was "Indiscretion About Discretion," *Emory Law Journal* 31, no. 4 (Fall 1982), pp. 747–84. On Roberts and Friendly, see Brad Snyder, "The Judicial Genealogy (and Mythology) of John Roberts: Clerkships from Gray to Brandeis to Friendly to Roberts," *Ohio State Law Journal* 71, no. 6 (2010), pp. 1149–1243.

141 **was soon back in court** The court's decision from May 2020 is South Bay United Pentecostal Church v. Newsom, 140 S. Ct. 1613 (2020).

141 **After losing in the lower courts** The church's application for an injunction is posted on the Supreme Court's website, supremecourt.gov, under docket number 20A136. The petition is docketed under 20-746.

141 **In an unsigned order** supremecourt.gov/opinions/20pdf/20a136_bq7c.pdf #page=3 (order and opinions).

144 **With the execution hours away** Alabama's application to vacate the Eleventh Circuit's stay of execution, Dunn v. Smith, is posted on the Supreme Court's website, supremecourt.gov, under docket number 20A128.

144 **The case touched a nerve** The first Alabama case was Dunn v. Ray, 139 S. Ct. 661 (2019). Alabama's application to vacate the Eleventh Circuit's stay of execution is posted on the Supreme Court's website, supremecourt.gov, under docket number 18A815.

145 **A few weeks later** Murphy's application for a stay of execution, Murphy v. Collier, is posted on the Supreme Court's website, supremecourt.gov, under docket number 18A985.

146 **The court, ruling in *Dunn v. Smith*** Dunn v. Smith, 141 S. Ct. 725 (2021), supremecourt.gov/opinions/20pdf/20a128_e1pf.pdf.

148 **In October, when the court refused to expedite** The case name at that time was Republican Party of Pennsylvania v. Boockvar, 141 S. Ct. 643 (2020), supremecourt.gov/opinions/20pdf/20-542(1)_3e04.pdf.

148 **The Republicans' petition argued** The petition and all other filings, including Trump's motion to intervene, are posted on the Supreme Court's website, supremecourt.gov, under docket number 20-542.

148 **But a concurring opinion in *Bush v. Gore*** 531 U.S. 98, 112 (2000).

150 **It was not until February 22** The case (with the same docket number) was now called Republican Party of Pennsylvania v. Degraffenreid, supremecourt .gov/opinions/20pdf/20-542_2c83.pdf.

152 **The next voice to be heard** The transcript of Trump's speech to the Conservative Political Action Committee is at rev.com/blog/transcripts/donald -trump-cpac-2021-speech-transcript.

CHAPTER EIGHT: MARCH · PRESSURES

153 **Erwin Chemerinsky** Erwin Chemerinsky, "Love Ya Ruth, but It's Time to Go," *Politico Magazine*, Sept. 24, 2014, politico.com/magazine/story/2014/ 09/love-ya-ruth-but-its-time-to-go-111305/; "What Mitch McConnell Got Right," *New York Times*, Feb. 11, 2021.

154 **Paul Waldman** Paul Waldman, "Opinion: It's Time for Justice Breyer and Senator Feinstein to Retire," *Washington Post*, March 18, 2021.

154 **But a liberal academic** Noah Feldman, "Stop Telling Stephen Breyer to Retire," *Bloomberg*, March 16, 2021, bloomberg.com/opinion/articles/2021 -03-16/stop-telling-stephen-breyer-to-retire.

154 **In December, before the retirement** Dahlia Lithwick, "Justice Breyer on Whether Judges Get More Liberal as They Get Older," *Slate*, Dec. 22, 2020, slate.com/news-and-politics/2020/12/stephen-breyer-interview-dahlia -lithwick-80-over-80.html.

154 **In mid-March, the National Judicial College** Marcia Coyle, "Supreme Court Brief," *National Law Journal*, March 17, 2021.

155 **"You have a lot of people"** Ariane de Vogue, "Conservatives with High Expectations Anxious for Justice Amy Coney Barrett to Show Her Hand," CNN, March 24, 2021, cnn.com/2021/03/24/politics/amy-coney-barrett -conservatives/index.html.

155 **Barrett issued her first majority opinion** United States Fish and Wildlife Service v. Sierra Club, Inc., 141 S. Ct. 777 (2021).

157 **The court had one last piece of business** Trump v. Wisconsin Elections Commission. The petition and procedural records of the case are posted on the Supreme Court's website, supremecourt.gov, under docket number 20-883.

157 **The court's silence was not matched** Jonathan Easley, "Trump: Supreme Court Should Be 'Ashamed' for Not Reversing Biden Win," *The Hill*, March 16, 2021, thehill.com/homenews/news/543543-trump-supreme-court-should-be -ashamed-for-not-overturning-election?rl=1.

158 **At any time in recent years** The consolidated cases are Brnovich v. Democratic National Committee, No. 19-1257, and Arizona Republican Party v. Democratic National Committee, No. 19-1258. The briefs are posted on the Supreme Court's website, supremecourt.gov, under docket number 19-1257.

158 **In one particularly flagrant** Stephen Fowler, "Why Do Nonwhite Georgia Voters Have to Wait in Line for Hours? Too Few Polling Places," NPR, Oct. 17, 2020, npr.org/2020/10/17/924527679/why-do-nonwhite-georgia -voters-have-to-wait-in-line-for-hours-too-few-polling-pl.

159 **But Chief Justice Roberts's opinion** Shelby County v. Holder, 570 U.S. 529 (2013).

159 **The U.S. Court of Appeals** Democratic National Committee v. Hobbs, 948 F. 3d 989 (9th Cir.) (en banc) 2020.

160 **For example, although the question of Sunday voting** The argument transcript is posted on the Supreme Court's website at supremecourt.gov/ oral_arguments/argument_transcripts/2020/19-1257_1b7d.pdf.

162 **In a 1980 decision** City of Mobile v. Bolden, 446 U.S. 55 (1980).

162 **By 1982, when the issue came to a head** For Roberts's background on the voting rights issue, see Ari Berman, "Inside John Roberts' Decades-Long Crusade Against the Voting Rights Act," *Politico Magazine*, Aug. 10, 2015, politico.com/magazine/story/2015/08/john-roberts-voting-rights-act -121222/.

164 **A decision in early March** Uzuegbunam v. Preczewski, 141 S. Ct. 792 (2021).

166 **A brief from the Foundation for Individual Rights in Education** The briefs in the case are posted on the Supreme Court's website, supremecourt .gov, under docket number 19-968.

167 **It may be hard to believe** Torres v. Madrid, 141 S. Ct. 989 (2021).

168 **Dissenting from a majority opinion by Ruth Bader Ginsburg** The case was Perry v. Merit Systems Protection Board, 137 S. Ct. 1975 (2017).

168 **"At the end of the day"** Roberts's reference was to Scalia's majority opinion in California v. Hodari D., 499 U.S. 621 (1991).

CHAPTER NINE: APRIL · AGENDAS

170 **That the country had just experienced a third** Sarah Bahr et al., "In Indianapolis, 3rd Massacre in 3 Months," *New York Times*, April 16, 2021.

170 **That 5-to-4 decision** District of Columbia v. Heller, 554 U.S. 570 (2008).

171 **A mobilized social movement** For background on the development of the gun rights movement's constitutional claims, see Reva B. Siegel, "Dead or Alive: Originalism as Popular Constitutionalism in Heller," *Harvard Law Review* 122, no. 1 (2008), pp. 191–245.

171 **By 2015, Thomas** See, e.g., Friedman v. Highland Park, 136 S. Ct. 447 (2015); Peruta v. California, 137 S. Ct. 1995 (2017); Silvester v. Becerra, 138 S. Ct. 945 (2018). See also Linda Greenhouse, "A Call to Arms at the Supreme Court," *New York Times*, Jan. 3, 2019.

171 **On the D.C. Circuit, Kavanaugh** Heller v. District of Columbia, 670 F. 3d 1244 (D.C. Cir. 2011).

171 **Finally, in January 2019** N.Y. State Rifle & Pistol Association, Inc. v. City of New York, 140 S. Ct. 1525 (2020).

172 **It did not take long** N.Y. State Rifle & Pistol Association, Inc. v. Corlett, No. 20-843, pet. for cert. filed Dec. 17, 2020. The petition and all other filings in this case are posted on the Supreme Court's website, supremecourt .gov, under docket number 20-843. The name of the case changed after the retirement of Keith Corlett, the superintendent of the New York State Police, and his replacement by Kevin Bruen. The case is now N.Y. State Rifle & Pistol Association, Inc. v. Bruen.

172 **Their applications were denied** The Second Circuit precedent from 2012 was Kachalsky v. County of Westchester, 701 F. 3d 81 (2d Cir. 2012). It was appealed to the Supreme Court as Kachalsky v. Cacace, No. 12-845, pet. for cert. den., April 15, 2013.

173 **Within weeks of taking his seat** Peruta v. California, 137 S. Ct. 1995 (2017).

174 **In her brief time on the Seventh Circuit** Kanter v. Barr, 919 F. 3d 437 (7th Cir. 2019).

175 **This quotation was from a 2010 opinion** McDonald v. Chicago, 561 U.S. 742 (2010).

175 **On April 2, an "emergency application"** Tandon v. Newsom, No. 20A151. The filings are posted under that docket number on the Supreme Court's website, supremecourt.gov.

176 **A panel of the Ninth Circuit** Tandon v. Newsom, 992 F. 3d 916 (9th Cir. 2021).

177 **While the court did not give him absolutely everything** Tandon v. Newsom, 141 S. Ct. 1294 (2021), supremecourt.gov/opinions/20pdf/20a151_4g15 .pdf.

179 **The case, *Montgomery v. Louisiana*** 577 U.S. 190 (2016).

179 **In *Roper v. Simmons*** 543 U.S. 551 (2005).

179 **In *Miller v. Alabama*** 567 I.S. 460 (2012).

180 **A Mississippi prisoner** Jones v. Mississippi, 141 S. Ct. 1307 (2021), supreme court.gov/opinions/20pdf/18-1259_8njq.pdf. The petition and filings in this case are posted on the Supreme Court's website, supremecourt.gov, under docket number 18-1259.

182 **A headline in an account** Ed Whelan, "Vindicating Scalia's Last Opinion," *National Review Bench Memos*, April 23, 2021, nationalreview.com/bench -memos/vindicating-scalias-last-opinion/.

182 **On April 15, Rep. Jerrold Nadler** The text of the bill is online at congress. gov/117/bills/hr2584/BILLS-117hr2584ih.pdf. Nadler's statement: nadler. house.gov/news/documentsingle.aspx?DocumentID=394602. Nadler's press release: nadler.house.gov/news/documentsingle.aspx?DocumentID=394601.

182 **The ink on the proposed** Sarah Ferris, "Pelosi Dismisses Progressive 'Court Packing' Legislation," *Politico*, April 15, 2021, politico.com/news/2021/ 04/15/pelosi-dismiss-progressive-court-packing-bill-481895.

183 **The "court-packing" epithet** There are numerous books and other published accounts of the episode. See, e.g., William E. Leuchtenberg, *The Supreme Court Reborn: The Constitutional Revolution in the Age of Roosevelt* (New York: Oxford University Press, 1995). For a recent journalistic account, see Gillian Brockell, "FDR Tried to Pack the Supreme Court During the Depression. It Was a Disaster for Him," *Washington Post*, Sept. 24, 2020.

183 **Proponents of the modern court** Robert Barnes and Ann E. Marimow, "Justice Breyer Warns Proponents of Packing Supreme Court to 'Think Long and Hard' About the Risks," *Washington Post*, April 7, 2021.

183 **"I wish that he would just stop talking about that"** Madison Adler, "Progressives Push Back on Breyer for Court Packing Comments," *U.S. Law Week*, April 8, 2021, news.bloomberglaw.com/us-law-week/progressives-push -back-on-breyer-for-court-packing-comments.

184 **On April 9, he signed an executive order** whitehouse.gov/pcscotus/.

CHAPTER TEN: MAY · THE QUESTION

185 **The titanic battle** The most complete account of the Bork nomination is Ethan Bronner's *Battle for Justice: How the Bork Nomination Shook America* (New York: Union Square Press, 2007). The book is unfortunately out of print, but it is available from marketplace sellers. A useful academic treatment of the confirmation process is Paul M. Collins and Lori A. Ringhand's *Supreme Court Confirmation Hearings and Constitutional Change* (New York: Cambridge University Press, 2013).

185 **Subsequent nominees** The transcript of Ruth Bader Ginsburg's confirmation hearing is on the Government Printing Office website: govinfo.gov/ content/pkg/GPO-CHRG-GINSBURG/pdf/GPO-CHRG-GINSBURG .pdf. The GPO site also provides links to other recent confirmation hearing

transcripts. The Library of Congress has posted extensive files on recent Supreme Court nominees beginning with John Roberts in 2005: guides.loc .gov/supreme-court-nominations. Other resources are available through the Georgetown Law Library's "Supreme Court Nominations Resource Guide," guides.ll.georgetown.edu/c.php?g=365722&p=2471068.

187 **The full D.C. Circuit, voting 6 to 3** Garza v. Hargan, 874 F. 3d 735 (D.C. Cir. 2017) (en banc). For an account of the litigation, see "Recent Cases," *Harvard Law Review*, vol. 131, pp. 1812–19 (April 2018).

188 **In "Catholic Judges in Capital Cases"** John H. Garvey and Amy V. Coney, "Catholic Judges in Capital Cases," *Marquette Law Review* 81, no. 2 (Winter 1998), pp. 303–50, at 306, 307, 350.

189 *June Medical Services v. Russo* 140 S. Ct. 2103 (2020).

189 **The Fifth Circuit upheld the law** Whole Woman's Health v. Cole, 790 F. 3d 563 (5th Cir. 2015), overturned by Whole Woman's Health v. Hellerstedt, 136 S. Ct. 2292 (2016).

189 **To apply the "undue burden" standard** Planned Parenthood of Southeastern Pennsylvania v. Casey, 505 U.S. 833 (1992).

190 **The balancing test that Breyer employed** For the debate among judges on how to apply the "undue burden" test, see Linda Greenhouse and Reva B. Siegel, "Casey and the Clinic Closings: When 'Protecting Health' Obstructs Choice," *Yale Law Journal* 125, no. 5 (March 2016), pp. 1428–80.

190 **Samuel Alito, a judge** Planned Parenthood of Southeastern Pennsylvania v. Casey, 947 F. 2d 682 (3d Cir. 1991).

191 **The Fifth Circuit's decision to uphold** June Medical Services v. Gee, 905 F. 3d 787 (5th Cir. 2018).

192 **Almost immediately, lower courts** See, e.g., Hopkins v. Jegley, 968 F. 3d 912 (2020); EMW Women's Surgical Center, P.S.C. v. Friedlander, 978 F. 3d 418 (6th Cir. 2020); Whole Woman's Health v. Paxton, 972 F. 3d 649 (2020).

192 **Americans United for Life** Americans United for Life, 2020 State Legislative Sessions Reports, at 3, aul.org/wp-content/uploads/2020/10/2020-State -Legislative-Sessions-Report.pdf.

193 **Ginsburg was still on the bench** The petition in the Dobbs case as well as all subsequent filings are posted on the Supreme Court's website, supreme court.gov, under docket number 19-1392.

193 **The state was appealing a decision** Jackson Women's Health Organization v. Dobbs, 945 F. 3d 265 (5th Cir. 2019).

193 **But as U.S. District Judge Carlton** Jackson Women's Health Organization v. Dobbs, 349 F. Supp. 3d 536 (S. D. Miss. 2018).

194 **"There are few additional babies"** Gerard V. Bradley, "An Opportunity to Overturn *Roe*," *First Things*, April 27, 2021.

194 **Some 90 percent of abortions** Guttmacher Institute, "Induced Abortion in the United States," September 2019, guttmacher.org/fact-sheet/induced -abortion-united-states.

194 **Consequently, by the time** These cases are collected at Note 23 of the Fifth Circuit's opinion.

197 **"I hope I am proved wrong"** Ed Whelan, "The Supreme Court Is *Still* Sitting on Important Certiorari Petition in Abortion Case," *National Review Online*, March 22, 2021, nationalreview.com/bench-memos/supreme-court-is -still-sitting-on-important-certiorari-petition-in-abortion-case/.

198 **The court's first encounter** Baze v. Rees, 553 U.S. 35 (2008).

199 **Seven years later** Glossip v. Gross, 576 U.S. 863 (2015).

199 **In another 5-to-4 decision** Bucklew v. Precythe, 139 S. Ct. 1112 (2019).

200 **In August 2020, another Missouri death row inmate** Johnson v. Precythe. The petitions and filings are posted on the Supreme Court's website, supreme court.gov, under docket number 20-287.

200 **After the eighth conference** Monday, March 29, 2021, Orders in Pending Cases, supremecourt.gov/orders/courtorders/032921zor_nmip.pdf.

200 **Sotomayor dissented, joined by Breyer and Kagan** Johnson v. Precythe, 141 S. Ct. 1622 (2021), supremecourt.gov/opinions/20pdf/20-287_8mjp.pdf #page=3.

201 **The term would include** United States v. Tsarnaev, No. 20-443.

201 **The First Circuit, while upholding the jury's guilty verdict** United States v. Tsarnaev, 968 F. 3d 24 (1st Cir. 2020).

CHAPTER ELEVEN: JUNE–JULY · RELIGION, ESTABLISHED

203 **In a succinct sixteen pages** California v. Texas, 141 S. Ct. 2104 (2021), supremecourt.gov/opinions/20pdf/19-840_new_5hdk.pdf.

203 **His first major dissenting opinion** Massachusetts v. Environmental Protection Agency, 549 U.S. 497 (2007).

204 **During the Trump years, Democratic state attorneys general** Jacqueline Thomsen, " 'Ready for a Fight': How Republican Attorneys General Prepared to Go After Biden in Court," *National Law Journal*, Jan. 27, 2021.

204 **In March, Trump's former adviser** Brent Kendall, "Stephen Miller's Next Act Finds a Stage in the Courts," *Wall Street Journal*, April 7, 2021.

205 **These included the *Massachusetts* case** Department of Commerce v. New York, 139 S. Ct. 2551 (2019).

205 **In his dissenting opinion in the *June Medical* abortion case** June Medical Services v. Russo, 140 S. Ct. 2103 (2020). The 1976 precedent on doctors' standing is Singleton v. Wulff, 428 U.S. 106 (1976).

205 **He was still fighting the outcome** The 2012 Obamacare case was National Federation of Independent Business v. Sebelius, 567 U.S. 519 (2012).

207 **In 2019, for example, he used a woman's** New York Times v. Sullivan, 376 U.S. 254 (1964). Thomas's opinion was a concurrence in the denial of review, McKee v. Cosby, 139 S. Ct. 675 (2019), supremecourt.gov/opinions/18pdf/17 -1542_ihdk.pdf. On July 2, 2021, Thomas and Gorsuch, in separate opinions this time, dissenting from a denial of review, elaborated on the critique of

New York Times v. Sullivan in Berisha v. Lawson, supremecourt.gov/opinions/
20pdf/20-1063_new_6j37.pdf. The D.C. Circuit opinion was by Judge Silberman in Tah v. Global Witness Publishing, Inc., 991 F. 3d 231 (CADC
2021).

208 **Fulton was the oldest argued case** Fulton v. City of Philadelphia, supreme
court.gov/opinions/20pdf/19-123_new_6kg7.pdf.

208 **That was the 1990 precedent** Employment Division v. Smith, 494 U.S. 872
(1990).

208 **Fulton was unlike the shadow docket cases** Roman Catholic Diocese of
Brooklyn v. Cuomo, 141 S. Ct. 63 (2020); South Bay United Pentecostal
Church v. Newsom (South Bay II), 141 S. Ct. 716 (2021); Tandon v. Newsom,
141 S. Ct. 1294 (2021).

209 **This was Church of Lukumi** Church of Lukumi Babalu Aye, Inc. v. City of
Hialeah, 508 U.S. 520 (1993).

210 **As Philadelphia's lawyer, Neal Katyal** The argument transcript is posted on
the Supreme Court's website at supremecourt.gov/oral_arguments/argument
_transcripts/2020/19-123_0758.pdf.

211 **After all, when the court granted the case** The petition and all other filings in Fulton are posted on the Supreme Court's website, supremecourt.gov,
under docket number 19-123.

212 **With that case now added to the docket** The Mississippi abortion case is
Dobbs v. Jackson Women's Health Organization, No. 19-1392.

215 **The petitioner, an Idaho building contractor** Ricks v. Idaho Contractors
Board. The petition and all other filings in the case are posted on the Supreme
Court's website, supremecourt.gov, under docket number 19-66.

215 **Arlene's Flowers** Arlene's Flowers v. State of Washington. The petition and
all other filings in the case are posted on the Supreme Court's website,
supremecourt.gov, under docket number 19-333.

215 **In 2017, after the Washington supreme court had ruled against** State of
Washington v. Arlene's Flowers, 389 P. 3d 543 (Wash. 2017).

215 **The justices then held the petition for Masterpiece Cakeshop** Arlene's
Flowers v. State of Washington, docket number 17-108; Masterpiece Cakeshop, Ltd. v. Colorado Civil Rights Commission, 138 S. Ct. 1719 (2018).

216 **The Washington court reinstated nearly all** State of Washington v. Arlene's Flowers, 441 P. 3d 1203 (Wash. 2019).

216 **The case the court granted** Carson v. Makin. The petition and all other
filings in the case are posted on the Supreme Court's website, supremecourt
.gov, under docket number 20-1088.

217 **The first decision in the series** Trinity Lutheran Church of Columbia, Inc.
v. Comer, 137 S. Ct. 2021 (2017).

217 **The federal district court and the Eighth Circuit** Locke v. Davey, 540
U.S. 712 (2004).

218 **Roberts wrote the majority opinion** Espinoza v. Montana Department of
Revenue, 140 S. Ct. 2246 (2020). The petition and all other filings in the case

are posted on the Supreme Court's website, supremecourt.gov, under docket number 18-1195.

218 **"The religious education and formation"** Our Lady of Guadalupe School v. Morrissey-Berru, 140 S. Ct. 2049 (2020).

219 **In that case, the court had for the first time** Hosanna-Tabor Evangelical Lutheran Church and School v. Equal Employment Opportunity Commission, 565 U.S. 171 (2012).

219 **John Roberts, product of an elite school** Scalia's "faux judicial modesty" charge came in Federal Election Commission v. Wisconsin Right to Life, 551 U.S. 449 (2007). See also Linda Greenhouse, "Even in Agreement, Scalia Puts Roberts to the Lash," *New York Times*, June 28, 2007.

220 **The lawsuits had failed** The two earlier cases were Bagley v. Raymond School Department, 728 A. 2d 127 (Me. 1999), and Anderson v. Town of Durham, 895 A. 2d 944 (Me. 2006).

220 **The Maine parents had lost** The lower court opinions (both titled Carson v. Makin) are at 979 F. 3d 21 (1st Cir. 2020) and 401 F. Supp. 3d 207 (D. Me. 2019).

222 **He managed to move the law** Scalia's most notable property rights opinion was Lucas v. South Carolina Coastal Council, 505 U.S. 1003 (1992), which held that a ban on coastal development was a taking.

222 **The classic definition of a "regulatory taking"** Pennsylvania Coal v. Mahon, 260 U.S. 393 (1922).

222 **Scalia's effort ran aground** Tahoe-Sierra Regional Council, Inc. v. Tahoe Regional Planning Agency, 535 U.S. 302 (2002).

222 **At their conference on November 13** Cedar Point Nursery v. Hassid. The petition and the other filings in the case are posted on the Supreme Court's website, supremecourt.gov, under docket number 20-107.

223 **When *Cedar Point* was argued** The argument transcript is posted on the Supreme Court's website at supremecourt.gov/oral_arguments/argument _transcripts/2020/20-107_n758.pdf.

223 **By a vote of 6 to 3** 141 S. Ct. 2063 (2021), supremecourt.gov/opinions/ 20pdf/20-107_ihdj.pdf.

224 **CEDAR POINT NURSERY V. HASSID QUIETLY REWROTE** Josh Blackman, "Cedar Point Nursery v. Hassid Quietly Rewrote Four Decades of Takings Clause Doctrine," *Volokh Conspiracy*, June 25, 2021, reason.com/volokh/2021/ 06/25/cedar-point-nursery-v-hassid-quietly-rewrote-four-decades-of -takings-clause-doctrine/.

224 **Alito's opinion for a 6-to-3 majority** Brnovich v. Democratic National Committee, supremecourt.gov/opinions/20pdf/19-1257_new_4g15.pdf.

227 **Guinier's 2008 article** Lani Guinier, "Foreword: Demosprudence Through Dissent," *Harvard Law Review* 122 (Nov. 2008), pp. 4–138. Breyer's dissent came in Parents Involved in Community Schools v. Seattle School District No. 1, 551 U.S. 701 (2007).

228 **An indication of its power** Jason Richwine, "Justice Kagan's Rhetoric Di-

minishes the Court," *National Review Online*, July 6, 2021, nationalreview
.com/corner/justice-kagans-rhetoric-diminishes-the-court/. Scalia's dissent was
in Obergefell v. Hodges, 576 U.S. 644 (2015).

228 **When she became dean** For Kagan's reputation as a conciliator at the time
of her nomination, see Laura Meckler, "Kagan's Harvard Stint Could Be Sell-
ing Point," *Wall Street Journal*, April 27, 2010.

228 **Earlier in the term, for example** Kagan's dissent was in Edwards v. Vannoy,
141 S. Ct. 1547 (2021). The earlier case was Ramos v. Louisiana, 140 S. Ct.
1390 (2020).

229 **By mid-June, with vaccinations increasing** Centers for Disease Control
and Prevention COVID Data Tracker, covid.cdc.gov/covid-data-tracker/
#trends_dailytrendscases.

229 **A group of Alabama landlords** Alabama Association of Realtors v. Department of Health and Human Services. The emergency application and other
filings are posted on the Supreme Court's website, supremecourt.gov, under
docket number 20A169.

229 **Of the nine justices** Alabama Association of Realtors v. Department of
Health and Human Services, Kavanaugh concurring, 141 S. Ct. 2320 (2021),
supremecourt.gov/opinions/20pdf/20a169_4f15.pdf.

230 **On August 3, with some renters** Centers for Disease Control and Prevention, "Temporary Protection from Eviction," cdc.gov/coronavirus/2019
-ncov/covid-eviction-declaration.html. The Biden administration's struggle
to respond to the evolving situation is described in detail in Michael D.
Shear, Charlie Savage, and Alan Rappeport, "White House Scrambled
to Find Solution on Evictions to Satisfy Pelosi," *New York Times*, Aug. 8,
2021.

230 **Conservative scholars predicted** Ilya Somin, "A Takings Clause Lawsuit
Against the CDC Eviction Moratorium," *Reason*, August 3, 2021, reason.com/
volokh/2021/08/03/a-takings-clause-lawsuit-against-the-cdc-eviction
-moratorium/.

230 **On June 30, Attorney General Merrick Garland announced** Office of the
Attorney General, "Moratorium on Federal Executions Pending Review of
Policies and Procedures," July 1, 2021, justice.gov/opa/page/file/1408636/
download.

230 **in 2020, the federal government carried out ten** Death Penalty Information Center, "The Death Penalty in 2020: Year-End Report," deathpenalty
info.org/facts-and-research/dpic-reports/dpic-year-end-reports/the-death
-penalty-in-2020-year-end-report.

231 **"I was disappointed"** The comment is in the transcript of a podcast interview of the former president conducted by David Brody, June 21, 2021, just
thenews.com/government/white-house/read-full-water-cooler-interview
-president-trump-here.

231 **At a campaign-style rally in Ohio** Josh Marcus, "Trump Says He Will 'Never
Stop Fighting' 2020 Election Results at Campaign-Style Rally," *The Inde-*

pendent, June 27, 2021, independent.co.uk/news/world/americas/us-politics/trump-ohio-supreme-court-election-b1873447.html.

EPILOGUE: THE BROKEN FOURTH WALL

232 **The year was 2007** The case was Gonzales v. Carhart, 550 U.S. 124 (2007). The earlier case from Nebraska was Stenberg v. Carhart, 530 U.S. 914 (2000).

233 **This construct enabled Chief Justice John Roberts** Trinity Lutheran Church of Columbia, Inc. v. Comer, 137 S. Ct. 2021 (2017). Espinoza v. Montana Department of Revenue, 140 S. Ct. 2246 (2020).

234 **In an April 2021 Harvard Law School lecture** Rachel Reed, "Breyer Cautions Against the 'Perils of Politics,'" *Harvard Law Today,* April 7, 2021, today .law.harvard.edu/supreme-court-justice-stephen-g-breyer-cautions-against -the-peril-of-politics/.

234 **It was a concern that John Roberts had long shared** Roberts's majority opinion in 2013 was Shelby County v. Holder, 570 U.S. 529 (2013).

235 **The case,** *Students for Fair Admissions* The petition and other filings are posted on the Supreme Court's website, supremecourt.gov, under docket number 20-1199.

235 **The claim, which two lower courts had rejected** The district court decision is reported at 397 F. Supp. 126 (D. Mass. 2019). The appeals court decision is at 980 F. 3d 157 (1st Cir. 2020). Both are titled Students for Fair Admissions v. President and Fellows of Harvard College.

235 **Directly aimed at Chief Justice Roberts** League of United Latin American Citizens v. Perry, 548 U.S. 399 (2006).

236 **Eight students sued** The complaint is posted on the Bopp Law Firm's website at bopplaw.com/wp-content/uploads/2021/06/iu-vax-complaint.pdf.

236 **A federal district judge in South Bend** Klaassen v. The Trustees of Indiana University (USDC N.D. Ind., July 18, 2021).

237 **The legal authority he invoked** Employment Division v. Smith, 494 U.S. 872 (1990).

237 **A panel of the Seventh Circuit** https://media.ca7.uscourts.gov/cgi -bin/rssExec.pl?Submit=Display&Path=Y2021/D08-02/C:21-2326 :J:Easterbrook:aut:T:op:N:2741753:S:0.

237 **Bopp turned immediately** Bopp's emergency application is posted on the Supreme Court's website, supremecourt.gov, under docket number 21A15.

238 **Her instincts were strongly against** O'Connor had served as majority leader of the Arizona senate, the first woman in the country to hold so high a position in a state legislature. For a recent biography, see Evan Thomas, *First: Sandra Day O'Connor* (New York: Random House, 2019).

238 **One of O'Connor's last opinions** McCreary County v. American Civil Liberties Union of Kentucky, 545 U.S. 844 (2005).

239 **A Gallup poll** Jeffrey M. Jones, "Supreme Court Job Approval Dips Below 50%," Gallup, July 28, 2021, news.gallup.com/poll/352895/supreme-court -job-approval-dips-below.aspx.

240 **Neither did the truck** The organization's press release described the truck: demandjustice.org/demand-justice-launches-breyer-retire-push-on -anniversary-of-stevens-retirement/.

240 **On July 15, the journalist** Joan Biskupic, "Exclusive: Stephen Breyer Says He Hasn't Decided His Retirement Plans and Is Happy as the Supreme Court's Top Liberal," *CNN Politics*, July 15, 2021, cnn.com/2021/07/15/politics/ stephen-breyer-retirement-plans/index.html.

INDEX

Abbott, Greg, 59
  *Planned Parenthood Center for Choice
    v. Abbott*, 60, 252n60
abortion, xxii, xxviii, 3, 60, 90, 185–98
  abortion exceptionalism, 60
  Alito and, 28, 62, 131, 190, 191,
    192, 205
  Barrett and, xxvi–xxvii, 68, 188–89,
    239
  Bopp Law Firm and lawsuits, 236
  Casey, 27, 29–30, 67–68, 132,
    189–92, 194, 198, 232
  Catholic justices and issue of, 19
  Dobbs, ix–x, 193–96, 267n212
  *EMW Women's Surgical Center,
    P.S.C. v. Friedlander*, 249n30
  Ginsburg's position, 43, 185, 193
  Gonzales v. Carhart, 41, 134, 232,
    250n41
  Hopkins v. Jegley, 249n30
  Hyde amendment, 61, 252n61
  June Medical, 28–31, 189, 191–93,
    198, 205, 246n3, 249n30, 266n205
  Kavanaugh and, 28, 186–87
  Louisiana ban, 27–28
  March for Life rally (2020), 73
  medication abortion and *FDA v.
    American College of Obstetricians
    and Gynecologists*, 60–62, 131–34
  "partial-birth" abortion, 41, 134,
    232, 250n41, 270n232
  Partial-Birth Abortion Ban Act, 232
  phrase "abortion on demand" and,
    187
  *Planned Parenthood Center for Choice
    v. Abbott*, 60, 252n60
  Roberts's dissatisfaction with court's
    abortion jurisprudence, 27, 29
  Roe, 68, 185, 194, 196–97, 198
  Roe v. Wade overturned, ix–x, xii
  Scalia and, 27, 68, 189
  spousal notice requirement, 190
  state legislatures and antiabortion
    measures, xxi, 193–94, 196
  Stenberg v. Carhart, 232, 270n232
  Supreme Court divided on, 193, 196
  Texas ban, 59–60
  TRAP laws, 190, 192, 193–94
  "undue burden" standard, 27,
    29–30, 189–90, 192, 194–95
  viability question, 194, 196, 198
  Whole Women's Health v. Cole (Fifth
    Circuit case), 189, 265n189
  Whole Woman's Health v. Hellerstedt,
    27, 28, 29, 189–92, 196, 198
  Whole Women's Health v. Paxton,
    249n30
  See also Roe v. Wade

LINDA GREENHOUSE has reported on and written about the Supreme Court for *The New York Times* for more than four decades, earning numerous accolades including a Pulitzer Prize. She currently writes frequently on the court and teaches at Yale Law School. She lives in New Haven, Connecticut, and Stockbridge, Massachusetts.

ABOUT THE TYPE

The text of this book was set in Janson, a typeface designed about 1690 by Nicholas Kis (1650–1702), a Hungarian living in Amsterdam, and for many years mistakenly attributed to the Dutch printer Anton Janson. In 1919, the matrices became the property of the Stempel Foundry in Frankfurt. It is an old-style book face of excellent clarity and sharpness. Janson serifs are concave and splayed; the contrast between thick and thin strokes is marked.